THE URBAN COMPLEX

Robert C. Weaver was born in Washington, D.C. and has lived for extended periods in New York and Chicago. He received his B.S., M.A., and Ph.D. degrees from Harvard University and has been awarded numerous honorary degrees. From 1933 to 1937 he served as Adviser on Negro Affairs to the Department of the Interior, after which he became a special assistant to the U. S. Housing Authority. An economist, Mr. Weaver has held visiting professorships at Columbia Teachers' College and the New York University School of Education, as well as served as program director to the John Hay Whitney Foundation and as a consultant to the Ford Foundation. Intermittently from 1954 to 1961, he served in various governmental capacities with the cities of Chicago and New York, including membership in Governor Harriman's cabinet.

At present Mr. Weaver is Administrator of the Housing and Home Finance Agency and President Johnson's chief adviser on matters regarding city planning and development, housing and real estate codes and practices. In this capacity he is responsible for the Federal Housing Administration, the Urban Renewal Administration, the Federal National Mortgage Association, and the Public Housing Administration.

Mr. Weaver is the author of numerous magazine articles and papers, as well as three other books, *Negro Labor: A National Problem* (1946), *The Negro Ghetto* (1948), and *Dilemmas of Urban America* (1965).

THE URBAN COMPLEX

Human Values in Urban Life

ROBERT C. WEAVER

Generously Donated to
The Frederick Douglass Institute
By Professor Jesse Moore
Fall 2000

ANCHOR BOOKS
DOUBLEDAY & COMPANY, INC.
GARDEN CITY, NEW YORK

THE URBAN COMPLEX was originally published by Doubleday & Company, Inc., in 1964. The Anchor Books edition is published by arrangement with Doubleday.

Anchor Books edition: 1966

Copyright © 1960, 1961, 1963, 1964 by Robert C. Weaver
All Rights Reserved
Printed in the United States of America

All rights reserved including the right to reproduce the parts of this book covered by previous copyrights as detailed below and other parts of the book not explicitly put in the public domain. The author has indicated that the fourth section of Chapter II, the first and second sections of Chapter IV, and the first three sections of Chapter V are in the public domain.

Portions of this book have previously appeared, usually in somewhat different form, in various periodicals and books as follows:

Journal of the American Institute of Architects: "Some Planning and Design Considerations," Chapter II (under the title "The Metropolitan Frontier").

Journal of Housing: "The Role of the Federal Government," Chapter IV (under the title "Growing Metro Areas Make Case for Department of Urban Affairs"). This article is based upon testimony of the author before a Congressional committee. The testimony and the article as revised are now in the public domain.

Journal of Intergroup Relations: "Southern Comfort," Chapter VI (under the title "Southern Comfort: A Possible Misapplication of Federal Funds"); "The Most

Recent Newcomers," Chapter VI (under the title "The Changing Status of Racial Groups").

Land Economics: "Color, Class, and Urban Renewal," Chapter II (under the title "Class, Race, and Urban Renewal"), © 1960 by the University of Wisconsin; "The Economic Consequences of Open Occupancy," Chapter V (under the title "The Effect of Anti-Discrimination Legislation upon the FHA- and VA-Insured Housing Market in New York State"), © 1955 by the University of Wisconsin; the first four sections of Chapter III, "Urban Renewal Today" (under the title "Current Trends in Urban Renewal"), © 1963 by the University of Wisconsin.

Proceedings of the Academy of Political Science: "Human Values in Urban Life," Chapter I (under the title "Human Values of Urban Life"), © 1960 by the Academy of Political Science.

Proceedings of Canadian Council on Urban and Regional Research: "Urban Growth and Research," Chapter IV (under the title "Urban Growth Problems and Research"), © 1962 (Canada) by Canadian Council on Urban and Regional Research.

Phylon: "A Transitional Period of Population Movement," Chapter VI (under the title "Recent Developments in Urban Housing and Their Implications for Minorities"), © 1955 by Atlanta University; "An Early Appraisal," Chapter II (under the title "Non-White Population Movements and Urban Ghettos"), © 1959 by Atlanta University.

Wayne State University Press: Arnold Rose, ed.: *Assuring Freedom to the Free:* "The Impact of Urbanization," Chapter VI (under the title "The Changing Structure of the American City and the Negro," a chapter in the book identified above), © 1964 by Wayne State University.

CONTENTS

PREFACE

This is an urban age. And the United States is in the vanguard of nations which are undergoing the process of urbanization. As a consequence almost every aspect of our lives is affected by the rapid movement of people from rural to urban communities. Of course, a contemporary urban community is composed of suburbs as well as cities and towns. Indeed, some of the most pressing problems confronting us stem from this mixture of small and large communities, incorporated and unincorporated areas, central cities and outlying residential developments. It is this mix, fraught with economic, political, and social problems, that comprises the metropolitan complex.

In a Nation where many institutions and attitudes have strong roots in a predominantly agricultural past, it is inevitable that much passion and emotion are involved in discussions of urban matters. Thus, it is incumbent upon anyone who writes in this field to set forth his value judgments. The most important of these relate to the virtues of urban versus rural living and the relative desirability of home ownership versus rental. Although, in certain quarters, I am said to be central-city oriented, I do not share the attitude of those who believe that the suburbs are undesirable per se. In the first place, I was born and reared in a suburb, and as far as my conscious mind can recall, I had a happy and exciting childhood. Secondly, I am convinced that it is no less narrow-minded to affirm blanket condemnation of suburbs than it is to state that cities are evil, destined to, and deserving of, destruction.

Of course, I am involved in the revitalization of our cities, but there is little nostalgia in this commitment. Rather, I believe that the urban complex cannot remain healthy and grow unless its core areas are strong and vibrant. At the same time, I am equally concerned about, and involved in, the provision of good housing in the suburbs. I am probing to develop better and more efficient land utilization in the fringe areas and the provision of more adequate public facilities in all parts of the urban community. It is my hope that the American people will have the maximum choices in an adequate inventory of housing, both in the central city and in the suburbs, both rental and sales. And I am dedicated to the principle that our citizens, regardless of ethnic origins, should have access to the total housing market for which they have an effective demand.

As in all social, economic, and political issues, the subject discussed in this book is fraught with myths. I hope, in the pages which follow, to identify some of these and challenge "conventional wisdom." Only by recognizing facts can we hope to approach sound and desirable solutions.

Throughout this book I shall be discussing urban renewal. The phrase "urban renewal" expresses two concepts. The first, and more comprehensive, refers to many activities—slum clearance and redevelopment, highways and public works, demolition and construction privately financed—all of which change the structure of a city. The second usage relates to an institutional form and is restricted, primarily, to the types of activities facilitated by the Federal Government's urban renewal program. The second concept is the one used in this book.

This book, as its subtitle indicates, addresses itself primarily to human values. While the orientation is toward people, there is recognition of the economic realities in housing and community development. An underriding principle throughout is that governmental action should be directed toward the public interests and that both the community and the consumer, no less than industry, are basic elements. Thus, there is a discussion of the physical structure of urban communities; the economic and fiscal policies of government and their effect upon the home building industry and the economy, as well as the urban setting, and its housing problems; the planning concepts and practices which affect this environment; the research needs and the values basic to urban living. The role and reactions of a still unassimilated element in the population—its non-white citizens—is probed.

Much of what appears on the pages which follow has been extracted from published articles or lectures prepared over the last decade. Some—indeed the majority of the articles—were written when I was a critic rather than a practitioner in the field. Others were prepared either during the period that I was a codirector of New York City's urban redevelopment program or in my present position as Administrator of the Housing and Home Finance Agency.

The materials which were published have been edited and revised so as to avoid repetition and to update or supplement earlier analyses with more current illustrations. For the most part, I have avoided modifying the original analysis. And, of course, I have supplemented earlier evaluations with more recent ones.

The copyright statement at the front of the book identifies the published materials from which I have drawn. I appreciate the permission granted for the reproduction of the materials involved. In addition, mention should be made of certain of my lectures which have supplied materials appearing on the pages that follow. The list includes The Shepard Memorial Lecture delivered at Ohio State University in April, 1962; The Herman G. James Memorial Lecture delivered at the University of Ohio in December, 1962; a lecture before the Department of City and Regional Planning at Harvard University in May, 1961; and the Commencement Address at Hunter College in New York in June, 1962.

Inevitably, in light of my current responsibilities, I have summarized what the Kennedy Administration has done to meet some of the problems I had delineated prior to my returning to Washington and the Federal Government. This manuscript was completed in late October, 1963. Subsequently President Kennedy was assassinated. In light of the fact that President Johnson is continuing the policies and expanding the programs of the previous administration, the progress delineated in the pages which follow will continue.

I am deeply indebted to my present associates for the development of my thinking about much that appears in those parts of this book which were written in 1961 and subsequently. While it is impossible to identify the contributions of each one of them, several deserve special mention. Wayne Phillips has been a constant source of stimulation and assistance. The Office of Program Policy, under the able direction of Morton J. Schussheim, has contributed much to my thinking about planning and economic policies. Special appreciation goes to Dr. Schussheim, Henry B. Schechter, and Marian Perry Yankauer.

Of course, my ideas reflect many influences. First, they have been stimulated, in part, by conversations and discussions with those mentioned above and scores of others. Also, they are influenced by the articles and books I have read over many years. While I shall not be able to identify all of these sources of inspiration and knowledge, I do want to express appreciation for their contributions. Naturally, I assume full responsibility for what appears on the pages which follow.

R.C.W.

Washington, D.C.

THE URBAN COMPLEX

I THE URBAN FRONTIER

The Problems before Us

Any discussion of the future of the American city must have two aspects: consideration of the changes that will come about as a result of the forces of growth and migration, over which we have little control, and consideration of the best way to accommodate to those changes by utilizing the forces which we do control.

Projections of growth and migration can be made, operating on the assumption—which is not necessarily valid—that the trends of the past will continue into the future. The Census Bureau estimates that by 1970 the United States will have a population of 214 million, and by 1980 a population of 260 million. Other projections indicate a population by the year 2010 of over 400 million—nearly equal to that of present-day India.

While the size of our total population continues to grow, so, too—it is believed—will the migration from rural to urban areas that has brought about the transformation of our cities. Nearly all the future growth in our country is expected to take place in the urban sector of our population. And within not too many years 85 per cent of our population may be living in urban areas.

Together with this concentration of growth in the urban segment of the population, however, we can expect to see the dispersal of this population over wider and wider urban areas. The 70 per cent of our population that is now urban is concentrated in only 1 per cent of the country's total area. Within the last decade

alone the urbanized areas recognized by the Census
Bureau increased from some 13,000 square miles to
about 25,500 square miles. At the same time the density
of population within those urbanized areas declined
from 5000 persons per square mile to 3000.

This pattern of growth has drastically altered our concept of the American city. There was a time in our
history when cities were readily identifiable urban concentrations serving as the political, economic, and social centers for a surrounding rural area. Today these
urban concentrations have blended one into the other
and have lost much of their individual identity. When
we speak of "the city" we usually are thinking of those
cities of 50,000 population or more that are the centers
of the 212 metropolitan areas in the country—areas that
form social and economic units, ranging in size from
the 24 square miles around Meriden, Connecticut, to
the 27,000 square miles around San Bernardino, California.

Even this concept of the city has begun to change,
however. For it has become apparent that the expansion of these metropolitan areas is so great that they
have begun to evidence a potential merging into even
more complex social organisms. And these have come
to be called "strip cities"—vast areas of urban development stretching sometimes for hundreds of miles and
encompassing cities, towns, and metropolitan areas in
one interdependent area. There are thirteen such strip
cities readily identifiable in the United States. Combined they include 119 of the 212 metropolitan areas,
and half the population of the United States.

A detailed study of the largest of the thirteen strip
cities—that area stretching from Boston to Washington
along the northeastern seaboard of the United States—
was recently completed by a French scholar, Jean Gottman, with the help of the Twentieth Century Fund.[1]

[1] Jean Gottman, *Megalopolis, The Urbanized Northeastern
Seaboard of the United States* (New York: The Twentieth
Century Fund, 1961), 810 pp.

He called the area "Megalopolis," borrowing the name of a city the ancient Greeks had hoped would be the most powerful in the world. And he approaches it as though it were a laboratory for urban growth, where the outlines of the future can be detected.

"Tomorrow's society," he writes, "will be different from that in which we grew up, largely because it will be more urbanized. . . . So great are the consequences of the general evolution heralded by the present rise and complexity of Megalopolis that an analysis of the region's problems often gives one the feeling of looking at the dawn of a new stage in human civilization. . . . Indeed, the area may be considered the cradle of a new order in the organization of inhabited space." When we talk of the city of the future, therefore, we can no longer think of an independent urban community, or even one that is just the focal point of a metropolitan area. Rather we must think in terms of urban communities that must function as one of many nerve centers in a vast, complex, and delicately interconnected social organism.

If this is the function which the future American city will assume, as a result of certain forces of growth over which we have no control, it is certainly time we began considering the changes that will be necessary in its form. We can control the form of the American city, and thus influence, even though we cannot control, its growth. When we design and build and rebuild cities with a form suited to the growth we can expect, we will be creating a better life for those who choose to live in them.

A fundamental concern of Metropolitan development is recognition, in the process, of the responsibilities of a democracy. The guiding principle is simple: it is that Americans should have the maximum choice in where they live and how they move about in the urban complex.

The introduction to a book on municipal problems published in this country in 1891, said in part,

. . . What shall we do with our great cities? What
will our great cities do with us? These are the two problems which confront every thoughtful American.

For the question involved in these two questions does
not concern the city alone. The whole country is affected,
if indeed its character and history are not determined by
the condition of its great cities. . . .[2]

Those words were written in connection with a trea-
tise on conditions existing more than seventy years ago,
when the urban problems in this nation were not nearly
as acute as they have now become. Yet decades ago it
was already apparent—as it certainly must be now to us
all—that on the future of the American city depends
the future of America itself. Our country will continue
to grow in the years ahead, and so will the concentration of Americans in urban areas. We have created, or
we are in the process of creating, some of the tools of
government for dealing with the physical problems this
growth will produce. It is up to each community to use
those tools intelligently and wisely, while we constantly
evaluate and supplement them.

We still have a long way to go, however, in finding
ways to deal with the human problems this growth will
bring upon us. But we have taken the first steps toward
solution when we recognize the issue. America today is
taking a new and inquiring look at its urban communities. At the same time, we are attempting to reshape
and improve them. What we do now will affect the lives
of our children and our children's children.

While we must act, we must think also.

The Development of Our Cities

The idea of urbanization not only implies and connotes
the process of moving from rural to city life, or to some-

[2] Lyman Abbott, "Introduction," Helen Campbell *et. al.*,
Darkness and Daylight (Hartford, 1891), pp. 40, 42, cited
in Arthur M. Schlesinger, *The Rise of the City, 1878–1898*
(New York: The Macmillan Co., 1933), front matter.

thing approaching city life, but it also carries with it a change in how people live. The usual agricultural life, with the exception of some variations which have been instituted in recent years, has been in a rather self-sufficient, individual economy where people are dependent largely upon themselves and their family and much less dependent upon their neighbor or upon the society of which they are a part.

Urban areas conceived of in this context are quite distinct from villages and towns that rely on the rural economy about them. Because of the Homestead Acts, which required farmers to live on the land they were cultivating, this country did not develop—except in the older areas along the East Coast—the form of agricultural village found in Europe and some other parts of the world. In those areas, farmers lived in the villages while they tilled the surrounding land.

Most of the towns of this Nation, however, developed as commercial centers for surrounding agricultural areas. They were the places where farmers went to market their produce, and where they stayed on after they had gotten the returns and spent some of the money—first for the necessities of life, and then for the enjoyments of life. They were dominated by the small businessmen who controlled the commerce which was the basis of their very existence. Once very common in the United States, these towns are beginning now either to be transformed into cities or to disappear—because the truck and the automobile have made it easier for farmers to reach larger and more distant markets.

In all of this process, technology has been important—not in determining what has happened, but in extending and in limiting the possibilities of what *could* happen. One could not conceive of modern urbanization, for example, without modern technology. Today we are able to produce more than enough farm goods with a much smaller part of our labor force in agriculture. The present great productivity of agriculture, which does not

require and which does not even afford a good liveli-
hood for a large number of those persons who are rural,
has thus been an enormous factor in the development
of our cities.

Originally this Nation was developed largely by offering people absolute control over wide areas to facilitate
the rapid improvement of the land. Now we are trying
to recover control of the way land is used so as to
achieve a proper type of development of our urban
areas and of our whole country. Our current objectives
are to secure the open space needed both for urban
and rural recreation, to protect wildlife, to promote
conservation, to eliminate scatterization, and, of course,
to provide sites for the shelter required by our population. Thus, we seek to recapture control of the use of
land, most of which the government has already given
to people.

Recently a land economist was discussing some of
the problems of a so-called backward nation. Looking
at these issues in the perspective of contemporary
America, he advised the people of this emerging nation: "Don't give your land away. Hold your land real
tight, and then when you get to the point where we are,
you won't have the problems we have."

Actually, this may not be good advice. For there is
always a danger in counseling people in terms of one's
own experience and one's own situation. A method by
which the country under discussion, with its agricultural and mineral and other resources, could develop
itself—and it needs to be developed—is by having a land
policy somewhat similar to ours. Or perhaps it should
effect a compromise somewhere in between, not giving
the land away, but certainly getting it into use through
conditional release, restriction upon use, or some other
way short of total individual control. For the present,
if the central government continues to hold all the
land it will not have the resources and the people may
not have the motivation to develop the country rapidly.

Land policy, like so many other policies, needs to be approached from an evolutionary point of view. At one period, a policy of getting the land into private ownership and private control, absolute control, may be extremely desirable for the economic and political development of a country. If this policy is effected, and the nation matures, other socio-economic situations and problems arise, and they become more complicated if there is a tradition of absolute private control of land use.

Those who have traveled in Western Europe probably have noted the relative ease with which the Scandinavian countries, or Great Britain, or France, can control land use in the periphery of the central city. In the United States this is practically an impossibility.

There are institutional reasons for the greater facility with which the European nations meet this aspect of land policy. In the first place, the nations are small and homogeneous. Secondly, their system of government usually involves only two layers: the federal (which they call, of course, the state) and the local. Their tax system is sometimes quite different, with the local governments often more dependent upon income than property taxes. Under our system of government and taxation, there are serious impediments to annexation by central cities. Some are institutional, reflecting rivalries for political control and tax dollars between central cities, suburban areas, and counties. Others reflect the hesitancy of state governments to accord greater local control or relinquish tax powers. Still others, to be delineated in greater detail subsequently, are a hangover from our rural past.

In this Nation, we have a multiplicity of problems involving central cities and their suburbs: mass transit is an example; open space is another; land utilization is still another; and housing and many of the public services are involved. Also we have a system of local governments so proliferated that it is almost impossible to deal effectively with these matters. Thus, our situation is much more difficult and complex than that of many other Western nations.

This illustration points out that, as far as land use is concerned, the technology and the structural nature of government and of the economy are limiting factors. It also depicts the principle that no matter how wonderfully something may operate in one country, it is not going to operate that effectively in another country unless it is adapted to the second country's cultural and governmental background, traditions, and institutions.

There are certain functions which cities are uniquely designed to perform. One of them is medical research. A university hospital seeks a location where there is a large population, where economic diversity exists, where there are people of various ethnic, physical, and social backgrounds affording the opportunity to do the experimentation and clinical work that would be extremely difficult to do in a small community. There are additional advantages, usually found in a large city, in having access to museums, libraries, government agencies, and the like.

Raymond Vernon in his study of New York[3] has pointed out that it is in the city where there is the greatest degree of specialization. Perhaps this can be demonstrated best by considering the garment industry. Certain sectors of this industry have stayed in New York, and segments of other sectors have moved out —and again, the Vernon study explains why.

Those parts of the garment industry which have moved from New York City most readily involve mass production of cheap shirts or cheap dresses, where there are multiple reproductions of a given style. This production frequently moves to low-wage areas and low-overhead areas. For the products are mass produced

[3] Raymond Vernon, *Metropolis 1985; An Interpretation of the Findings of the New York Metropolitan Region Study* (Cambridge, Mass.: Harvard University Press, 1960), 252 pp.

and can be shipped very easily. The part of the garment industry that stays in New York City is the sector related to changing styles, where creative people are a necessity. The typical operator is located within a very small area of Manhattan, where he has a little showroom for his models, as well as his factory. He must have a place where the buyers can come, and the buyers in this branch of industry not only want to go to one city, but they want to go to one area in one city.

This industry, which is one of the most competitive industries in the United States, is confined to a little strip in mid-Manhattan and anybody who is anybody in it can survive only if he operates in this area. This is because those involved are small operators and a tremendous number of services have to be provided for them. People who can repair sewing machines, and people who can give various other specialized services are required. These services are supported jointly. Also, if one man runs out of green thread, his competitor will lend it to him, because the competitor knows that if he runs out of green thread, he wants to be able to borrow it. The result is that neither has to keep enormous inventories, thereby cutting down on overhead. Of course, too, there are "trimmings jobbers" who stock small items like thread and maintain sales and stock rooms of cloth which they will sell in small quantities. Those are the sort of thing that can be done only by a close association and can be done best in an area which is large enough to have the diversity to support the services and the facilities that are needed.

The analogy in the professions is very simple. If a lawyer in a large city has a complex, peculiar case, instead of needing a specialist in his firm, he knows there is one in the city whom he can call upon. This is important in the highly specialized economy and highly specialized society in which we live. And it is one of the reasons why large central cities survive and have a unique economic function.

The process of urbanization is continually extending over increasing areas. Starting in the eastern Mediterranean in ancient times it spread to northern Africa, to Europe, to the Far East, and to the Americas. Now it is extending to the so-called underdeveloped areas. The thing that is so striking about the phenomenon today is that it occurs in highly industrialized areas and in underdeveloped countries, under capitalism, and in areas of socialism. It seems to be an inescapable product of growth and population increase. Though land resources are limited, population is not, and the excess of people over land opportunities causes them to congregate in cities to seek employment and a better life.

Urbanization in this nation is different only in degree and detail from what is going on in nearly every other country in the world. Here we have built a massive ring of suburbs around our central cities, and it is in the outlying areas that we have the greatest growth. In other Western countries the same process is a little different because they have a larger degree of control over land use and greater participation of the government in the development. The new towns in Great Britain, and the very exciting new town, Tapiola, in Finland, are striking examples of this situation.

A large part of the migration to the cities in the United States has been by Southern Negroes. Less than fifty years ago the majority of Negroes lived on farms. Today over 70 per cent live in urban areas. Significantly, the proportion of the non-white population resident in central cities increased from 39 to 51 per cent in the last decade. In the District of Columbia 54 per cent of the population is colored; in Baltimore 35 per cent, in Atlanta 39 per cent. This is an extremely high concentration of non-white population when one realizes that non-whites constitute only about 10 per cent of the total national population and have remained fairly steady at that figure over the last hundred years.

The migration of white people, on the other hand,

has been not only from the rural areas but also away from the central cities. Both whites and non-whites have moved away from rural areas. The non-whites have tended to go to the central city where they have joined others who were already there because they have not had access to the suburbs. The whites have come from rural areas, some to the central cities, but many directly to the suburbs. Other whites who were already in the central cities have tended to move out to the suburbs.

This has resulted in some rather interesting population distributions, as far as age is concerned, generating economic as well as social and political implications. In the last decade the only age groups that increased among the white population in five of our large cities are those from 10 to 14 years old and those over 65. In New York City, for example, the white population declined more than 475,000 between 1950 and 1960. But the number of whites aged 55 and over increased by more than 265,000.

A similar pattern can be found in other large cities. In the metropolitan areas of the country the number of persons 65 years and over, without distinction to race, increased 45 per cent. Outside the metropolitan areas the number of persons in that age bracket increased only 25 per cent. The families which have the most children, whose adult members are in the prime of life and have the greatest economic productivity, are concentrating in the suburban areas. At the same time there has been a sizable increase in the number and the proportion of senior citizens in our population, bringing with it additional problems. Much of this increase of senior citizens is concentrated in the central cities.

There is another recent development worthy of note. It is the movement of some of our people from the suburbs back to the central city. This has been a very interesting phenomenon because a few decades ago there were two schools of thought among land economists and sociologists. Those of us who felt that people might move back were decidedly in the minority. Our feeling was that people would return to the city if desirable accommodations were available. Those articulating the opposite point of view cited past behavior and opinion polls.

The behavior of people is dependent upon their experience, and there is little use of taking polls to decide what people *think* they will do. A man cannot realistically answer the question as to whether he would buy a compact car, as we discovered in this country, until he sees one. Behavior patterns are unpredictable unless there are real choices and real possibilities of experience.

It is, of course, far too soon to assert that the movement back to the central city is a major trend. It is something that I believe will continue to the degree that we are able to do a good job in making the central cities more attractive. But it does not provide a basis for believing that the growth of suburbs will abate.

We are developing heavy concentrations in the central cities of the poor, the old, and the discriminated against. As a result, problems of crime, social unrest, and other ills which are associated with urban living have become accentuated. These things cost a great deal and place an extremely heavy burden on tax resources because, with the movement of population, the higher taxpaying people have been moving away from the central city. People who require greater public expenditures for certain services are remaining or moving in without the taxpaying ability to meet these costs. But this is not completely a central-city problem. The suburbs, too, are getting a large number of people with moderate income who can pay some taxes but bring with them tremendous tax burdens—to wit, children. For one of the great tax problems of modern times is the support of adequate schools.

All this has serious implications for federal policy.

The state and federal governments should intervene to transfer tax revenues from the more affluent areas to the less affluent ones. Various fiscal devices are being, and have to be, used. Federal and state programs for aid to education are an example. Theoretically and traditionally education in this country is a responsibility of local government. But now it is often impossible to support an adequate school system out of local tax revenue. This is why we have large programs of state aid, and why there is the issue of federal aid to education.

Our cities, by their very nature, tend to inhibit the mobility essential to their existence. If we continue to depend almost exclusively upon the automobile and the truck for movement of people and goods into and out of the central cities we are in for difficult times. Someone has said that in New York City, where fortunately there is a good rapid transit system, if all those who use it came in automobiles, we would have to take all Manhattan Island south of Sixtieth Street and make a parking lot of it. This would solve the problem because then most people would have nothing to come to.

We have made studies and know that, with present facilities, the fare box will not support an adequate mass transit system. This is a vicious cycle, because when the fare box does not support a good transit system, service is cut back. When this occurs less people use it; when less people use the transit system, income goes down and service is reduced further. The result is that in the last decade about fifty or sixty cities have lost all forms of mass transit. In this situation, the Kennedy Administration proposed grants to assist the cities to get the capital equipment they needed.

This is an example of where the tax power of the areas which are involved are not adequate to do the job, and where the Federal Government is therefore proposing to help out. This example also has a very interesting twist. Obviously there cannot be an effective rapid transit system that stops with the city line.

Thus, we have proposed that, to be eligible for this assistance, a transit plan must cover the majority of the district which would be served by the transit system.

The economic resources of this Nation are concentrated in the urban areas. The controls are there, and the financial determinations are made there. The economic brainwork of the country is concentrated in these urban areas. The pattern of this concentration is changing, however. The large industrial concentrations of the past are being decentralized and moved into smaller communities. But the managerial functions are shifting more to the central city.

At the same time there are concurrent developments. There has been a tremendous increase in the amount of space that is needed by management, and this was, for a time, accentuated by the limitations upon construction imposed by World War II and the Korean War. Increasingly, a good front for many businesses is quite important, while air conditioning and all the other conveniences that a modern office building provides take up room. A tremendous amount of managerial activity is incident to record-keeping, utilization of electronic devices, communication, and in the planning and processing work of a large business. Office space per worker is also increasing.

All of this is a reflection of the concentration of managerial functions in the central city at the same time that they are becoming more complex and require more space and more money. Certainly we see this in occupational distribution. Our working population is shifting from blue collar to white collar. For it is in the managerial, clerical, and the professional occupations that the increase in employment is concentrated.

The growth in urbanization will mean an even more rapid increase in the demand for the comforts of living. The extent to which our people expect, demand, and get certain amenities of life is one of the things that has been uniquely evident in this country. Doubtless the consumer credit system is in part responsible. The resulting expansion in purchasing power goes far in explaining why our productivity in consumer goods, such as washing machines, refrigerators, bathroom equipment, and kitchen equipment, is so superior to that in any other place in the world.

The concentration of an increasingly large proportion of our population in urban areas also will bring about the need to devote an increasingly larger proportion of our national income to the public sector of the economy. The sort of thing that John Kenneth Galbraith talked about in *The Affluent Society* is happening of necessity. We have a population dependent as never before upon public facilities—public schools, public sewage disposal, public water supply systems, fire departments, police departments, bridges and highways, and welfare departments. These facilities and services are taken for granted without thought as to their economic implications. When we compute the millions and millions of dollars that are put into our highway system and when we consider the cost of our schools, we come to realize that an increasing proportion of our national income and our national productivity flows into the public sector. In 1951 new public construction expenditures accounted for 2.8 per cent of the gross national product; ten years later the figure was 3.3 per cent.

We have done a phenomenal job of housing certain population groups in this country. For middle- and upper-income families, living in the suburbs, we have gone far toward meeting the demand. New family formation is at a plateau. A new breakthrough in new marriages —new marriages produce new families and new families produce a demand for new homes—was formerly expected in the latter half of the 1960s. Now there is a question as to the nature of its impact upon the housing market during this decade, since most recent demographic projections suggest that the age group 20 to 29 will increase almost by a third between 1960 and 1970, but the number of those 30 to 49 years old will remain stable. It is this latter group which constitutes the basic home buyers in our economy. Yet, the increase in the number in their twenties should sustain and possibly expand the demand for multi-unit accommodations during the decade, while augmenting the expansion of demand for new one-family homes.

There is a great need for housing for certain sectors in the population. We have not, we do not, and apparently we cannot produce an adequate amount of housing for low-income families without some form of public assistance. The filtering-down process, discussed in more detail in Chapter II, does not filter down fast enough. In addition, filtering has its problems. Much of the housing that filters down was built for an earlier period. It is architecturally obsolete, providing big rooms with high ceilings that poor people cannot afford to decorate or heat.[4] There is also physical deterioration. After a house acquires a certain age, the plumbing, the heating, the electrical system, the mechanical parts of it which are the most expensive, just get to the point where they can no longer be patched. At that time real expenses are required to make the structure usable.

There is the additional problem of lower middle-income housing. Here are the forgotten people of housing. They are those who have too much money to get into public housing and not enough to get decent housing in the private market. Finally there is a large unmet

[4] The writer was struck in a recent visit to a rehabilitation area in Baltimore to see that a prudent investor who was gutting an old building which had high ceilings was lowering them by some twenty inches, since the new user group will be lower middle-income families for whom high ceilings would spell uneconomic heating and decorating costs.

demand for shelter designed to meet the needs of our senior citizens.

Urbanization has political implications too. The tradition in this country has been, for several centuries, that of an agricultural nation. Our state legislatures and our Federal Legislature have been heavily weighted by persons representing rural districts at the same time that our urban districts have been grossly underrepresented. There are certain states where it takes twenty times as many votes to elect a representative from a city or a suburb as it does from a rural area. But this is changing. In fact the change is taking place at a more rapid pace than could have been anticipated a decade ago.

The concentration of certain ethnic and economic groups in the central cities has complicated the issue. We have had, for a very long time, the dichotomy of interests between rural and urban areas. We also have the conflict of interest between the central city and the suburbs. Yet many problems demand coordination and cooperation between the central city and the suburbs. If we have economic, class, and color lines where the suburbs represent one set of either real or imputed interests (and it doesn't make any difference whether they are real or imputed) and the central city another, then the day of cooperation is going to be delayed. As a consequence there will be competition and conflict within the urban complex. We face this situation today.

Urban problems are difficult and vital. They are basic to most Americans and they will not fade away. By the same token, these issues are as exciting as is urban living. Those who deal with them face many frustrations but seldom are they bored.

The City College and the Urban University

In many respects the city colleges of New York are the prototype of urban institutions of higher education.

They have accelerated the urbanization of newcomers. In the process the city colleges facilitated economic mobility and the attainment of higher social status for the sons and daughters of immigrants.

It is therefore significant that this extensive system of municipal higher education has entered into a new era. In 1962, there finally was brought into being the City University of New York. This new institution unites the seven municipal colleges. By this step formal recognition was given to the emergence over the past 115 years of a group of municipally supported institutions of higher learning distinguished by their diversity and yet united by their dedication to educational opportunity for all who live in the municipality.

The City University of New York, which consists of City College, Hunter College, Brooklyn College, Queens College, and the three community colleges, is truly a university in the same tradition as the great urban universities of medieval Europe. The doors of these colleges have been open to all who came with the desire and capacity to learn. Representatives of all nations, members of all races, and believers in all faiths have been attracted to them.

Many of the medieval universities began as schools, clustered about the cathedral which was the intellectual and cultural center of the medieval towns. Today the university has become such a center for the modern city. As the cities gave birth to universities, so the universities have spawned the ideas and the energies which have enriched the city and brought forth nations.

As each immigrant group has come to New York, it has seized the opportunities to be found in the public schools and municipal colleges to move rapidly upward in social and economic status. Sometimes this was a family endeavor, as mother and father, sisters and brothers pooled their industry and their resources to enable one of the sons or daughters to get a higher education. Sometimes it signified rebellion against the family, as younger persons turned their backs on their cultural heritage to struggle for a place in a world their parents found strange and unfriendly.

Often, so often, the cost of an education, involving menial labor to stay alive, grinding study to maintain grades, physical and emotional exhaustion, was enormous, even though the tuition was free. The sum total of all the sacrifices made to achieve the "free" education offered by the colleges in the City University of New York probably is far greater than that exchanged for the instruction at our most expensive institutions.

Some of the most outstanding graduates of these colleges have been the children of immigrants. Bernard Baruch was the son of a surgeon who came to this country from Posen in the Polish Corridor. Felix Frankfurter was brought to this country by his parents in 1894 from Vienna. Gustave Rosenberg, Chairman of the Board of Higher Education that governs these colleges, is also the son of immigrants. In one of his recent addresses he said, "To the immigrant child, to the child of the slums, education is at once the key to a better life and a key to service. The early recognition of public responsibility for higher education has helped to make and keep New York the great city that it is. The whole nation is now waking up to the fact that higher education must be for the many—all those who have the capacity to profit from it—not for the few."

The students at the colleges in the City University of New York have accurately reflected over the years the shifting source of newcomers in New York. Thus, as immigration to this country has declined in recent years, there has been a decline in the proportion of students at the municipal colleges who are the children of immigrants. In time, we can expect to see in their places the children of those who have been swept into the city by the vast wave of migration from Puerto Rico and the South. The children of these migrants face barriers higher than those of language and culture, however.

When the children of immigrants had broken with the customs of their past, had adopted the behavior patterns and values of middle-class America, and had achieved an education that enabled them to earn a middle-class income, they moved into the mainstream of American life. But the sons and daughters of nonwhites, even when they have achieved higher education, are still set apart by the barrier of color. And many of them, realizing this, have not felt the drive for a higher education that seized the children of immigrants.

Oscar Handlin, who comes from an immigrant family and was graduated from Brooklyn College, has written of the newcomers. In a recent book with that title,[5] he delineates the special problems which face Negroes and Puerto Ricans in New York City. Noting the new ecological patterns of the city, the changing labor market, and the differences in backgrounds, he says that for them migration was not the decisive break it had been for the European. He relates this to our inability to view these people in the perspective of the city's earlier experience. They are, historically, but the most recent in a long and uninterrupted stream of newcomers. Our reluctance to view them as such is both a cause and a consequence of their less rapid rate of assimilation into the dominant culture.

The problems of urban areas are of increasing scope and complexity. They demand a new partnership, involving government, business, charitable foundations, and institutions of higher learning. Out of this must emerge centers where there will be accumulations of the best data and analyses available: sources of information as to the status of projects, proposals, and plans; and current information on the nature of research completed, under way, and in the planning stages. Our universities must not only be major participants in these

---

[5] Oscar Handlin, *The Newcomers* (Cambridge, Mass.: Harvard University Press, 1959), 171 pp.

centers but also actively engaged in the training of men and women who will be the future practitioners in urban matters. Colleges and universities have a responsibility for exposing the maximum number of their students to the urban culture and its problems.

There are many fields where more needs to be known. All areas which provide shelter and employment need an economic base and that base is constantly changing. City-oriented colleges and universities should therefore be active participants in maintaining and providing the research required to meet this need.

There are no problems in America as baffling or important as those relating to government and urban growth. By now it is a truism that the geographic boundaries of effective governmental units and those of urban problems do not coincide. A few decades ago much discussion was centered upon metropolitan government, a device designed to bring all parts of an urban complex, its central city or cities and its suburbs, under the jurisdiction of a single local government. It was a simple, logical proposal. Only one thing was wrong. The people involved did not, and have not, accepted it. Perhaps it was too logical to be workable.

In the abortive efforts to establish metropolitan government, we learned much about our urban areas. One of the things made crystal-clear is that there are fears of subservience on the part of suburban areas toward central cities and vice versa. Some of these fears are justified, some are imaginary, and others are not yet understood.

Today, a most crucial and apparently difficult function of the teacher in our public schools is to reach the children of the most recent newcomers. The city-oriented colleges can and should devote their efforts to understanding this phenomenon. They should analyze the situation and then prepare future teachers to comprehend the social, economic, and cultural factors involved. These teachers should be able to appreciate the fact that people who have limited opportunities do not, and will not, adopt dominant values which are, unfortunately, meaningless to them. There is need for research into, and appreciation of, the values which deprived peoples develop. New and more realistic teaching materials are required. We need men and women in our schools who comprehend that people of all ages are the products of the experiences, hopes, and aspirations with which they can identify.

This problem of adequately prepared teachers is but one of the challenges which lie before us. It is, indeed, a specialized segment of a larger sphere. Our urban communities, with their economic, social, cultural, governmental, and educational problems, will require a large corps of trained people. This is a field of employment which should and can have real attraction to urban college students. Since their roots are in the city and its environs, and most of them know what urban life means, they have seen or experienced the process of urbanization. For many of these students, there are less impediments to recognition, and greater opportunities for full participation, in public service than perhaps any other professional area.

Those students dedicated to improving the urban environment enter a thrilling and rewarding experience.

The urban university today functions in a situation which is unique and difficult. This is primarily a consequence of the population explosion. Some notion of the magnitudes involved can be derived from a few statistics. For example, since 1920, the number of our people at college enrollment ages and their proportion in the population have been steadily increasing. From 8,805,020 in 1950, the number had increased to 9,167,-783 in 1960 and was projected to grow to 13,761,302 by 1970. Thus, while only 52,000 students were in college in 1870, today over 3.5 million are enrolled, and it is estimated that the figure will be 7 million in 1970.

President Kennedy stated that if the colleges and universities are to accommodate such a level of enrollment, they will need twenty-three billion dollars in new facilities by 1970. Today, those concerned with higher education are asking: "How are our colleges and universities going to meet the demands we see ahead of us? How much can they expand; how quickly can they do so?" There is little question that the publicly supported institutions, both urban and non-urban, will have to absorb most of the expansion. However, the urban colleges and universities will be expected to make the major contributions.

Most urban universities are located in the older sections of cities, close to neighborhoods where urban decline has occurred, both physically and socially. These are the areas of high land costs and high densities. Expansion of physical plant by the university will occasion the dislocation of families and small businesses, and many of the latter are marginal with inadequate resources to absorb the disruptive consequence of moving.

To add to these problems is the long-standing conflict between town and gown. Thus many colleges and universities are viewed with distrust or hostility, or both, by the townspeople or those who live in their shadow. Unfortunately, some of these institutions traditionally neglected to offset the adverse opinion of themselves in the community. But now it is clear that they are a part of their communities, whether they like it or not. Today, the town and gown have got to get together if either is to survive. Thus, our institutions of higher learning face problems of public relations. Some are solving them.

Unless the city which contains the university is healthy and vigorous, it is a threat to the institution. Unless the institution better serves the city, it will not merit or receive the type of cooperation it needs to expand and prosper. In city after city, under the urban renewal program, expansion of university campuses has provided a significant part of local matching funds required by the Federal Government for urban renewal. The number of colleges and universities participating in such programs increased from less than half a dozen in 1960 to almost seventy as of July, 1963. At the same time the local redevelopment agency facilitates acquisition of acreage for university expansion it provides public responsibility for relocation of uprooted families and businesses. There is an additional dividend to the communities where universities expand with the aid of the urban renewal program. Such action assures that the growth of the universities will occur within the framework of the over-all development of the cities.

There is also a pressing need for development of the generalist, who, for want of a better term, we call "urbanist." This is a person who has a real comprehension of the urban process. In my opinion this person needs more than a smattering of general knowledge: rather, training in a particular discipline with orientation toward the problems of the city. I am confident that the need for such thinkers and operators will continue to expand and that we must develop better techniques for identifying and preparing such people.

One of the places where this training and its perfection can and should be nurtured is in the urban universities. This is because of the nature of the problems involved and because of the backgrounds of many of those who attend these institutions. This training will in no way divert these universities and colleges from their current activities, for there are few of them that are not now involved with operating problems of the very type that urbanists must face.

An increasingly important role of the urban university is, in fact, no more than an expansion of a service it has long provided in varying degrees. A *raison d'être* of all institutions of higher learning and of most urban areas is the development and preservation of our culture. Today, as never before, the urban universities have to participate in this process. In one area, it may involve music for young people, in another it may be community drama or a little theater; elsewhere it may involve the display of new forms of art. Such activities are important—and they always have been—as a part of the normal functioning of a university. Now they are crucial as a means of assuring that our city colleges and universities become a part of the community where they are located.

These centers of learning need the cooperation of local government in almost everything they do. No less important is the understanding and participation of all local media of communication. Certainly the leadership of the community can be a real asset in accelerating the development of local educational institutions. One of the ways of attracting and encouraging community support is to involve increasingly the activities indigenous to a real university with the life of the community.

The urban areas of America must flourish. This involves more than just building pretty apartment houses or attractive town houses, as important as that is. It requires decent neighborhoods, served by adequate public facilities and adequate transportation. It calls for improved and more comprehensive planning. But most important it is a matter of developing communities that stick together and have a personality. Part of that personality, in my opinion, is a great university which serves the community and serves humanity.

Human Values in Urban Life

Man has gravitated to cities for many reasons. In early times, a principal motivation was protection. At a period when physical survival was basic, the city dweller walled himself and his neighbors into a veritable fort as a means of defense against human enemies. Subsequently, the city began to provide certain economic and cultural bases for a fuller and more meaningful existence. Long after it had served as a haven, the city survived as a center of trade and industry and as the focus of learning and culture.

Since the dawn of the Industrial Revolution man has migrated to cities in the Western world primarily in search of economic opportunities. In the urban areas, he has found more remunerative employment, superior investment opportunities, higher horizons of hope for his children, and a more varied and fuller life.

It is in the urban areas that social reform has had its incubation and most rapid progress. Cities have made the greatest advances in the development of education, and they have been the places where democratic participation and democratic institutions have flourished. Cities have usually been characterized by diversity in economic, ethnic, and class status. They also have afforded a greater degree of status mobility than the more stratified and static rural areas. These characteristics are due primarily to a basic historic role of urban centers, especially in the New World, where they have served as a point of induction for migrants of diverse backgrounds. The human values of urban life in America reflect the impact of old and new cultures and their mutual modification.

Cities have always been threatened. A few, like Pompeii, have been wiped out by natural forces. Others have suffered from destruction by man. Human enemies from without and dissension and revolution from within have frequently destroyed or captured and transformed them. They have always been harassed by social problems. For centuries, some men have considered cities as centers of evil and sought to destroy this symbol. More recently, we have been told that many urban residents develop guilt feelings about their association with cities. Thus, the recent escape to suburbia may have deep historical and psychological roots. Be that as it may, when technology perfected means of mass transportation, man was able to participate in the city's economic activities at the same time that he centered his family life beyond its borders. Once this occurred, a new concept of urban life, a central city with suburban satellites, developed. The metropolitan area became a reality, and with its rise there appeared a new cluster of urban problems.

In all of the city's problems, the key element has been human beings. People conceived and developed cities. People have constantly threatened them. People, congregating into urban centers, made them the complex social organism we contemplate when the word city is used. It is human beings who, today, are shaping the vast metropolitan areas which house some two-thirds of the population in this Nation. Consequently, it is in terms of people that urban problems must be conceived and their solutions developed.

We express our current concern for cities largely in terms of slum clearance and urban renewal. Most of the discussion deals with questions of the degree of federal responsibility, the amount of money that Congress should appropriate for the preservation and improvement of cities, the desirability of a cabinet post on urbanism, coordination of the highway program with city planning, and associated matters. In all of this, there are only occasional references to the human values of urban life.

The very semantics of our approach is sometimes unrealistic and frequently incomplete. We speak of slum eradication and ridding the city of all slums in a decade. Seldom do we pause to consider the human elements in the rise, development, and perpetuation of slums or the human costs of their clearance. Thus, emphasis is placed upon the buildings in the slums and little attention is paid to the people who inhabit them or to the reaction of the rest of the population to these people. Yet the values of slum dwellers are of crucial importance. They determine, in large measure, the behavior patterns of those who dwell in blight and influence the reaction of others to slum dwellers. The values of the dominant elements in urban areas, in turn, determine, in large measure, the opportunities and mobility of the present residents in slums and blighted areas. These and associated values, if understood and taken into account, would make efforts to preserve the city more realistic and successful.

As long as there were large waves of immigrants coming to this Nation, slums provided an inevitable port of entry. When these groups matured in America, individual members and their children moved out of the slums as they progressed economically and socially. In response to the opportunities and mobility available to them, many rapidly adopted dominant middle-class values and middle-class occupations and behavior. Those who remained in the slums—and there were far too many—were unable to make the adjustment and often displayed anti-social behavior. However, slums were no longer generally associated with immigrant origins.

With the cessation of large-scale European immigration during and after World War I, new groups were substituted to supply the labor requirements of an expanding economy. The majority were readily distinguishable by physical attributes. In addition, they were denied the degree of occupational and residential mobility afforded to earlier migrants. Slum occupancy, an inevitable first step in urbanization of most newcomers, became a permanent identification for most urban Negroes, Mexican-Americans, and Indians, as well as a large portion of Puerto Ricans. More important is the fact that non-white families with high levels of achievement and aspiration were, and frequently still are, forced to remain in slums and blighted areas. Thus the population of these areas has become inflated, and the number of individuals conditioned by a slum environment has been artificially augmented.

Slums in American cities today house families which hold a wide range of values and evidence a variety of behavior patterns. Some are households with female heads and are stable nonetheless; others may be ungrammatical but adhere to high moral standards; still others evidence all the attributes of middle-class behavior and are dedicated to its values, if not recipients of its rewards. All three groups have ambition and talent, but fight an uphill battle in maintaining respectability and achievement for themselves and their children. It was from these families that public housing made its earlier selections and its initial successes. It is these families which, if they have access to decent shelter in good neighborhoods, will immediately respond to the new environment.

In addition, there are many among the residents in slums and blighted areas who, with a minimum of assistance and guidance, could and would adjust to better housing and neighborhood facilities. One has the feeling that in the current emphasis of social work upon problem families, the individuals and households of this type are neglected. Yet their numbers are large and concern for their rapid assimilation into the mainstream of city life would materially facilitate slum clearance.

Certain elements now concentrated in the slums, however, present clear and well-defined problems. They include the confirmed middle-aged winos, the established prostitutes, the overt homosexuals, the hardened criminals, and the like, who either resist rehabilitation or require long-term assistance of a most intensive type. They are multi-ethnic and constitute the real "hard core." In addition, the classical problem families which usually evidence some form of anti-social behavior are well-represented among slum residents. If blight is to be arrested, there must be more effective community action to minimize the anti-social behavior of these families and individuals and to accelerate the rehabilitation of as many as possible.

Slum eradication is a very costly objective. Already we have seen how many millions of dollars are involved in clearing a few square miles in a given city. That is only the down payment. In addition, if urban areas are to be rendered desirable for living, large sums must be spent for good schools, better transportation, better street lighting, adequate police protection and the like. But the costs do not end here. They include recognition of the potential of cities for family disintegration, assumption of responsibility for assisting migrants to adjust to urban life, willingness to offer real equality of opportunity to all ethnic groups so that all will feel wanted and be able to develop a sense of responsibility. Most important, effective slum clearance and meaningful urban renewal involve a new attitude toward low-income peoples who constitute the bulk of those now concentrated in slums.

Most social scientists, writers, teachers, and social workers, as well as public officials, belong to the middle-class and frequently assume, unconsciously perhaps, that any values or patterns of conduct which do not conform to their standards are undesirable and should be changed. These opinion-influencers and operators often confuse adjustment with conformity, believing that only middle-class-oriented families can make an effective adaptation to urban life. We need to examine critically these postulates, recognizing that our newer concepts of the city and social consciousness will not permit a healthy urban society to ignore the least successful, nor will the disadvantaged accept their deprivations without protest and increasingly overt hostility. We shall not quickly create a vast number of households with middle-class values out of people who have been long neglected, misunderstood, and discriminated against.

Had slum clearance and neighborhood rehabilitation

been initiated at the turn of the century, they would have required public action to accelerate the assimilation of European immigrants. Today slum clearance and neighborhood rehabilitation call for far more action. Not only must we discover and provide techniques and machinery for rapid assimilation of the more recent migrants, but we must recognize that the social pathology of slums and blighted areas will persist as long as elements in our population are relegated to what seems to their members as an institutional submerged status.

Adolf A. Berle, Jr., has recently observed that "the working man . . . lives, thinks and feels not as an oppressed proletarian seeking to be saved by revolution but as a member of the middle class to whose children any position is possible." Our most recent migrants are not oblivious to this development. They, too, so far, have rejected proletarian revolution, but they react to a limitation on their mobility. The contrast between what America means to them and what it means to those who preceded them in the slums is a major factor in the inability of many to rise to middle-class status. It is also a basic cause of their frequent abandonment of hope and their expression of anti-social behavior.

Perhaps the most disastrous consequence of continuing discrimination and segregation is the conditioning of their victims to a submerged status. Individuals who face what seems to be a brick wall learn to stop hitting their heads against it. Only a few of them will believe it worth while to attempt to squeeze through an apparent opening. Most of them know, from bitter experience, that the breach may be only a path to another barrier. Others use the situation as a crutch and justification for not trying.

In the current wave, migrants who are non-white not only face restrictions because of color, but they, as well as low-income whites on the move, are entering urban areas which have changed drastically during the last quarter of a century. The United States has new insti-

tutions and new attitudes as it completes the transition
to a predominantly urban nation. This means not only
a shift from rural to urban values but a situation in
which urban values themselves are rapidly changing.
Even those individuals acclimated to, and familiar
with, life in a highly industrial society are forced to
make adjustments constantly. For an appreciable number of newcomers, the very dynamics of urban life present a striking and confusing contrast to a relatively
static rural background or an urban experience which
has been in a segmented and separated section of a city.
All of this complicates assimilation of newcomers at the
same time that lack of occupational and residential
mobility slows up the full development of earlier non-
white migrants and their children.

We can no longer ignore the growing number of individuals and families who are unprepared for urban
living or have given up trying to escape from the limitations of ghetto life. A major problem is to discover
how the migrant can be reached and what can be done
for the normal families, as against the problem ones, in
our slums and blighted areas. We need to communicate
where and how these families can avail themselves of
essential governmental and other services, identify the
nature of the most important of these services, indicate
the basic individual and family behavior required by
city life, and teach the minimum of skills in house-
keeping and environmental sanitation that are called
for in an urban setting.

We may not be prepared to meet these problems.
If so, the cities are in for further decay. Tearing down or
upgrading substandard housing alone will not solve
the problem of urban deterioration. Without a coordinated program for human rehabilitation and re-exami-
nation of the human values of urban life, demolition of
slums and rehabilitation of deteriorating areas will
probably result in greater dispersal of blight.

The flight of the middle class to the suburbs has been much discussed. It is an escape from changing neighborhoods, lower-class encroachment, inadequate public services, and inferior schools. It is also a drawing of status-conscious, socially mobile people to prestige areas where they feel their upward movement will be accelerated. But it is more. It is running away from the ugly facts of urban life; facts that have always existed but never for long on the doorstep of "nice people" who had the option of escape.[6]

In a middle-class-oriented society, slums serve an important role. By housing the most obvious of the deviants as well as the disadvantaged, the discouraged, and most individuals identified with groups marked for discrimination regardless of individual characteristics, they solace those whose values dominate the social order. Many are able to talk impersonally about "the poor unfortunates" or damn the "brutes." Others identify delinquency with certain ethnic or geographic origins and enjoy a double dividend of racial superiority and social irresponsibility. For some people the imperfections of society have no significance; the key is biological inferiority. Clearly, they must run away from any and all who belong to the "inferior" groups and thereby escape from any personal responsibility for, or involvement in, the rehabilitation of slum occupants.

There is a striking parallel between the exodus of middle-class families from the central city and the abandonment of public housing by the more stable households. On the surface, both phenomena appear to be racial, reflecting the flight of whites from non-whites. Careful analysis, however, casts doubt upon the adequacy of such an interpretation.

[6] The movement of middle-class families to the suburbs obviously involves more than flight from the central city. There are real and positive attractions of suburban living which would be operative were there no core area problems from which one might escape. Without the motivation of escape, suburbanization would be less rapid than it is.

Chicago, which is a most productive laboratory for the analysis of Negro-white relations, offers an impressive case study which cannot be accommodated within the racial theory. In the northern part of the city, the in-migration of mountain whites is blamed for the same social problems that are generally associated with the arrival of non-whites in urban centers. Similar situations exist in Detroit, Cincinnati, and Columbus, to mention but a few of the cities affected. It is clear, however, that this is a cultural problem, involving the adjustment of low-income rural people to a complex urban environment.

Middle-class families and low-income families with middle-class orientation are running away from households with social problems and deviant behavior. This situation cuts across racial lines. In the private housing sector, whites resent and flee from some other whites as well as from Negroes, Mexican-Americans, and Puerto Ricans. In public housing, whites and non-whites resent and flee from some non-whites. In those few instances where they have the opportunity, middle-class Negroes move away from whites, Mexican-Americans, and Puerto Ricans as well as from other Negroes whose values and patterns of living are incompatible with middle-class standards. Fair-skinned, middle-class Puerto Ricans quickly desert areas which are congested with new arrivals from the Island. Foreign-born and the children of foreign-born, who yesterday were the victims of class and ethnic prejudice, are often its perpetuators today. In the process, racial and cultural characteristics become confused.

Oscar Handlin, in *The Newcomers*, reminds us that running away from, and abandoning neighborhoods to, migrants is no new phenomenon in America. Generations ago the older settlers in our cities considered contact with foreigners a threat to their status. At that time, however, the urban environment was somewhat different. Cities were still young and undeveloped so that most of the out-movement of the established middle class took place within the city's limits, and its borders afforded the physical possibility of expanding space for all. But the process, its motivation and basic manifestations, was the same regardless of whether the repudiated group was German, Irish, Jewish, Polish, Italian, or Negro, Mexican-American, and Puerto Rican. Color complicates the matter principally by extending in time the period of group repudiation.

Revitalizing cities is more than a real estate operation. It involves reaching and assisting the residents of slums and blighted areas, and learning more about them and society's attitudes toward them in the process. In doing so, we will doubtless come to appreciate that some of their values, although strikingly different from those of the dominant groups in our society, are not only utilitarian but worthy of emulation. Many of their patterns of behavior, while unacceptable to the majority, may well be compatible with successful urban living. Some of their other patterns of behavior will require modification. To the degree that society discovers how to encourage these adjustments, it will develop tools to arrest the spread of blight and accelerate urban renewal.

Most of those who would save our cities have long been hesitant to face up to the problems outlined above. By doing this, they failed to comprehend the real nature of the institution they want to preserve. Cities, by definition, are cosmopolitan areas composed of a diversity of economic and social classes. In the United States rapid urbanization inevitably involves an increase in the ethnic diversification of our cities. We have a choice: minority groups can be contained in the central city, where they will increasingly displace middle-income families, or they can, as earlier migrants have done, move out of the core areas as they progress economically and socially. The choice we make will reflect and condition the human values which will characterize this Nation's urban communities of tomorrow.

If American cities are to be healthy, their inhabitants must have the tolerance of difference that urban life implies. Should we fail to give substance to such tolerance, current investments to renew our cities will prove to be most unproductive. Perhaps they should fail, because unless the human values of urban life are recognized and stressed, the city has no *raison d'être*.

Goals for Urban Development

America is unusual in that many of its cities were founded with, or soon acquired, some form of rational plan. Boston, of course, is an exception. The gridiron pattern, which has strait-jacketed the growth of Manhattan, was designed just 150 years ago. L'Enfant's plan for our Nation's Capital seemed as extravagant to some of his contemporaries as it does today to Lewis Mumford. The original street plans of many of our cities— from Buffalo to Omaha to Denver—were designed by land promoters who were certainly no less qualified than the designers of some of our more recent suburban subdivisions.

If there is one thing our city planners have learned, however, it is that people will not be imprisoned by their plans. In time the best of plans will be outgrown and will no longer meet the need for which they were intended. Even so, communities, like individuals, should have the intelligence to plan for their futures, and the sense to realize that the future will not necessarily conform to their plans. Planning is a continuous process. To be effective, an urban plan must have the participation and the agreement of those who live in the community. The only means of mobilizing this participation and reaching this agreement is through government.

The economic implications of planning for urban development are, of course, disturbing to some people.

Effective planning requires effective control of resources. Community planning means necessarily the substitution of public for private decisions in the use of land resources. The public interest in these decisions has always been recognized in this country. From the primitive town plans of the Colonial period up to the zoning regulations of today, the community has consistently asserted its right to regulate the use of privately owned land. Gradually the community has developed, as well, the principle that land may be taken and used for the general benefit of the community; for the construction of schools and public works; for slum clearance and low-rent housing; and, more recently, for improving the housing, industrial, commercial, and cultural resources of the community. Now we have reached a point in this evolution where communities need to be able to control the use of their remaining vacant land.

In our society, there still persists a strange suspicion of government, a sort of anarchic hang-over from the old frontier. To conquer that frontier, as the pioneers discovered, it was necessary to have machinery to arrive at community decisions. This meant creating the machinery of government. To conquer the new frontiers of the 1960s and the 1970s we also need government —not a government that tells people to do things they do not want to do, but a government that enables people to decide what they want and helps them to accomplish it.

Those of us in the present Administration have certain basic convictions about what the American people want in their urban environment. These are not convictions formulated in a closet. They are convictions forged in the heat of many controversies, and reflecting a consensus of all of them.

One of our convictions is that the small-town atmosphere of the nineteenth century has disappeared from our major cities and cannot be reclaimed. We believe, for example, that the city is a good place, that life in it can and should be desirable, and that what people like about it is the challenge of its concentration.

Another of our convictions is that Americans are not interested in living in a series of suburbs surrounding the ruins of their old central cities. We can see the steady movement of industry and offices and people away from the congestion and dirt and deteriorating services of the downtown to new suburban centers. Around most of our larger cities today are a series of such centers, all of them growing at the expense of the central city. We could, if it were what the American people wanted, design our course of urban development to continue and accelerate this trend.

To abandon our central cities, however, would be to forsake the cornerstones of our culture. A great city is far more than the sum of its parts. To fragment that city, and scatter its energies through a score of communities, would destroy the institutions that give it greatness and the culture they make possible. We are convinced, therefore, that the central city is far more than an underground control center. We are convinced that it is the cultural, commercial, and political nerve center of our metropolitan civilization.

Through planning and urban renewal programs we want to revitalize the central city. We want to open it up, by surgery if need be, so that it is accessible to all. We want to facilitate, not extinguish, the flow of people and ideas through the downtown area. We want to make it a place where people come not only to work and to shop, but to seek out the highest intellectual and cultural experiences available in their communities.

With the power to meet our destiny, however, goes the responsibility to resist the temptation to demand uniformity. The essence of urban culture has always been its diversity. This has involved many peoples and many cultures, and they have left their imprint upon the physical structures that surround us. Thus our cities have a wide variety of architecture. Today we attempt to build the best of contemporary design, beside the best of yesterday. It takes courage to do this and to refuse to be bound by little minds seeking consistency as we design the cities of our future.

Social diversity is another heritage that must be preserved. There is no place in the cities of our future for ghettos of any kind—ghettos of religion or of race. The ghettos that exist must, in time, be disintegrated. In their place must be built cities open to all Americans, whatever their differences. Our goal is not equality or leveling or wiping out the differences between Americans. Our goal is to enable Americans to live and work together so that their differences will become the strength, rather than the weakness, of America.

II THE RISE AND DEVELOPMENT
OF URBAN RENEWAL

The Rise of Urban Renewal

We have heard many suggestions about what has caused
the movements of peoples toward urban areas. Some
such suggestions are better fertilizers and improved
agricultural methods which have increased production;
technological discoveries which have made mass industries possible; improvements in transportation and communications which have made our populations more
mobile. The more one sees and learns of recent population movements, the more they suggest that, for reasons
far more complex than anyone has so far delineated,
our civilization has entered a new stage of development. One of our responsibilities is to analyze and attempt to understand the process.

In 1917 the Communists rode to power in Russia on
a wave of national revolution. Soon thereafter they
embarked on a program of forced industrialization and
collectivization of agriculture. For years all the energies
and resources of that Nation were poured into that
effort. The cost in violence and misery was enormous.
What were the accomplishments? Agricultural production was reorganized. Millions of persons moved from
the farms to cities, and with their labor a great new
industrial power was created. All of this was held up to
the world as an example of how an underdeveloped
nation can lift itself up by its bootstraps.

A similar development occurred much earlier in England where, in the eighteenth century, the Enclosure
Acts provided a great impetus to the growth of indus-

trialization and urbanization. In this Nation, the laissez faire economic policies of the nineteenth century facilitated large profits which contributed so much to the investment basis of our industrialization and concurrent urbanization.

The Communist program in the Soviet Union called for industrialization, industrialization required an urban labor force, and collectivization of agriculture brought about forced urbanization. But capitalist laissez faire in the United States, a country which, incredible as it may seem, is still in many ways dominated by its rural areas, produced much greater industrialization, urbanization, and depopulation of the countryside. Greece, which was a world power when Russia and America were the domain of savages, but now is considered an underdeveloped nation, has been swept up in the same process of urbanization although its political and economic policies cannot be equated with those of either the United States or the Soviet Union.

The indication seems to be that urban development, as we witness it throughout the world, does not depend in any fundamental way upon the economic philosophy of a people. However, any country, whether it be communistic, socialistic, or capitalistic; democracy, monarchy, or dictatorship, must reflect the impact of this vast, world-wide shifting of peoples.

By 1960 one-third of the world's population lived in towns or cities with populations of 2000 or more; this involved approximately one billion people. And it was a comparatively recent phenomenon because it is estimated that in 1800 the aggregate urban population could hardly have exceeded 5 per cent of the total, which would have meant 45 to 50 million people at that time. Thus, today the urban population exceeds the entire population in 1800, estimated at 960 million.

Some concept of the degree of concentration of population in larger cities can be illustrated by citing the percentage living in cities of 100,000 or over in 1960. In England and Wales, the figure was 60.2 per cent; for USSR 23.9; for the United States 61.8; for East and West Germany combined 43.9; for France 26.4. Other principal European nations varied from 42.5 per cent for Belgium and the Netherlands to 20.7 for Portugal. A country such as Ireland, which is thought of as agricultural, had 30.4 per cent of its people in cities of 100,000 or over in 1960. Argentina had over half its population in cities of 100,000 or more in 1960, and Japan only slightly less than half. Three additional South American countries had a third so concentrated. In addition to Egypt, several African nations had a quarter of their people living in cities of 100,000 and over in 1960.

It is worth reflecting, however, that there were cities long, long before there were nations. Many of today's nations are, in fact, the creations of cities. The Soviet Union is largely the vast extension, over centuries and continents, of Moscow, a trading post on the river routes from Scandinavia to Byzantium. The British Empire, in the same sense, is the reaching out around the world of the vitality of London, a river port and provincial capital of the Roman Empire. The United States, too, is but the effluence of a federation formed in part by a handful of colonial cities scattered along the Atlantic shore.

The "original thirteen colonies" were greatly influenced by bustling ports which provided a core for some surrounding farm land. Between the cities and the surrounding rural areas was wilderness. In those days the national government's lack of concern with urban affairs was not because those affairs were insignificant. If anything, those affairs were a basic and often integrated part of the total community. Even the legislative assemblies of our colonies were occasionally dominated by the cities, and the city dwellers made a significant contribution to the American Revolution.

But the cities were widely scattered, and the national government concerned itself only with the few things they had in common, namely, national defense, foreign relations, and commerce between the states.

In the nineteenth century a new nation emerged. Colonial and Revolutionary America were agricultural in outlook and economy. Yet they were also anchored securely to the urban areas. From every part of the world immigrants came to this country, 42 million of them, funneling through our port cities and pouring out across this vast vacant land to stake out farms and homesteads. It was not until the First World War that it became unmistakably apparent that the population tide had turned from the farms toward the cities. But long before this, there were straws in the wind. The proportion of homebuilding in urban areas was 57 per cent in 1890–1899, 65 per cent in 1900–1909, and 73 per cent in 1910–1919.

Our Congress began looking into the problems of slums in 1892 when less than 16 per cent of our people lived in cities of 100,000 or over. However, the national concern with urban problems really did not begin in this country until the depression of the 1930s, when the United States had to face a choice between doing something about urban unemployment or risk a complete economic breakdown. In Washington, D.C., in the early 1930s, an army of the unemployed, demanding government assistance, was dispersed by federal troops. Only a few months after that President Franklin D. Roosevelt was elected, and for the first time our National Government became involved on a large scale in urban affairs.

The primary purpose of what was done, however, was to stimulate the economy. We launched a large-scale public works program, which built courthouses, post offices, bridges, highways, and parks that are still landmarks in our cities. We began demolishing our slums, building public housing, and experimenting with model towns. We created a system of government insurance of home mortgages, and we established an agency to provide a secondary market for mortgages. This was as far as our National Government went until after World War II, when the country was faced with an unprecedented housing shortage. Then we acted, through a series of measures liberalizing mortgage credit, to induce the private housing industry to meet that shortage. And we undertook a new program of slum clearance, tied primarily to private redevelopment rather than public housing.

There was nothing very original about this new form of slum clearance. Denmark had undertaken an almost identical program in 1939, and had run into exactly the same difficulties we proceeded to encounter. In both countries the cities were encouraged to use their power of eminent domain to condemn slum areas, clear them, and sell them to private redevelopers. In both countries, the national government paid a share of the loss resulting from the resale, and the new owners had government assistance in obtaining mortgages at favorable rates of interest for rebuilding.

Despite all this, however, in both countries, areas were redeveloped with luxury apartments or commercial structures. In both countries the program was severely condemned for displacing the poor to provide facilities for the rich. And in both countries it became apparent that slum clearance is difficult, if not impossible, to achieve when there is a housing shortage. What a sobering testimonial it was, for us, to the folly of ignoring the experiences of other countries. What a dramatic demonstration of the wisdom of utilizing the channels of communication provided by international conferences and the exchange of information between nations.

In recent years Congress has gradually broadened the activities of our National Government in urban renewal. Our government has accepted its responsibility to assist cities, through loans and grants, in planning their future development and expanding the public facilities that are essential to that development. Our national budget now includes grants to local governments for urban planning, highways, hospitals, airports, and sewage treatment plants. Government loans are made for nearly every other kind of public facility, if private financing is not available.

The discussion now going on in this country over the creation of a Department of Urban Affairs and Housing and the general expansion of our national activity in the field of urban affairs are pretty good evidence that urban development *is* still emerging as an issue of national policy in this country. The reason that it is still emerging at this late date in our national development is because of the peculiar pattern of that development.

This Nation, to a very large extent, was settled by rural refugees from war and revolution. Many of them paused in our cities only long enough to push on toward the frontier and the promise of land. They had a very real distrust of that city, its morality, and its political turbulence; but, perhaps, more important is the fact that they saw economic opportunity in the frontier. Because of the long-standing fear of cities and the lure of land, the seat of our National Government was planted in a place far from any major city. Likewise, the capitals of some of our states were removed from the cities, often to slumbering country towns. It is apparent to all that our National Government has created, by its very presence in Washington, a city where none had existed before. In many other parts of this country state capitals, originally rural communities, have now also become cities.

In the older areas of the world, however, urban development has ebbed and flowed as great tides of population moved inward toward the cities, then dispersed again in the wake of great disasters such as invasions, earthquakes, plagues, famines, or fires.

The history of Amman, now the capital of Jordan, is an interesting example of this. For centuries it was only a pleasant village, hidden in an arroyo in the midst of what was once a fertile plain. Then the Romans conquered the country and transformed the village into a great provincial capital, called Philadelphia, serving a vast grain-growing region. In time their empire collapsed, the climate turned dry, the fields became dust, and nomads came to water their flocks amid the ruins of a deserted city. Then, about a century ago, Circassian refugees from the wars in the Caucasus between Russia and Turkey found their way to Amman and made it a village again. At the time of the First World War, Hussein, Hashimite King of the Hejaz, led an Arab army out of the peninsula that is now Saudi Arabia against the Turks. After the war he made Amman his capital.

Even then it was but a small city, with mud huts huddled among the crumbling ruins of the Roman amphitheater and palaces. When the war came between Israel and the Arab countries, thousands and thousands of refugees from the fertile plains of Palestine poured out across the desert and settled in Amman. And with their coming began a renaissance that has transformed the city again into a cultural and commercial center of the Middle East.

The lesson of Amman and many another of the ancient cities of our world is that they are far more durable than the nations of which they have been a part.

The national governments in the older areas of the world are a far more recent development than cities. They were, in fact, created in cities, by cities, and often for cities. They have usually been dominated by those who lived in cities. These governments have created a climate of political and economic stability which has enabled the city to flourish as never before.

Urban renewal, with which our National Government has been experimenting for the past dozen or so years, is an old, old story for the governments of many nations. When London was all but destroyed by fire in 1666, the rebuilding of the city was carried out under acts passed by Parliament and supervised by a board of six commissioners, three of them appointed by the King, and three chosen by the city. It was in every way a major national effort. The rebuilding of Paris by Baron Haussmann, a century ago under Napoleon III, was also a national effort, not unrelated to political realities. The wide avenues of that city, which still charm all who view them, were designed in large part to facilitate the movement of troops in the event of civil disturbance.

At the end of World War II, many of the cities of Europe and Asia were left in ruins. Almost two decades have flown by since then, and today the gaunt devastation has been swept away and magnificent new cities have arisen like a phoenix from the ashes. In nearly every case this, too, was accomplished with the guidance and assistance of national governments.

Urban development has been an issue of national policy in most countries for a long time. What impresses us today is the fantastic acceleration of national activity in this field. Urbanization is not new. The things that are being done to cope with it are not new. The means by which these things are being done are not very new, either. What is new *is* the great momentum which has developed behind this movement of urbanization—a momentum which has been building up for centuries, and shows every sign of continuing to build, and build, and build in the decades ahead.

An Early Appraisal

It is perhaps indicative of a significant trend in American governmental policy that by the mid-1950s discussions of housing and slum clearance in central cities dealt for the most part with privately-financed construction. This was in striking contrast to earlier concern with public housing and its problems. There was, however, no less need for low-cost housing than there had been in the past, and much of what is termed privately-financed construction enjoys some form of public assistance. One of the great apprehensions I had at that time was the tendency of advocates of various programs to imply or state that one special tool or one identified approach offered the answer to the housing problem of America.

The housing requirements of the Nation are so complex and so vast in magnitude that they cannot be conceived of in terms of public housing versus private housing or urban renewal versus construction in the suburbs. Of necessity, any successful approach must be a synthesis of these various devices. This synthesis had become difficult to effect in the post-World War II period since each element had already become identified with its own proponents and the principal champions of each were often the most deadly foes of some of the others.

No doubt, the then prevalent segmented-approach orientation reflected failure to outline clearly and categorically the goals of a housing program for America. It seems obvious, however, that certain elements must be involved. First and foremost, housing is for people, and it is adequate housing only when and if it meets the needs and suits the paying ability of the population. Secondly, a sound housing program must be developed within a concept of effective city planning. Of course, in 1954 most professionals in the field gave lip service to the importance of planning. However, there was far from complete agreement as to what good city planning involved, although progress had been made in realizing that it must be concerned with land use and the provision of those services and institutions which are needed in a modern community.

Discussions of slums and blight at that time reminded me of the general condemnation of sin. Few, if any, were in favor of these social ills, but there was, and is, a vast difference between being against sin and knowing what to do to eradicate it. Similarly, opposition to slums was, and is, far from commitment for their eradication or realization of the painful and slow process that is involved in effecting this objective.

There was one significant contribution which had been made by emphasis upon urban renewal. We had for the first time thought and spoken in terms of preventing blight as well as wiping out and controlling substandard housing. This had its advantages and its disadvantages. Among the former was the obvious one that more than a piecemeal job was implied, while the stage was set for demonstrating the need for a combination of the various tools and approaches to achieve the announced goal. By the same token, a tremendous potential of public support was created since the more comprehensive approach inspired and aroused local pride in its achievement. Finally, there were possibilities in this program for securing the maximum cooperation between local, state, and federal governments in carrying out urban renewal. Theoretically, at least, there should also have been a favorable climate for cooperation between public and private housing.

Among the disadvantages, the major one was already apparent by 1954. Because of the very magnitude of this undertaking, it could, and often did, bog down in execution. We were, therefore, faced with the possibility that urban renewal might be talked about rather than executed; that it could become the subject of a tremendous promotional program which would excite the imagination of the people without simultaneously providing effective vehicles for its execution. Actually, our horizons had been lifted and our concepts had been broadened. At the same time initial results had not been commensurate with the thinking, the planning, and the hopes which had brought urban renewal into the foreground as a program for housing in American cities.

In my analysis of residential segregation, published in the late 1940s,[1] I devoted a chapter to "Urban Redevelopment—A Threat or an Opportunity." The situation in the mid-1950s could have been summarized by substituting "Urban Renewal" for the term "Urban Redevelopment." Then, even more than in 1948, the threat in urban renewal loomed large and had been documented by experience. On the other hand, the opportunities under this program remained as a possibility and a challenge to those concerned with good housing and sound human relations.

Such progress as had been made in urban renewal raised serious questions and created serious problems for the disadvantaged. As one would expect, the displacement of the low-income recipients, the aged, and the non-whites under the program of slum clearance and rehabilitation had been disproportionately high. While this was almost an inevitable consequence, it had been accentuated because of the basic law and the administrative policies adopted by the Federal Government and by local authorities. We were developing a program which reduced the supply of low-cost housing at a time when there was an existing shortage of shelter of this type.

The idea of slum clearance germinated during the depression when there were many vacancies, so that substandard properties could be torn down and families relocated with a minimum of difficulty. That concept was carried over and still persisted in the mid-1950s, despite the fact that the Defense Production Program, World War II, and their aftermath occasioned large-scale migrations to urban centers and created an entirely different housing supply situation, a situation typified by a tight housing market.

Thus relocation had been facilitated under the public

[1] Robert C. Weaver, *The Negro Ghetto* (New York: Harcourt, Brace and Co., 1948), 404 pp.

housing program by the demand and supply relationship in the housing market. That relationship complicated the process as urban renewal got under way. Regardless of how much effort might have been expended and how socially oriented it might have been, the sheer lack of vacancies in standard dwellings would have militated against a successful relocation program at that time. In addition, of course, the emphasis of urban renewal was more on real estate than people. The reverse had been true of public housing.

One must not forget that during the Great Depression we had mass unemployment involving all class and occupational groups in our society. Today, we face class unemployment which directly affects but a segment of our people. Thus the initial stages of public housing were initiated at a time when a large proportion of the American people were living in dilapidated and substandard housing. Those displaced by the program represented a large occupational, ethnic, age, and color cross-section of the Nation. In more recent years, those displaced by urban renewal have been concentrated in lower-paid occupations and disproportionately composed of the aged and minority groups. Consequently, in its initial stages urban renewal felt less effective political pressures to do a good job of relocation at the same time that the housing market complicated the process.

During the early phases of urban renewal we were faced with a housing picture which made slum clearance workable only if it were coordinated with a large construction program and if that construction program were of such a nature as to provide additional units for low- and middle-income families of both sale and rental types. Many of the champions of urban renewal attempted to get around the situation by reviving a somewhat crude version of the filtering-down, or upgrading, concept, which asserted that any increase in the supply of housing immediately eases the pressure for dwelling units in all segments of the market. The October,

1953, issue of *House and Home*, which contained a comprehensive statement on urban renewal at the time, described the filtering concept.

> This high volume of new construction [required to facilitate urban renewal] need not necessarily mean building any great number of new homes specifically for occupancy by the people moved out of the slums. With more than 31 million people moving from house to house each year, the entire US population changes homes on an average of every five years, and surveys show that every good new house makes it possible for as many as 13 families to play musical chairs and each move to a nicer home. The end of this upgrading process is that for each good new home built one less family will have to live herded into an overcrowded slum tenement, or one more unit unfit for human use can be junked.

One difficulty with this concept is that it disregards the problem which faces minority groups in their quest for shelter. The filtering-down process is based on the existence of a free competitive housing market. Enforced residential segregation repudiates the basic idea of free competition in the housing market and, to the extent that any segment of the population is denied free access to the total housing market, the filtering-down process must suffer. If a large element of the population is so restricted, the process will bog down. Also, filtering becomes sticky if there is a housing shortage in low- and moderate-cost shelter, because, under these circumstances, there are wide gaps in the qualitative gradations in the market. This, clearly, prevents or impedes the easy movement of families from bad to slightly better or from medium to somewhat superior shelter. The magnitude of degree in upgrading, and sharp increases in rents or prices that may be required in individual moves, then become so great that economic forces require overcrowding or other undesirable occupancy patterns. They also occasion high rents.

Slums and blight are not the lone reflections of

physical decay. Occupancy patterns and standards are equally important. As a matter of fact, they often precede and forecast the physical deterioration. The type of overcrowding and improvised living which follows in the wake of the geographic expansion of the racial ghetto into surrounding areas of housing ill-designed to meet the pocketbooks of low-income families has been and remains a principal factor in the spread of blight and generation of slums.

This, too, was in part a reflection of administrative inadequacies in the early execution of urban renewal. A program which in theory would expose the need for, and require the creation of, additional housing units for displaced families had, in practice, proceeded without occasioning the prescribed increase in dwelling accommodations.

There is also another basic consideration which must be kept in mind. It is the fact that in most instances urban renewal has involved a major change in cost of housing. Slum clearance and rebuilding by private enterprise on the land made available through urban renewal usually produced much higher-priced housing. Thus, urban renewal generated two major problems: it created the need for relocation housing for those families which were initially displaced, and it involved permanent displacement of a large class of families formerly living in the areas affected by the new program.

From the beginning of the urban renewal program relocation has been a major issue. Problems of large dimensions developed in cities like Chicago, Detroit, and New York, where low-income families were either forced out by economic and political pressures, required to purchase second-hand properties at inflated prices, or were further overcrowded in contiguous areas already substandard or in the process of becoming substandard due, primarily, to over-occupancy. With the exception of those families which qualified for the available public housing (in which they had priority), the relocation experience could be, and was often, unfortunate and fraught with extreme hardship for many of those involved.

Occasionally areas subjected to renewal were occupied either by families which had created socially viable, if physically blighted, neighborhoods, or by a large number of homeowners, or both. Clearly, relocation of those who had been long identified with an area, who were attached to their neighborhood, and who had long utilized its institutions, created real psychological problems. For homeowners, both psychological and economic problems were involved. The former are obvious —the threat to security incident to displacement from a home that was owned by a family. The second was more complex—loss of real or imputed value incident to leaving an area which had sentimental and imputed great economic worth. This, too, was complicated by the difficulty of acquiring, in a tight housing market, a comparable dwelling with the equity derived from the old house.

Of course, as real as these costs were to some families, there was, and continues to be, a false assumption that every renewal area was a tightly integrated and socially stable neighborhood and that all relocation extracted, and extracts, major psychological and economic costs from those affected. While any forced displacement occasions inconvenience and a feeling of outrage incident to being forced to move on the part of many involved, especially the older residents, the areas selected for renewal in the larger cities were occupied predominantly by renters, most of whom move frequently. These were basically the same people who had been dislocated by public housing. There was little written about the latter's displacement, perhaps because the new housing was for low-income occupancy and because the loose housing market facilitated relocation.

At the same time, priority for displaced families in public housing projects, when combined with concentration of urban renewal areas on sites inhabited largely by non-whites, increased the proportion of colored tenants in subsidized projects. As a consequence, many racially integrated public housing projects in the North became predominantly or exclusively Negro developments largely as a result of the pressures created by the displacement incident to urban renewal. This development will be discussed in greater detail in Chapter VI.

Relocation often created additional slums and brought blight into new areas. This was particularly true where minority group families were concerned, since contrary to the filtering-down theory, they do not have access to the total housing supply and were usually relegated to only a segment of the total housing market. By mid-1950, among minorities urban renewal was referred to as "Negro removal." There was a danger that unless and until additional housing, available at low rentals or selling prices and open to all ethnic groups, was provided simultaneously with the demolition of substandard houses, we would often tear down slums in one neighborhood only to spread blight and create slums elsewhere.

In Washington, D.C., for example, where relocation was carried out with care and adequate records were maintained reflecting where families moved, some of the older residential areas were adversely affected. Southwest Washington was cleared only at the price of creating the need for additional clearance in parts of Northwest Washington and the spread of blight in a segment of the Northeast.

There was still another development which had social implications. It was the result of selecting for urban renewal those sites in which whites and non-whites formerly lived side by side under substandard conditions. In some instances, especially in Southern and border cities and some small cities outside the South, it was planned to redevelop these areas for the exclusive occupancy of white families. Even when this was not clearly indicated in the local plans, it would sometimes become a *de facto* situation due to elimination of minority groups on economic rather than racial grounds. Where, in a few Southern cities, there had been a protest against this, a compromise was sometimes reached involving a proposed re-use for other than residential purposes. Thus, a slum area formerly housing both Negro and white families was proposed as the location for industry or a public institution. Urban renewal too often seemed to be an instrument for wiping out racially integrated living in one area at the same time that it failed to provide for an equal degree of racial integration on the site or in another section of the city.

In a situation where relocation was often poorly done and human suffering frequently occasioned, the other defects of renewal became magnified out of proportion to their true incidence. This, too, was a function of the fact that renewal, at best, is a slow process. As a new program, it was subject to mistakes and faulty execution. Thus one of the principal criticisms of it in the mid-1950s was the amount of vacant land that lay unused.

As pessimistic as this picture may have been, there were several rays of hope as early as the mid-1950s. One arose from the fact that a real job of urban renewal cannot be effected unless the defects which have been outlined above are corrected. It is significant that in Washington, D.C., where a total program had been envisioned and outlined, redevelopers were committed to open occupancy in the new housing which was to be built in renewal areas. This meant that white and non-white families would be living together in a limited amount of public housing adjacent to the redevelopment and in privately-financed, upper middle-income housing in the redevelopment. Actually, with the exception of the public housing developments in the area, the degree of non-white participation was expected to be relatively small, due to income distribution among

non-whites. It was contemplated to be significant, however, insofar as it represented the stamp of governmental approval on open-occupancy housing at the
higher income ranges where prestige values are important. By the same token, there was every reason to believe that elsewhere in the city the concentration of
lower-income non-whites in racial ghettos would probably increase under the new program. This, of course,
was facilitated and accelerated by the movement of
white families from the city to the suburban areas outside the limits of the Nation's capital at the same time
that the non-white population was increasing.

By 1954 there were unmistakable evidences that
urban renewal, while failing to solve the housing problems of minorities, was forcing public officials and
private redevelopers to face up to the issue. A few involved in urban renewal were realizing the impediment
to their objectives inherent in residential segregation
and its restrictions upon maximum utilization of the
housing supply. Others were talking and thinking in
terms of more and better Negro housing. All, or almost
all, had come to realize that something had to be done
in the realm of housing for minorities and for low- and
moderate-income households as a whole.

The earlier mistakes in relocation had also aroused
public anger and political pressure. Consequently, there
was evidence that many local agencies, particularly those
in large cities, were attempting to do a better job. All
involved in the program came to realize that valuable
time was lost and many problems were created when
sites remained vacant. Related to this, of course, were
the difficulties in securing competent redevelopers.
However, out of the mistakes and experience came
greater understanding of this new effort.

Even more important from the point of view of public acceptance of urban renewal was the fact that a few
developments were moving into the execution stage.
They were tangible evidences of the potential of the

program, indicating its capacity for revitalizing core areas, restoring economic health in the heart of the city, and affording an effective vehicle for advanced city and site planning. As an instrument for clearing slums, arresting physical decay, and providing attractive housing in the central city, urban renewal had evidenced real promise.

Color, Class, and Urban Renewal

Urban renewal has opened a Pandora's box in several fields. It has occasioned a fresh look at slums; it has given rise to renewed discussion of racial balance in neighborhoods; it has inspired new thought and approaches relative to the racial and class composition of schools in the central city; and of course it has intensified research in the fields of housing, city planning, and municipal government.

Since one of the principal objectives of urban renewal is to attract more middle-class families back into the central city and slow down the exodus of middle-class families from the inlying areas, much of the current discussion about color and class is oriented around these goals. There is, however, a tendency to treat current problems as though they were unique and devoid of historical precedents. Actually, this is not only untrue but dangerously misleading.

Since in many American cities a principal wave of low-income migrants is composed of readily identifiable members of color minorities, there is a tendency to identify the problem as one of race alone. This is inaccurate and unfortunate. Identification of the decline of central cities with the encroachment of non-whites (and in a few places Mexican-Americans or Puerto Ricans) upon established middle-class neighborhoods reflects our consciousness of color. It does more. Such superficial analysis weakens our capacity to deal effectively with the problems of our cities. The color and class aspects of these problems are frequently intertwined but neither should be ignored. Any effective program must recognize both and learn to deal with each.

On the other hand, it would be sheer sophistry to ignore existing demographic and ecological changes, long-standing racial attitudes, and the current economic forces which operate in the housing market. Because of these circumstances, the arrival of increasing numbers of non-white families may, and often does, lead to the departure of previous middle-class whites. This long-recognized phenomenon has recently been expressed in terms of a "tipping point" theory, which says that there is in any neighborhood a point at which whites will move out when the proportion of non-whites reaches a certain size. Unfortunately for planners and administrators, one recognizes the "tipping point" only when it has been exceeded.

Many factors are involved in the desertion of a neighborhood. First there is the economic climate. In a period of general prosperity, transition is accelerated. The same situation occurs in a loose housing market. The location of the neighborhood involved is also important. Factors tending to stabilize middle-class occupancy include proximity to, and identification with, institutional facilities, such as in the area around a university or college or around long-established religious facilities.

Access of minority and low-income families to a formerly white middle-class neighborhood is not always a consequence of whites' desertion of an area in the face of the encroachment of new user groups. Often it results from vacancies caused by the movement of earlier residents and failure of other middle-class whites to replace the former occupants. The cause of the desertion of such neighborhoods is usually the attractiveness of other areas. They may be suburban subdivisions or, as in the case of the East Side of Manhattan, a new prestige location in the central city. Once the vacancy rate becomes high, as it did in New York City's West Side, owners and property managers are happy to substitute new user groups rather than suffer greater losses.

From early days, middle-class Americans have wanted distance between themselves and the newcomer. That desire has been accentuated by two recent developments; the rise of prestige-laden, single-class, homogeneous suburban areas; and the identification of color with a large number of low-income migrants. The recent concern of Americans with the quality of education has, of course, occasioned increasing emphasis upon good schools.

As long as there was ample space within the city limits and no effective modes of rapid transportation, most of the outward movement of middle-class families occurred within the city proper. The streetcar, automobile, and bus, as well as under-utilized railroad lines, changed the situation, by opening large areas of virgin land removed from the central city for housing development. This process was beginning when the great impetus to Negro migration occurred during World War I. Low-income colored Americans from the South poured into many Northern cities, replacing, as the new source of unskilled and semiskilled labor, the earlier European immigrants who were no longer available during and after the hostilities. Not only were the newcomers mostly poor and ill-prepared for urban life, but they were also dark-skinned. Race and color joined class in rendering them forbidden neighbors.

Middle-class whites, led by the real estate fraternity, frequently resorted to racial housing covenants and zoning to contain non-whites in a restricted area. Low-income whites, only slightly less undesirable in the eyes of the middle-class, sometimes used intimidation, violence, and threats to assert their Americanism. On the part of the middle-class whites, this was a manifestation of class as well as racial prejudice; on the part of the low-income whites it was primarily racial. Yet lower-class whites and Negroes frequently shared the same residential areas and faced the same disabilities of poor neighborhoods. Class was often more important than color in neighborhoods which failed to offer prestige or adequate protection and public services to any residents, regardless of race.[2] The early governmental policy of segregation in public housing subsequently served to accentuate color consciousness in low-cost housing at the same time that it reflected the strategic role of authority in establishing racial patterns.

World War II brought in a new stream of Negro, Mexican-American, and Puerto Rican migrants to the urban North and West. It also brought greater residential segregation. Initially this too represented resistance to the expansion of land space available to non-whites and, most recently, abandonment of segments of the central cities to them. Several factors played an important part in this. The Federal Government through the Federal Housing Administration had facilitated phenomenal expansion of suburban construction. Low downpayments and a longer repayment period for mortgages had made a significant part of this available to white middle- and lower middle-income families. At the same time FHA accepted the concept of homogeneous neighborhoods and, until 1947, the instrument of the racially restrictive housing covenants. Higher incomes during the war enabled a vast number of families to accumulate downpayments, and sustained prosperity facilitated their meeting monthly carrying charges. At the same time government housing policy and federal income tax laws made home ownership more attractive

[2] Findings of recent research challenge the oft-repeated assertion that the source as well as the center of anti-Negro prejudice and discrimination in this country is in the lower socioeconomic classes. See Robert K. Merton, "Discrimination and the American Creed," in R. M. MacIver, ed., *Discrimination and National Welfare* (New York: Harper and Brothers, 1949), p. 111; and National Committee on Segregation in the Nation's Capital, *Segregation in Washington* (Chicago: The Committee, 1948), p. 38.

than rental and practically all new construction was in lily-white suburbs.

Not only was it possible for upper-middle-class whites to desert the central city but many of lesser means, if they were white, could follow suit. Even the low-income white family could hope for homogeneity, in the suburbs by spending a little more money or perhaps in the gray areas of the core city if the expansion of non-whites was contained. Racially homogeneous neighborhoods had achieved a new prestige and this was increasingly apparent in slums and blighted areas where residents sought to emulate dominant racial attitudes.

Rapid movement of whites to the suburbs was but a part of the population trend. While a large volume of long-term residents left the cities, an even larger number of individuals moved from non-urban areas directly to the suburbs. Meanwhile a much smaller number of whites moved into, than moved out of, central cities, while many non-whites entered the inlying areas. "The process of losing one net migrant to the suburbs actually was the end result of a larger process whereby for each two non-white persons moving into the central city about three white persons moved out."[3]

These movements have brought interesting changes in the housing market. Throughout the North and West, non-whites have acquired a much larger number of housing units and frequently more diversified and better quality housing. In the process they have expanded into many areas which were formerly all white. The Chicago experience of 1940–1950 suggests the human components of this development. Those who initiated the movement were long-term rather than newer residents of the city, resulting in no significant changes in socio-economic characteristics. The first arrivals had to "pay a premium rental, which they are able to finance only by using residential space very intensively, for example,

[3] Donald J. Bogue, *Components of Population Change, 1940–50* (Oxford, Ohio: Miami University, 1957), p. 34.

by doubling up families in the household or by including relatives or lodgers in the household."[4]

While it is true that only in a quite general sense has
succession in Chicago followed a pattern of radial expansion of the Negro community outward from the
center of the city, it is significant that

> . . . within both the Negro and the white community,
> high-status groups tend to share residential areas and to
> be residentially segregated from low-status groups. Ap-
> parently, the selective forces which produce differentia-
> tion of residential areas in the urban community operate
> in somewhat the same way upon the Negro and the white
> population. This is also in line with the finding that pat-
> terns of interarea differentiation with respect to physical
> characteristics of the area and social and economic charac-
> teristics of the residents tend to be maintained under the
> impact of succession from white to Negro occupancy.[5]

These developments in Chicago, which are fairly typical of larger Northern industrial centers, reflect the in-
teraction of many events. Such expansion of housing
accommodations for Negroes as took place was facilitated largely by the decline in the white population. It
reflected a growing demand for shelter on the part of
an expanding non-white population in which a significant number were able to pay higher rents and prices for
housing, and it enabled some whites to sell profitably
and buy new suburban houses. Even where sales were
not profitable the availability of Negro purchasers and
renters greatly accelerated the liquidation of property
in the central city, and the acquisition of new homes
elsewhere, on the part of previous residents in the core
areas. To a degree, this greater effective demand for
housing on the part of non-whites sustained property
values in many parts of the central city and accelerated

---

[4] Otis Dudley Duncan and Beverly Duncan, *The Negro
Population of Chicago* (Chicago: University of Chicago Press,
1957), p. 236.

[5] *Ibid.*, p. 298.

the purchase of new homes by whites who were replaced by non-whites. Many of the non-whites paid higher prices than could otherwise have been secured.

One upshot of residential segregation has been to contain most Negro middle-class families in the core cities. Another, and much more serious consequence for the cities, has been the concentration of demand for housing on the part of the growing middle-class Negroes on certain city areas. This too has often sustained property values but it has tended to accelerate the exodus of middle-class whites. Were middle-class Negroes able to compete freely in the total market, their volume in most neighborhoods would have been so slight as to have occasioned little concern. Indeed, in those cities where the numbers of Negroes entering new neighborhoods were small and the participants of comparable economic and social status to the original residents, non-white neighbors were absorbed. Had this been prevalent there would have been much less premium payment incident to initial non-white occupancy and white owners would have had less economic incentive to forsake attractive neighborhoods and homes. Even the real estate operators would have had slight impetus to engineer flight of middle-class whites since the principal source of effective demand—the middle-class Negro purchaser—would be more discriminating and less available for any one neighborhood.

There can be no better illustration of the confusion between emotion and economics than the implications of this analysis. Without a color line, housing in certain areas of the central city would probably have fallen in value. This would have been accounted for in economic terms—architectural obsolescence, loss of neighborhood prestige, age of structure, competition of more desirable facilities and neighborhood location, and resulting weakness in demand for the affected housing. Under conditions of color concepts the experience in these areas when values are sustained is cited (and rightfully) as evidence that non-white occupancy does not necessarily adversely influence property values.[6]

For the process described above to have taken place, there would have had to have been a much larger volume of low-priced housing available to non-whites in metropolitan areas. Without such a supply the sheer pressure of numbers occasioned the growth of non-white areas of concentration. In some instances this involved expansion of one or several major Negro ghettos, engulfing surrounding housing regardless of its price or suitability. In other instances it involved the development of new pockets of non-white residential concentration. Invariably, it occasioned overcrowding, undesirable high densities, and blight.

However, in a situation where the supply of low-cost housing available to non-whites is limited, the entrance of middle-income, non-white families into a neighborhood and its subsequent desertion by whites has benefited the mass of colored home-seekers. For, had there been less turnover, there would have been less filtration. This, in turn, would have delayed the improvement in the quality of housing occupied by non-whites. In the present situation of enforced segregation in many segments of the housing market, rapid racial transition of desirable housing in parts of the central city has made a larger amount of physically good housing available to non-whites. Where those entering the transition area could obtain housing only by paying a price that was too large to be amortized by the individual family income, it has also resulted in more intensive and often socially undesirable occupancy patterns in the areas recently accessible to non-whites. This, in turn, has made it difficult to sustain the middle-class characteristics of the affected areas, even when higher-income non-whites have attempted to do so. Relatively high vacancy rates

[6] See Luigi Laurenti, *Property Values and Race* (Berkeley, Calif.: University of California Press, 1960), for a definitive analysis of the effect of color upon property values.

have accelerated racial transition in certain neighborhoods with the result of substantial upgrading in the quality of the occupied housing stock and instability in some middle-class housing areas.

Modern cities can absorb a large supply of low-income migrants without subjecting the newcomers to economic exploitation and greatly augmenting slums and blight only by providing more low-rent housing, solving the problems of rehabilitation without excessive costs, and providing a free housing market. The central city has a stake in open occupancy throughout the metropolitan area because it is necessary in order that the market may operate most efficiently. Under conditions of open occupancy a much smaller number of areas of middle-class housing need be threatened by inundation by non-whites and it is possible to make the most effective use of the existing supply of housing—particularly the low-rent sector. This is the economic rationale for open occupancy (fair housing) legislation. As in all non-discriminatory legislation, enactment of a law is but a first step. To be effective, such laws need implementation—and that not only involves enforcement but also positive action on the part of minority groups. Thus, the Philadelphia Commission on Human Relations encouraged Negroes to seek homes in all-white neighborhoods, saying: "To break the stubborn pattern of segregated housing many Negro citizens must have the courage to live in 'new' neighborhoods."

It is against this background that urban renewal programs' efforts to attract and maintain middle-class families in the central city must operate. Regardless of any social, political, or moral considerations, the economics of the situation require concern for retention of white middle-class families in central cities because their numbers far exceed those among non-whites. In any given locality the problem has three manifestations: creation of new areas in which middle-class families will establish stable communities, rehabilitation or partial renewal of areas which will attract and hold middle-class families, and arresting or preventing the desertion of middle-class families from existing areas of residence.

In the larger cities of the South new, segregated middle-class Negro communities have been developed. This has been possible for the reasons delineated in Chapter VI. In some instances it results from annexation of new areas by the central city after informal agreements have been made concerning the color identification of land. Atlanta is a prime example.

Clearly, by creation of new segregated areas in most of these cities and restriction of Negro encroachments upon middle-class white neighborhoods to a few locations in others, the impact of the non-white market has had but limited effect upon the desertion of the central city by middle-class whites. In Houston, where there seemed to have been a rather loose housing market in 1960, Negro expansion into one good neighborhood served to sustain values and thereby accelerated movement of the older residents to the suburbs. However, some of those who sold to Negroes may have replaced other central city whites moving to the suburbs and thereby supported property values elsewhere in the central city.

In Northern cities the establishment of all-Negro suburbs is usually impossible. This is due to the spatial distribution of non-whites and rejection of segregated patterns by non-whites in the North.

> In certain ways, the North presents more problems for upper-income Negroes than the South, for here the problem is not only to get good housing—and if Atlanta can supply a Negro market for extensive Negro subdivisions, unquestionably this can also be done in northern cities —but to get good, *unsegregated* housing.[7]

[7] Nathan Glazer, "Introduction," Glazer and McEntire (eds.), *Studies in Housing and Minority Groups* (Berkeley, Calif.: University of California Press, 1960), p. 6.

The latter objective is, of course, supported by legislation. Also, the capacity and willingness of Negroes to pay for better housing in middle-class neighborhoods has increased significantly during the last decade at the same time that the low-income non-white population has grown appreciably. Indeed, the growth of non-white urban populations has been much greater in border and Northern cities than in their Southern counterparts. Thus, the pressure of Negroes for more housing has had greater impact in the North than in the South. Also, it has had less outlet via expansion into new, vacant areas. The consequence is that Negroes have expanded to a much greater degree into areas formerly occupied by whites in Northern than in Southern cities.

Efforts to attract and retain middle-class families in the central urban centers of the North and border states must recognize the pressure for housing occasioned by a growing Negro population. Some of these cities also face the arrival of large numbers of Appalachian Mountain whites, Puerto Ricans, and Mexicans. Since the Negro often presents problems of class and almost always those of color, concentration upon his impact is fruitful. Glazer, in the study cited, while minimizing the problem of the dark-skinned Puerto Ricans and Mexican-Americans, has set forth the peculiar disabilities of the Negro in American society:

> . . . it may seem far-fetched to consider the implications of a social situation in which Mexicans, Puerto Ricans, and Negroes show roughly the same social constitution as the rest of us. However, in the case of the Negroes such large middle-class groups are already developing. They will change greatly the whole character of anti-Negro prejudice in America. But—and this is the point of this last observation—the Negroes will still be a long way from taking up the status in American society of assimilated European ethnic groups. The Mexicans and Puerto Ricans, because of their physical characteristics, will find it easier to achieve this status.

Survival of healthy central cities requires recognition and solution of this problem. First, as was set forth above, there needs to be an acceleration of the size of the middle-class among non-whites. Second, this will be achieved in large measure in proportion to the degree that the middle-class Negro is accepted as his immigrant prototype was accepted. Third, unless the achievement of American norms of success on the part of Negroes is rewarded, as it has been among others who started at the bottom of the economic and social scale, there will be a loss of motivation (already apparent among Negroes) with consequences which are inimical to the economic, political, and cultural health of the central city. Fourth, such results would be tragic for the Nation —and Western democracy—in the world of the cold war and the emergence of Asian and African nationalism.

Cities in the United States, and Northern cities in particular, if they are to maintain a sound economic base, must strive to adjust to growing low-income Negro, Puerto Rican, Appalachian white, and Mexican populations. A first step in this direction is to understand the nature of cities and the historical precedents. A second step is to face up to the unique problems of the present migrant groups. These can be summarized in a simple statement: All of certain ethnic groups, because of their physical identification, are assumed to be a threat to a middle-class neighborhood, regardless of the individual's or the family's income, education, or behavior. Centuries of slavery, generations of color discrimination, repeated instances of economic disadvantage via perpetuation of a color line, and a liberal amount of guilt have perpetuated color concepts. These are most apparent and effective in situations involving areas of living and schools.

Most liberals and many social scientists advocate heterogeneous neighborhoods. The majority of them would favor a community of homes in which low-, medium-, and upper-income groups lived; as a minimum, they would mix low- and medium-income people. Some have equally strong feelings about racial heterogeneity, affirming that in the modern world it behooves us in the United States to learn and demonstrate how the members of a multi-racial society can live together under democracy. Recently an outstanding land economist has dissented, questioning the innate superiority of multi-income neighborhoods.[8] No attempt will be made here to pass moral, social, or political judgments on this issue; rather, the problem will be treated from the point of view of the survival of central cities. Our orientation will be primarily economic, recognizing that enforced racial residential segregation is under attack and in the process of change in the Nation.

From this point of view, it must be recognized that the middle-class in America is keenly conscious of the

[8] "It is not clear why economically heterogeneous neighborhoods are innately superior to the homogeneous. We do not really know whether economically diverse groups truly mix or merely live side by side. And casual observation indicates that many exclusively high-income or middle-income neighborhoods seem to have withstood neighborhood decline extremely well while many economically-mixed neighborhoods have proven quite vulnerable. The social gains of mixture and the social losses from homogeneity have yet to be demonstrated." (Louis Winnick, *Facts and Fictions in Urban Renewal*, p. 12. Mimeographed: a speech delivered before the Forum of the Philadelphia Housing Association, January 28, 1960.) Most planners, however, believe that there are such social gains. A recent forum composed of citizens and professionals who met to consider what neighborhoods should be like "pleaded for variety—variety of housing types . . . available at a variety of prices and rentals so that a varied neighborhood population could result, all races, young and old, rich and poor, and people falling between these extremes." Ironically enough, zoning as currently practiced was considered a chief deterrent to such mixture. (Howard W. Hallman, "Citizens and Professionals Reconsider the Neighborhood," *Journal of the American Institute of Planners*, August, 1959, p. 123. For a somewhat similar point of view, see Arthur L. Grey, Jr., "Los Angeles: Urban Prototype," *Land Economics*, August, 1959, pp. 237–238.)

threat of lower-class encroachments. As was pointed out above, this has long been a national characteristic, perhaps an inevitable consequence of a socially mobile people who are status conscious. During the last quarter of a century, it has become more acute. This leads to the conclusion that many middle-class families will not long voluntarily remain in an area which they believe threatened by lower-class engulfment; few will migrate to such areas. The second fact that has to be recognized is that the white middle-class fears neighborhood deterioration on the entry of non-whites—an attitude that has partial roots in the history of decline in city services, lax enforcement of housing codes, and overcrowding in areas inhabited by non-whites. Actually, the degree of this fear is often a function of the speed and intensity of non-white penetration, although it is often an almost immediate reaction upon the first evidence of non-white entry in urban areas with large colored populations. But, as indicated in Chapter VI, it can be, and is being, modified by effective community action. Most white middle-class families will not long remain in a neighborhood where they are a decided racial minority. Should they fear this eventuality, they usually act so as to assure its fruition. On the other hand, as will be set forth subsequently, there are many evidences of whites' accepting a few Negro neighbors, particularly if they are of comparable economic and social status.

Urban renewal activity concerned with attracting and holding middle-class households in the central city must be geared to creating neighborhoods which offer good schools, a reasonable degree of cleanliness, protection from violence, and physical attractiveness. They need not be single-class neighborhoods. But there is a limit— a class tipping point—to which they can *at the present* be heterogeneous from a class point of view. Similarly, they can absorb some minority-group families of middle-class attributes as well as some of lower-incomes. The class and color mix will vary from new urban redevelopment sites, partial redevelopment and rehabilitation efforts, and conservation areas. The greatest flexibility is in the newly reconstructed redevelopment areas—if for no other reason because new areas and new houses have a snob appeal in themselves.

Proximity to an established blighted non-white slum complicates or deters white occupancy in redevelopment projects. Either large-scale demolition, or extra value for the housing dollar, or both are required to offset this circumstance. Chicago illustrates well this situation. The New York Life Insurance Company financed and constructed Lake Meadows, a large redevelopment, medium-cost rental project in the heart of what had been some of the worst of the city's Negro slums. Although the sponsor announced open occupancy from the start and, despite the scope of the redevelopment and its inherently desirable location in relation to downtown and in proximity to city-wide health and educational institutions, the attractive new housing failed to appeal to a large number of white tenants. Intensive efforts and tangible evidences of a new neighborhood achieved 20 per cent white occupancy and then shifted to 25 per cent white tenants.

Prairie Shores was subsequently constructed on the site of a former Negro slum and on the edge of the Negro ghetto. But it was adjacent to Lake Meadows and the upgrading of the neighborhood was well under way. Indeed, the promotion of Prairie Shores describes it as "an entirely new community immediately adjacent to the Michael Reese Hospital campus." In the words of its developer—who incidentally evidenced his commitment to the project by selling his house in the suburbs and moving into Prairie Shores—"people just recognized a hell of a good buy when they saw it." The nature of this buy is indicated by the fact that apartments rented for an average of $33 a room as against $45 to $65 for comparable new accommodations elsewhere in the city. And the first 342 units in the initial structure of this five-building development rented quickly. Seventy-seven per cent of the occupants were white but most households were childless and none had children of high school age. In May, 1960, when two buildings in Prairie Shores had been completed, they were fully rented and leases were being signed on a third which was scheduled to be ready for occupancy in late summer. The racial mix remained about 80 per cent white and, while few families with school-age children were in occupancy, there were many with pre-school children.

There is striking evidence that the Lake Meadows–Prairie Shores complex in Chicago is a stable racially integrated neighborhood. As of April 15, 1963, of the 3700 odd families in the area, some 2900 were white and the remainder non-white. The problem of maintaining mixed racial occupancy was complicated in Lake Meadows because the first five buildings were 100 per cent non-white occupied from the start. The rest of the project was 64 per cent non-white occupied. A small luxury building was 25 per cent non-white occupied. Prairie Shores was 80 per cent white occupied and had a large waiting list, primarily of whites.

With rare exceptions a small island of medium-cost redevelopment housing in a sea of non-white slums will not attract whites. This was the experience of the attractive—but not relatively competitively-priced—Longwood Redevelopment in Cleveland. On the other hand, redevelopment in an area which is fairly large and marked for total treatment can attract middle-class whites when a minority of non-whites are housed in it. This has been demonstrated in architecturally attractive Capitol Park Apartments and the subsequent redevelopment of the Southwest Redevelopment in Washington, D.C. and in the Gratiot Redevelopment in Detroit. Both of these are fairly high-rent and that fact initially limited greatly non-white participation.

Partial redevelopment and rehabilitation present

more difficult problems. In the first place, frequently the old neighborhood which is the symbol of the threat of lower-class and minority families is not destroyed. Even if a new type of area is planned the physical evidences of the old remain. Where, as in the neighborhood around the University of Chicago, there is a sizable amount of good housing and an enduring institutional base, the possibilities of success are enhanced. The urban renewal plan for the West Side of New York, which also involved spot clearance and a great amount of rehabilitation, is also favorably located. On the north is a completed large upper middle-income redevelopment project, on the east an attractive predominantly upper middle-class and high-income residential strip on Central Park West, on the south a middle-class strip on 86th Street, and on the west a traffic artery.

In the Chicago and New York projects there has been great controversy as to how much public housing would be provided. In both instances the amount was originally drastically limited so that low-income families would be a definite minority of those in the areas. This situation long existed in Chicago and occasioned much resentment on the part of the original occupants and their champions. In New York, the pressure of resident protest resulted in a significant increase in the proportion of low-income housing. New York's West Side will also have a sizable amount of new lower medium-rent facilities or reasonably priced cooperatives and a somewhat lesser amount of new high-rent housing, but the tone of the area will be middle-class. These redevelopment areas will have non-white, low-income families and some non-white, middle-income households, as well as a limited number of higher-income non-whites and whites of these income groups. They will have economic as well as racial diversity, and the stability of the New York City area will be greatly enhanced by a program of tenant education undertaken by the local redevelopment agency in cooperation with federal agencies, described in the next chapter.

Since conservation areas are subjected to the least amount of physical change, they share characteristics with most of the standard areas of existing housing. While the structures in such areas of the old city may be imposing in size and appearance, frequently they are architecturally obsolete. This, as has been noted above, may occasion new property uses—rooming houses, conversions to apartments of varying degrees of adequacy, or other forms of multi-family occupancy. Seldom are they suited for small families and their utilization by low-income households usually involves undesirable economic and social consequences.

In some instances the location of conversion areas (in terms of proximity to present concentrations of nonwhite families) inspires acute fear of minority inundation on the part of present residents. Thus, the possibility of panic selling is real and immediate upon the entrance of non-whites. There is another complicating factor. Present residents of some of these areas may not have elected to live with non-white neighbors. The latter have come in after the neighborhood has been established as a racially homogeneous one. Thus, there may be a feeling on the part of old residents that they have lost the opportunity to exercise freedom of choice in selecting non-white neighbors. In this regard they differ from those who move into a new or existing bi-racial community. However, as open-occupancy legislation and executive action become more prevalent the possibility of moving into an assured lily-white neighborhood declines. The physical attributes of conservation areas and the process of change involved in establishing racial mixture complicate the process in such neighborhoods.

Thus, conservation areas present perplexing problems to those who would attract and hold middle-class whites in the central city. At the outset it must be recognized that many parts of the core city are destined to be occupied by non-whites. These areas will continue to provide the principal supply of housing for Negroes and other non-whites who seek better shelter and are achieving or have achieved sufficiently high earnings to pay for it. In addition, if the past is any indication of the future, many areas of this type will, should they lie in the path of the geographic expansion of existing racial ghettos, be occupied by house-hungry lower-income non-whites.

The degree to which low-income minority families enter these areas depends upon several things. If there is an alternative supply of good housing which better fits the family needs and pocketbooks of non-whites, the process will be delayed. If housing and occupancy standards are enforced, a thing that is unlikely unless there is an alternative supply, due either to a loose housing market or a sizable low-income housing program, this, too, will slow up racial displacement. And, of course, the extent to which the central city becomes more attractive to whites will lessen the availability of such housing to non-whites. At the same time, however, the volume of migration of non-whites to urban centers and the natural population increase of non-whites will be major factors in determining the demand for housing on their part. Finally, in proportion as we concentrate upon clearing slums inhabited by non-whites, the process of racial displacement will take place elsewhere in the city.

In recent years there has been a series of attempts on the part of middle-class neighborhoods to stay the departure of whites with the arrival of colored residents. Until most recently, the majority, if not all, of these have been delaying tactics at best. Perhaps if such efforts become, as a few are today, a part of an over-all program involving new open-occupancy construction, action for spreading the non-white demand over a larger area of the central city, prevention of the engineering of panic selling by real estate operators, better enforcement of housing and occupancy codes and effective action to open the suburbs to non-whites, such programs might succeed in maintaining the bi-racial character of some well-located and attractive neighborhoods.

There is, however, another aspect of rehabilitation and conservation. It relates to areas which are, or were, bi-racial prior to their involvement in the urban renewal process. In this situation, realistic treatment which does not involve economic displacement can result and has (as set forth in Chapter III) resulted in the perpetuation of mixed racial patterns. Existing ethnic spatial patterns suggest that the greatest potentials in this sphere are in the urban South.

Up to this point little has been said of family composition and its implications for middle-class residence in the central city. The majority of the urban renewal projects mentioned are designed for small families and the most successful of them house few young people of school age.

Obviously, the needs and requirements of upper- and middle-income families without children are quite different from those who have youngsters. For the latter, schools are important. Among those of large incomes (and to some degree among the less prosperous) the possibility of using private schools may cause little concern for public educational facilities. In many Northern cities parochial schools serve a similar purpose.

Most knowledgeable observers consider schools a basic factor in attracting or holding middle-class families in the central city. Indeed in the Russel Woods area of Detroit, originally occupied predominantly by Jewish people, concern for education of children seemed to be the most important element motivating liberal families to leave their desirable homes. This, too, is often as much a class as a color phenomenon. In Cleveland, for example, middle-class Negroes entered the comfortable homes in the outlying Glenville section of the central city after World War II. Subsequently, as large numbers

of low-income non-whites entered the area, some of the
earlier Negro residents moved a second time, entering
the more exclusive and prestige-laden Shaker Heights
section. Many of those involved explain their action on
the basis of the superior schools in the latter location.
On the other hand, in Russel Woods and elsewhere,
the existence of synagogues and other institutions related to Jewish life and religion was a strong factor in
holding the original residents. Provision of similar facilities in the suburbs facilitated subsequent departure
of many of these families.

One student of the racial aspects of housing has proposed abandonment of the rule requiring children to
attend a neighborhood public school and provision of
special facilities for the middle-class oriented families.
Thus, heterogeneity in residential patterns would be
purchased at the cost of homogeneity in public schools.
It has been pointed out that special schools of the type
suggested might well fail to preserve or facilitate
heterogeneity in residential patterns, reinforcing islands
of upper-income white occupancy in an ethnic sea of
educational proletarianization. In light of the growing
political power of non-whites in Northern urban areas
such a consequence would sow the seeds of its own destruction—and that of urban renewal in the process.
And, of course, in view of the current attacks upon
neighborhood schools as an instrument of *de facto* educational segregation in the North, this proposal is totally
unrealistic today.

Public schools are a symbol and an instrument of
democracy. While their programs can and should be
tailored to meet the needs of students, the whole trend
in the Nation, as dramatized by the Supreme Court
decision of May, 1954, is away from racial segregation.
This, of course, is not to say that every child receives
the same training but it does call for no arbitrary assignment to schools on basis of color or class. It is compatible with an open system which, within a given

school, assigns pupils to educational programs which meet their needs (currently identified as the track system), provided that the system is fluid and based upon some universally applied criteria for assignment. The latter must be a reflection of ability and not social status.

Just as most middle-class families, if they have an alternative, will not long remain in a neighborhood where they are a minority so they will not long voluntarily send their children to a school where they are a minority. Middle-class whites with children will remain in the central city in large numbers only if they have access to a middle-class oriented, educationally satisfactory public school or can afford private or parochial schools. The degree of possible class and racial mix in a neighborhood is lessened, therefore, when school-age children are involved. It can be conceived, however, that as the number of stable bi-racial neighborhoods increases, tolerance for this type of living will grow. In light of the importance of prestige considerations in the selection of housing, it may well be that this process will be accelerated through the creation of attractive newly constructed, racially mixed neighborhoods in the central city. The efficacy of the latter will be minimized as long as the suburbs remain essentially racially homogeneous.

Public schools in the central city cannot compete with their suburban counterparts on terms of the latter. The city public schools can never match the snob appeal of many suburban ones. Seldom can they assure the same degree of class or racial homogeneity nor can they equal the spaciousness of the surrounding campus. But they can be good schools. Indeed if they are specialized high schools concentrating on specific fields, they can be better schools. This is demonstrated by certain technical schools, fashion schools, and performing arts high schools in New York City. Emphasis must be upon high scholastic standards, adequate discipline in the school, and exploitation of the opportunities for cultural enrichment which urban life offers. While these potentialities may not be given a chance to flower if middle-class white parents feel that low-income and minority group children are to be a large element in the student body, they are possible of achievement in a city school which is not homogeneous. Proof of this is the effort prestige private schools have made for years to attract and enroll children of poorer parents and from non-white households. The administrations and parents of many of these schools lament the fact that such enrollment is not larger.

At the same time the central city public school has a unique character to sell—a degree of class and racial heterogeneity which will teach young people to live with other children of varying backgrounds. Many middle-class families are acutely aware of the importance of this in a democracy; in the world today it has even more pressing international implications. Unfortunately, realization of its desirability is far from accepting situations in which there is heterogeneity. This is due largely to fear that some class and racial mixture will lead to an inevitable lowering of academic and discipline standards and an ultimate minority status for white children in the school. It is also manifestation of apprehension lest there may be loss of social status in living in a predominantly non-white neighborhood or having one's children in a school with large Negro enrollment. If, however, the public school is geared primarily to the educational goals of middle-class families, it can and will attract and hold many middle-class white children even though some lower-income and middle-class minority pupils are included.

Another attraction which the school in the central city can have is to afford a richer and more meaningful education. This suggests delineation and exploitation of the educational advantages of the central city. The many cultural institutions located in the central city—its

theaters, museums, concerts, and the like—are great assets. The school program should utilize fully and dra-
matically these facilities of the central city.

With all of this, there will be fear and apprehension
on the part of middle-class parents. Over the long run,
this can be met only as the living standards, opportunities, and assimilation of those least advantaged in the
city are increased. Here, too, the public schools have
a basic, but not an exclusive, role. In those areas where
the schools serve large numbers of migrant, low-income,
and minority families, programs need to be developed
to accelerate their adjustment to urban life. Included
among these are activities for remedial work, discovery
and nurture of talent, curriculum enrichment, reaching
parents and involving them in community problems related to schools, and the preparation of teachers who
understand the cultural problems involved.

All of these programs and activities will hold only
some of the middle-class families now in the central
cities. They will be more effective in attracting back to
the city others who are exhausted or disillusioned with
suburban life. But unless we begin now to deal with
them, the trend of certain groups away from the city
will continue—and probably at an accelerated rate. Certainly, in assessing the potential demand for medium-
priced housing in the central city, an important variable
is the success we have in creating and maintaining public schools which have an appeal to the families involved.

This analysis suggests that there can be a degree of
class and racial mixture compatible with attracting and
holding middle-class whites. In the expensive and upper
medium-rental apartments and sales houses this presents few problems of planning. The income structure
usually assures only token participation by non-whites
and, of course, eliminates the low-income group. If the
desirable mix (from the point of view of maintaining
large numbers of medium-income families) involves

limited participation of low-income households, this too can be achieved by redeveloping or renewing areas large enough to establish their own identity and limiting the amount of low-cost housing. This, however, implies the responsibility for providing in attractive locations an adequate supply of low-cost units and cessation of such widespread dislocation of families as had typified urban renewal in the past. It also assumes a deeper demand for high-cost shelter than currently exists.

It is at the level of medium-cost housing that real problems arise. The non-white, and particularly the Negro, housing market includes a growing number of families ready, willing, and able to purchase or rent such shelter. If the market is open to them in only a few locations at any one time the "tipping point" may soon be reached in any one or two developments. As was indicated above, opening the suburbs to non-whites is one of the necessary prices for attracting and holding middle-income whites in the central city. This is a complex matter. It would operate as suggested above by (1) siphoning off some of the middle-income demand for housing among non-whites from the central city; (2) removing the attraction of racial homogeneity from the suburbs; (3) reducing the snob appeal of racial exclusiveness since no area could assure it; (4) reducing the threat of "tipping" in any one racially open neighborhood.

Cessation of widespread dislocation of low-income families was suggested in the earlier discussion of high- and upper medium-cost housing. It was proposed there from the point of view of political expediency and equity. It is pertinent to the discussion of medium-cost housing for another reason. As long as large numbers of low-income families are uprooted by slum clearance they are a potential source for the displacement of middle-income families of all races elsewhere in the community. This is especially true when they are colored and limited to a racially restricted market.

A final approach, applicable chiefly to conservation areas, is to perfect techniques for stabilizing racially transitional neighborhoods. To be effective they must be an element in a comprehensive program for expanding the supply of housing available to non-whites at all price levels. Also, it must be realized that there are some neighborhoods which, because of location in relation to the growth of areas of non-white concentration, will not respond to this treatment. This only illustrates that cities are not static institutions. Their physical facilities change and their people move. The problems of class and color can never be solved in any one neighborhood. Today they cannot be solved in the central city. They are problems of metropolitan areas, where the effective demand on the part of non-whites is small.

If this analysis is valid, it has significance for the kind of cities we may expect in the next generation. While the size and squalor of slums may be decreased, we shall not clear all of them. Poverty, rejection, and a certain amount of individual choice will dictate their perpetuation. Through better schools—in terms of plant, quality of teaching, and effective programs to reach low-income families—the economic and social status of many slum residents can be raised. If we perfect and apply techniques to give the newcomers a feeling of belonging and provide meaningful assistance to the normal as opposed to the problem family, there can be greater occupational, educational, and residential mobility. For these approaches to work, our urban populations will have to be less color-conscious; and anti-discrimination legislation or executive action affecting the suburbs as well as central cities will be required. We need also to develop more tolerance of variations from established middle-class values and behavior.

American urban centers will not soon, if ever, become a total aggregate of class and racial heterogeneous neighborhoods. But we can expect to see a lessening of ethnic as well as economic ghettos. Still, most of our neighborhoods will be predominantly of one economic level; some will be almost exclusively non-white; a few will have a small number of medium-income non-whites; and others will be integrated in varying degrees.

The Progress of Urban Renewal

Discussions of urban problems evoke many points of view. There are those who question whether cities should or can be revitalized. At the other extreme are the uncritical proponents of urban renewal who attach magic significance to a phrase. They seem to believe that we have in that concept the final and inflexible answer to all the problems of the city. There is no one established and proven road to revitalizing our cities. Although we do not know all we should about how to accomplish this objective, we are learning how to do so through study, analysis, evaluation, and by doing.

One thing that needs to be done is to demonstrate how false are those who, under the guise of "individual initiative," "free enterprise," and "government economy," would let us drift into apathy. For freedom has never been reached through indifference. It can only be achieved with responsibility. In our desire to see more American cities accept their responsibilities, however, we must avoid dishonesty about the difficulties which have beset us in the past.

It is only a dozen or so years since urban renewal became a program of the Federal Government. In the history of our cities that is no more than a moment. In that period there have been some real accomplishments and some tragic failures. Too often those who are the advocates of bigger and better urban renewal talk only of the achievements; the new housing, the inspiring cultural facilities, the thousands who were moved from slums to better homes, the increased tax revenues. Just as often those who are the apostles of drift and do-nothing point only to the failures; the haphazard planning, the irresponsible or unsuccessful developers, the high rents, the destruction of housing which could have been saved, the indifference toward relocation, and the augmentation of ghetto patterns.

One of the most unfortunate mistakes which has been made in the past was simply a disregard for democracy. Planners and public officials have occasionally acquiesced in urban renewal projects to serve particular interests, without regard for the interests of the community as a whole. This particular mistake has attracted not only wrath but ridicule: witness the simulated greeting cards which have been circulated. On the cover they read: "Urban Renewal Is Good for You," and inside they say, "So Shut Up."

Since 1954 the Federal Government has required localities to have what is called a Workable Program for Community Improvement before they can receive urban renewal assistance.

Such a program has seven elements and they are as follows:

(a) Codes and ordinances establishing adequate standards of health and safety for a community's housing.

(b) A comprehensive plan for the community's future development.

(c) Analyses of the neighborhoods in the community to identify those where something should be done about blight.

(d) Administrative organization capable of coordinating and carrying out a community program.

(e) Financial resources to support the localities' share of an urban renewal program.

(f) Housing resources to meet the needs of those displaced by urban renewal.

(g) Assurance that the community as a whole is fully informed and has the fullest opportunity to take part in developing and executing an urban renewal program.

Critics of urban renewal have accused, with ample

basis, the Federal Government of being lax in enforcing these requirements. The Kennedy Administration resolved to correct the situation. For President Kennedy declared in his housing message to Congress that "only when the citizens of a community have participated in selecting the goals which will shape their environment can they be expected to support the actions necessary to accomplish those goals." In accordance with this statement of purpose, those who assumed responsibility for the Federal Government's housing programs initiated a review and re-evaluation of the Workable Program so as to determine its adequacy and the efficacy of its administration. Since it is the basic tool available to the Federal Government for establishing minimum standards for urban renewal, it must constantly be challenged and refined.

Relocation had become a dirty word in America. We took action to see that this was changed, resolving that relocation must no longer be the tragedy it has too often been, but the opportunity it should always have been. It can become, and in many instances it has become, a positive rehousing program for those now living in substandard homes.

William Slayton, the current Commissioner of the Urban Renewal Administration, reorganized the machinery for supervising relocation. In this connection he said: "I intend to look carefully at a community's relocation activities—that is, at its actual relocation operation, to make sure that the job is being done well before we permit a community to undertake new renewal activities." To implement this statement, he created within his agency a new position, Assistant Commissioner for Relocation. To fill this crucial post he recruited the man who had directed the successful relocation program in Washington, D.C.

During the early years urban renewal demolished a significant amount of good housing because it was intermingled with bad housing. The housing resources of

our country are far too valuable to be indiscriminately
destroyed if they can be rehabilitated satisfactorily. In
the past, however, rehabilitation often had been financially impossible. The owners of buildings in declining
areas lacked the resources to finance rehabilitation
themselves, and financial institutions were reluctant to
lend money on buildings in such areas.

The Kennedy Administration attempted to develop
and perfect programs to encourage and facilitate rehabilitation of our existing stock of housing. With these
tools, we hoped to be able to salvage a large number of
dwellings. This will enable our cities to blend the old
with the new, minimize the bulldozer approach, and
reduce the volume of economic and ethnic displacement incident to urban renewal. But one thing must
be made clear. The fact that many existing structures
which lend themselves to rehabilitation can and will
be preserved does not mean that local programs should
or will preserve all of them. Where there are some
sound buildings in a sea of hopeless ones, it is not
feasible or desirable to preserve the occasional structures at the cost of destroying a redevelopment plan
through inflexible application of a sound principle.

Urban renewal has been denounced because of the
high rentals for apartments in its redevelopments. We
cannot indefinitely go on redeveloping areas with housing which can be afforded only by families of substantial means. We must redevelop more of our slums and
blighted areas in such a way as to provide accommodations for families of modest means as well.

The Housing Act of 1961, in Section 221(d)(3),
permits the Federal Housing Administration and the
Federal National Mortgage Association, popularly
known as Fannie Mae, to join in a program of mortgage
insurance and purchase to make more moderate rentals
possible. Under this proposal, long-term loans below
the market interest rates can be made to non-profit organizations and cooperatives, certain public agencies,

or limited-dividend corporations to build housing which would be limited to those of moderate incomes. This makes possible rentals well below those formerly available in renewal areas. In order to facilitate the most reasonable rents or carrying charges, FHA waives its usual ½ per cent insurance premiums and insures loans for as long as forty years. The exact amount of rental or carrying charge reduction possible will, of course, vary with the size of accommodations, cost of construction, and duration of the loan, and would be materially augmented by partial tax exemption. State laws in Delaware, Massachusetts, Missouri, New Jersey, and New York provide for tax exemption or partial tax exemption for non-profit or limited dividend cooperatives. In Hawaii non-profit housing can be tax-exempt, and in Illinois the same is true of non-profit "old peoples' homes."

On the basis of 7586 dwelling units of Section 221 (d)(3) housing in thirty-seven localities for which cost figures were available in October, 1963, the average monthly rental per unit was $87.78. This was 57 per cent less than the average figure achieved in the regular FHA multi-family housing program. It reflected, of course, wide geographic variations—from $74.13 in the Southeast to $102.61 in the Northeast. The maximum incomes permitted at time of admission to the new moderate-income housing varied for a three- or four-person family from $4150 to $8400 in the continental United States.

The concept of economic diversity in urban renewal is a long-range, community-wide objective. It does not imply that each and every project must be multi-income, but that the city-wide approach must achieve such diversity. The economic realities and current consumer preferences, related as they are to prestige considerations, limit the tempo and extensiveness of economic mixing, especially in areas which have lost their attractiveness in the process of decline. (The previous section of this chapter dealt with this matter in greater detail.)

We have developed goals, and we shall pursue them without being so unrealistic and doctrinaire as to lose both the immediate objective and unduly complicate and endanger urban renewal. Nor have we ignored the economic realities of land use. There are some sites which, because of their location and value, should be used for housing that will produce high rents and correspondingly high taxes. But a local program composed exclusively of such sites is, in my opinion, unsatisfactory.

Another charge frequently leveled against urban renewal is that it suffers from "projectitis," a vision which does not extend beyond the limits of a single development. The Federal Government already provides assistance for planning comprehensive community renewal programs. These are programs in which urban renewal activities and capital improvements can be coordinated (to be delineated more fully in the next chapter). From the start we encouraged as many cities as possible to take part in this planning, because in order to be successful with urban renewal a city must know where it is going. A Community Renewal Program enables it to determine this, and associated, objectives.

The role of the Federal Government in all aspects of urban renewal, however, is a secondary one. It is the cities themselves which must take the initiative and must do the work. The Federal Government can only advise, assist, and offer financial aid. Each city has as its urban renewal program only what it deserves. Some take the easy path, and do nothing. As a result they have nothing, and for them the Federal Government does nothing. Others take the high road, but make the program, by their own ineptness, far more difficult than it need be. We hope, with advice and assistance, to make their way easier in the future. Happily there are cities which have always had wide vision, great vigor,

and the wholehearted support of their citizens. They
are the only ones that really know to what heights the
road marked "urban renewal" can lead. There are, however, phases of urban renewal, like the Workable Program and relocation, where the Federal Government is
directed to establish and secure compliance with minimum standards. We are resolved to accept these responsibilities.

Ours is a concept of a flow of change, the cadence
of which will be determined primarily by the aptness
of administration. We have our objectives, but we realize that we must pace our activity in terms of community understanding and community acceptance. Nor
do we think of the central city as separate and distinct from the metropolitan complex of which it is the
heart. The suburbs and the core areas are interdependent. Our responsibility is to articulate and emphasize
this fact at the same time that we encourage, to the
maximum degree, programs and approaches which assure metropolis-wide activities.

In order to arrive at guidelines and evaluate what
had been done during our first fifteen months in office,
the Housing and Home Finance Agency set up a conference in the spring of 1962. Among other things,
this meeting afforded the top officials of the Agency an
opportunity to pause and note where they were head-
ing. A small group of educators, businessmen, and government officials were called to Washington to discuss
some aspects of urban development. Papers were prepared on selected topics and circulated among participants prior to our convocation. They provided the
basis for the discussions which took place at the
meetings.

A basic objective of the conference was to appraise
the effectiveness of existing programs, particularly
those of HHFA, dealing with urban expansion. By identifying critical problem areas and those specific approaches offering the greatest opportunities for effective

action, a basis was sought for developing new strategies for public and private guidance of urban growth. The tone and wisdom of the conference were well stated by Catherine Bauer Wurster in her summary remarks when she concluded:

> . . . Our models will be hypotheses, not Utopias, but they will help us to assemble the bits and pieces of knowledge in a way that is meaningful, not only for expert understanding and judgment, but also for public communication and decision.

In any case, knowledge is no substitute for positive leadership, particularly in a field where science can never be more than a limited tool to improve the quality of judgment. "The vast process rushes on," in Charlie Haar's fine phrase, and we must understand it as well as we can. But those who know a little more than the rest will have to be brave enough to get out front and try to guide it.[9]

Some Planning and Design Considerations

Through our society today runs a dichotomy deeper than many of us realize: a division between urban and suburban thinking which, whatever the historical, economic, cultural, and sociological reasons, makes no sense in the future that we are seeking. A city is no island, entirely of itself. The city today is, or should be, the heart, and in a sense, the soul, of a metropolitan area. The suburbs around it, to a large degree, draw their life and their spirit from the city's economy and culture. The reason we are concerned at this stage in our history with redesigning urban America is not because of nostalgia for the "Greene Countrie Towne" of William Penn, or any other pioneer city planners. It is because we must revitalize the American city as the anchor holding together our metropolitan areas. At the rate that these metropolitan areas have been increasing,

[9] *Urban Expansion—Problems and Needs* (Washington: Housing and Home Finance Agency, 1963), p. 174.

this is a matter of concern to the large majority of Americans.

The 1960 Census recognized 212 metropolitan areas, where 113 million of the 180 million Americans lived. Eighty-four per cent of the country's population increase in the last decade took place in these areas. Three-quarters of the increase in the metropolitan areas was in the suburbs surrounding the central cities.

The land adjoining our cities has been engulfed at the astounding rate of a million acres a year. So rapidly have the metropolitan areas sprawled across the countryside that they have begun to merge, one into the other. Jean Gottman, who was cited in Chapter I, and others see the ultimate emergence of super-metropolises with populations ranging from five to twenty-three millions. This possibility should alert us to the need for more rational land utilization, the importance of open space, and the necessity for developing and preserving green belts around our centers of population.

At one time, it was sufficient to design a building capable of performing the function for which it was intended. Today architectural literature is filled with the call to design as well for the environment of which that building is a part. Too often, however, that environment is conceived within the narrow limits of adjoining buildings rather than the neighborhood, the urban renewal area, or the metropolis. Within these areas there should be unity of design. But it should also be a design that will integrate the neighborhood and the urban renewal area with the rest of the city, and the city itself with its metropolitan area. Too often, also, the architect has been content with designing in the patterns of the past. If we are to rebuild intelligently, the architect must be thinking in new urban patterns; patterns based not on the demands of today, but on the demands of tomorrow. Quality must be stressed, as well as scope. And at every stage of the redevelopment our standards must be high.

The Federal Government is already an active partner in rebuilding our cities. By June, 1964, we anticipate that the urban renewal program will involve about 1560 projects in 750 cities. The area encompassed by these projects will be about 120,000 acres (185 square miles) which is equal to the combined area of Atlanta and Louisville. In this gross area a little over half, 65,000 acres, will ultimately be acquired, cleared, and redeveloped. We estimate that communities will demand, and can intelligently use, under current conditions, 700 million dollars or more of federal assistance each year in their urban renewal programs. These communities must be assured of continuity in federal assistance if they are to work out long-range programs for their renewal. To give them this assurance, the President asked the Congress in his proposed housing bill of 1961 to authorize 2.5 billion dollars for urban renewal commitments to be used over four years. The Congress authorized 2 billion dollars which will be committed in three years.

One of the first acts of President Kennedy was to instruct the HHFA to work with local officials in every area to foster a broad approach to urban renewal, in which individual projects would be developed within the framework of an over-all program. This over-all program should clearly identify the city's long-term renewal needs and opportunities. By June, 1963, some 150 or more metropolitan and regional areas had been assisted by federal grants for area-wide planning. Through grants to state planning agencies more than 2800 smaller communities had received federal assistance for planning. Under the terms of the Housing Act of 1961 the federal share in the cost of urban and metropolitan planning was increased from one-half to two-thirds. This brought the federal participation up to the level of the urban renewal program, and closer to the level provided for interstate highway planning. The

authorization for urban planning grants was increased
from 20 million dollars to 75 million dollars.

One of our major concerns is to provide flexibility in
urban renewal programs, so they can be designed to be
of the maximum benefit to the community undertaking
them. Originally the urban renewal program was regarded exclusively in terms of slum clearance and housing construction. There was no thought given to the
industrial, commercial, and cultural needs of community renewal. As an awareness of these other needs has
grown, communities have been given increasing discre-
tion in their use of urban renewal. President Kennedy
asked that the percentage of urban renewal grant funds
which may be used for non-residential projects be increased from 20 to 30 per cent, and this was authorized
in the Housing Act of 1961.

Another planning problem which had hampered the
renewal of many communities is the Constitutional requirement for Congressional approval of interstate com-
pacts. Twenty-four of the metropolitan areas in the
country cut across state lines. The Camden-Philadel-
phia area is one of them. Over the years the Pennsylvania and New Jersey communities in this area have
worked together informally, but their effectiveness had
often been hobbled by this Constitutional provision.
The President's program which was enacted by the
Congress in 1961 removed that obstacle by a blanket
authorization for planning activities between states.

We, in the Kennedy Administration, stressed utilization of the existing stock of shelter and found many
problems in this area. One of the great difficulties in
rehabilitating the older structures in our cities has been
financing. Other difficulties have been lack of design
which is cost-conscious. We attempted, from the outset,
to deal with each of these deficiencies. New legislation
provided tools for financing rehabilitation, but it soon
became apparent that new legislation was not sufficient

to get the job done. Standards of rehabilitation, new concepts of valuation which envisioned the new community which would emerge, and successful experiences were needed.

We are on the threshold of some remarkable breakthroughs in urban design and development patterns concerning the relationship between land use and transportation, as well as construction. To facilitate these advances we are assisting communities with partial grants to acquire open land to meet the needs for open space consonant with their future development. We also sought legislative authority to make loans to enable communities to acquire land which would be used for future development as industrial parks, shopping centers, or housing in accordance with the needs of the community.

It is unnecessary to labor the point that unplanned and haphazard utilization of land in areas surrounding our cities gives rise to a multiplicity of problems. Transportation and highway requirements come to mind immediately. In addition, there is the wastefulness inherent in scattered developments. This manifests itself in matters such as water supply and sewage disposal. Equally important is the impact of unplanned and uncoordinated residential developments upon the costs of public facilities, principally schools.

For a land-use program to be successful it is essential that communities have a clear idea of how they want to develop. The President's proposals, therefore, required as a condition of federal assistance that the land be acquired by communities for future development in accordance with a comprehensive urban plan. Unfortunately the enabling legislation for this phase of a land policy was deleted by the Senate Committee on Banking and Currency. But the problems it was designed to meet remain and grow, and the legislative proposals for

1964 will, I am sure, readdress themselves to this problem.[10]

It is not often that a nation rebuilds its cities, and when it does it should do it well. The architects of this Nation will have in their hands, in the years ahead, a major part in shaping the urban life of the country. What they do will influence the lives of millions yet unborn for decades yet to come. No other generation of architects had before it such an opportunity or such a challenge.

America waits for their response.

[10] President Johnson's housing message of 1964 proposed federal aid for new communities and planned subdivisions, advanced acquisition of land for public purposes, and deferred amortization of federal loans for water and sewer facilities.

III URBAN RENEWAL TODAY

Workable Programs

In virtually every major city across the country, and in a great many of the smaller cities, urban renewal projects are under way or under consideration. In nearly every one of these cities there are heated debates going on about what has been done, what will be done, and what should be done. The passion and the volume of the resulting discussions are sometimes overwhelming. To a degree that is often surprising, urban renewal has become a focal point for the battles between intellectuals and materialists, liberals and conservatives, humanitarians and activists, and every other set of traditional rivals.

Urban renewal involves bricks and concrete and bulldozers and buildings and highways. It is also very close to people. It is something that is constantly being changed and shaped by the opinions of those who are interested. Controversies about urban renewal, unlike many other controversies of our time, are controversies that bring results. Therefore, they are healthy controversies.

Congress authorized urban renewal with two stated objectives in mind: a) to attract private financial resources to the enormous task of slum clearance; b) to help urban areas stop the downward spiral of decay with which local resources were no longer able to contend.

Urban renewal can claim credit for a number of solid accomplishments. By July 1, 1963, more than 650 com-

munities had programs under way, and the long years
of planning, acquiring properties, relocating families
and businesses, and redevelopment through private developers were beginning to show results. Some 22,000
acres of urban land had been acquired, and in scores
of cities new communities of attractive housing, impressive public buildings, commercial structures, and
industrial developments have been built. Numbers
aside, perhaps the major achievement of urban renewal
is that it has restored hope for older cities and worn-out
neighborhoods, providing local leaders and governments the tools for revitalizing their communities.[1]

From the outset it was clear to Congress and those
familiar with urban renewal that it could be subject to
abuses and that people could be unnecessarily hurt in
its operation. Thus, the Housing Act of 1949 contained
language to protect people from such injury. This was
subsequently strengthened when Congress established
the Workable Program for Community Improvement,
the elements of which were set forth in the preceding
chapter.

Congress stipulated that approval of Workable Programs and relocation plans be "nondelegable functions"
of the Administrator of the Housing and Home Finance
Agency, requiring that he give them his personal attention and certify that they were in proper order. But
even that requirement was not enough to see that this
responsibility would be carried out in much more than
a perfunctory and cursory manner.

The Kennedy Administration's responsibility, therefore, was clear. It was to establish machinery, promul-
gate regulations, and provide field reviews to promote
the effectuation of a Congressional intent. This we did
and, as a result, significant progress was made in se-

[1] For a description of the impact of renewal on a single city,
see "New Spirit of St. Louis Sparks Renaissance," *Engineering News-Record*, August 15, 1963, pp. 30–32, 34, 36–
38, 42.

curing compliance with the requirements and the spirit of the law.

One of the requirements of the Workable Program is citizen participation in a community's urban renewal activities. The vehicle for this participation, provided in the Workable Program, is an official advisory committee on which all the major elements of a community —businessmen, labor, the professions, religious leaders, educators, minorities, and others—should be represented. This committee is expected to have a number of subcommittees to deal with special urban renewal problems, including a subcommittee on minority housing.

When the Kennedy Administration took office it found that in community after community, where there was a Workable Program on paper, these committees had never been named or had rarely been convened. One of the most important accomplishments of recent months has been to show the communities involved in urban renewal how many needless controversies and conflicts can be avoided by having a committee of this sort and using it properly.

Many of the difficulties in urban renewal have developed because the leaders of a community have never had an opportunity to learn what is intended or to express an opinion about it before a formal proposal reached the local governing body. Too often, when that point was reached, the community found itself in a take-it-or-leave-it situation. Thus a tremendous struggle was necessary to introduce a change that could easily have been made if there had been a channel of consultation during the planning process.

As with other elements in the Workable Program, we first utilized educational and persuasive methods, which yielded some results. Then as communities applied for recertification of their Workable Programs, we became more insistent. In the case of a score of cities, HHFA delayed recertification until there was a Citizens' Advisory Committee. These methods were effective and now, with a few exceptions which will peril future re-certification, we have secured formal compliance with this key element in the Workable Program.

Not only was there compliance with the Agency's requirements for citizen participation, but there was also indication of acceptance of its importance on the part of local agencies. One example of this was the September 30, 1963, issue of the *Journal of Housing*, the official publication of the National Association of Housing and Redevelopment Officials. It was devoted exclusively to citizen participation, providing "a cross-sectional report of what's being done—and where—and how—to involve citizens meaningfully in public housing, urban renewal, and code enforcement programs."

Of course, as long as urban renewal was oriented primarily to complete demolition and resulting widespread displacement incident thereto, there was built-in resistance to citizen participation—especially at the neighborhood level. The most that could be hoped for was a city-wide committee; but even here there was resistance. The nature of this I delineated in a speech before the Better Housing League of Greater Cincinnati on May 15, 1963, when I observed that such committees "have a way of trying to promote themselves from advisory to operating roles, and try to seize control of the redevelopment program."

Once rehabilitation and conservation became real possibilities, citizen participation at the neighborhood level became an important and necessary factor in project execution. But there were problems. Perhaps the most serious is the inherent class cleavage in slums and blighted areas—especially in non-white ghettos where there is frequently class diversity among residents. In this situation, the middle-class-oriented elements are usually in favor of programs for upgrading the neighborhoods. Under current conditions, many of the low-income residents see in such programs dislocation or economic problems.

To make citizen participation more effective, it will be necessary to provide greater protection and aid for low- and medium-income households displaced or required to upgrade their properties by urban renewal. This will involve new legislation (alluded to subsequently) and better administrative procedures at the federal and local levels. The establishment of city-wide committees, therefore, is but the first step. It is a significant move, however, in that it reflects federal insistence upon, and general local acceptance of, some form of citizen participation.

Not unrelated to neighborhood citizen participation are the requirements of the Workable Program covering codes and housing resources for displaced families. Clearly, little is accomplished if a slum or blighted area is torn down only to occasion overcrowding, blight, and associated substandard housing conditions elsewhere in the city as a result of the relocation process. Codes and housing ordinances are a principal and indispensable instrument to prevent this (as well as to upgrade the quality of housing in a community), although, of course, an adequate supply of relocation housing is a *sine qua non*. Consequently, in October, 1961, HHFA established the policy that the four basic codes (building, plumbing, electrical, and housing) should be adopted within one year after initial certification and that systematic housing code enforcement be initiated within another year after adoption of the housing code.

Contrary to the past tradition in HHFA of not pressing too hard on code enforcement,[2] the Kennedy Administration secured a significant degree of compliance with the Workable Program's code standards. Results

[2] Even under earlier policy, urban renewal had been a somewhat effective instrument for encouraging adoption of housing codes. When the program started in 1954, there were some 60 such codes; by 1960 there were some 400 in existence.

for the two-year period ending June 30, 1963 are reflected in the following actions taken on the four basic codes:

TYPE OF CODE	NUMBER INITIALLY ADOPTED	NUMBER REVISED OR AMENDED
Building	168	114
Plumbing	161	111
Electrical	146	90
Housing	243	63

In accomplishing this we have used many approaches. Fact sheets, basic informational booklets, questions and answers, and guidelines on the Workable Program were prepared and distributed. Applications for initial certification and recertification of the program were revised. The regional offices of the Agency were strengthened so that now there are two persons in each region responsible for the Workable Program, and their efforts have been supported by frequent visits from those in the central office responsible for this phase of the Agency's activities. In addition, other personnel have assumed a responsibility for results, joining those specifically administering Workable Programs in visiting local officials and public agencies to explain and encourage cooperation. Finally, we have established cooperative relationships with organizations such as the Codes Division of the National Association of Housing and Redevelopment Officials; the Build America Better Committee of the National Association of Real Estate Boards; Action, Inc.; and federal and state government agencies. But the effort did not stop here.

The HHFA Administrator's office reviewed, during the Kennedy Administration, relocation plans for each urban renewal project. In that process another evaluation of codes was undertaken, and where progress was unsatisfactory deadlines were set forth for compliance with code requirements. This was done during the year ending June 30, 1963, in some twenty-five recalcitrant communities.

Under its new procedures, the Urban Renewal Administration requires code compliance before approval of a Loan and Grant contract, and administration of this requirement has been strengthened. Here, often, the standards are more stringent than those under the Workable Program. For example, when a dislocated family moves into a substandard house, refusing an offer of a standard dwelling, the local public agency (operating urban renewal) is required to notify city authorities of the circumstance. This facilitates inspection of the premises, and, as a result, the owner can be required, when necessary, to bring it up to standard conditions.

Of course, much remains to be done. By the very nature of our governmental structure, codes and their enforcement are local government responsibilities. We have resisted pressures for our establishing a national building code, and we are against the Federal Government's assuming financial responsibility for housing code enforcement. At the same time we accept responsibility for encouraging and, ultimately requiring, under the Workable Program, meaningful codes and their effective enforcement.

This is, in my opinion, a vital element in a successful urban renewal program. The initial impact of relocation in Southwest Washington upon housing and neighborhood standards elsewhere in the city was set forth in the section captioned "An Early Appraisal," in the preceding chapter. Since then, vigorous code enforcement has modified the situation. During the fiscal year of 1963, the 86 inspectors hired by the capital city made 124,600 inspections under the Housing Code and issued over 130,000 violation notices. Compliance was effected in some 121,000 cases. Largely as a consequence of this activity, there was in Washington, during the decade 1950 to 1960, a decline in the proportion of substandard housing, and this was fairly universal in most areas of the city.

In relation to submissions indicating the availability of relocation housing resources, HHFA has recently insisted upon a more realistic approach. Thus, indication of the volume of relocation broken down by rent-paying capacity and color, including those to be displaced by highway construction, public works, code enforcement, and the like, as well as by urban renewal, is required. The Agency also insists upon a breakdown of potential rehousing resources which reflects the cost distribution and availability by color.

Of the 748 applications submitted for initial certification under the Workable Program during the period April 1, 1961, through March 31, 1963, one-half were found acceptable, one-third became acceptable within three months, and slightly over one-tenth became acceptable in from three to six months. Two per cent had not been accepted within six months, and 6 per cent remained unacceptable for six months or more as of June 30, 1963. For those programs seeking recertification, where our standards were higher, 31 per cent were acceptable upon submission, and 14 per cent remained unacceptable six months or more after submission.

Not only is the Workable Program a prerequisite for new urban renewal activity but it is also a requirement for eligibility for public housing and mortgage insurance for moderate-income housing. Thus, at the end of the fiscal year 1963 (June 30), Indianapolis, Indiana, could not get a moderate-income project approved, and in a single region of HHFA, some 650 units of public housing, otherwise eligible, were rejected because of the absence of Workable Programs. Similar actions were taken in other parts of the Nation. These typical consequences of more stringent administration of Workable Program requirements explain why there had been hesitancy in the past to insist upon higher standards.

They also provide a basis for appreciating the significance of recent activities in this area.

Relocation and Rehabilitation

Although Congress has been very explicit in the requirement that those who are relocated as a result of urban renewal shall have "decent, safe, and sanitary" accommodations at rents they can afford, no aspect of the program has been subjected to more criticism than relocation. In some respects, as already set forth, this criticism has been justified, reflecting a disregard for human values and an earlier tight housing market. However, the inability of the public to differentiate between those displaced under urban renewal and those forced to move because of highway construction and various other public works projects resulted in *all* abuses being attributed to urban renewal. It must be remembered, too, that in this Nation some 12,000,000 families change their place of residence each year. Those forced to move because of urban renewal are but 2 per cent of this total and less than half of the households displaced by public action. These confusions were particularly unfortunate for the urban renewal program since it *did* provide relocation assistance and had established standards while the other programs usually lacked both.

Although the criticisms of relocation incident to urban renewal have sometimes been exaggerated, there were sufficient examples of abuses, failures, and maladministration to justify significant reforms. The new Administration was fully conscious of this and has taken steps to meet the situation. As indicated earlier, URA strengthened its administrative machinery for handling relocation requirements, established higher minimum standards, provided for more frequent field inspections and more stringent review of relocation plans and progress reports, and upgraded the quality of relocation statistics submitted by local public agencies executing programs.

Also, the Urban Renewal Administration has instituted a new data tabulation program which facilitates identification of problem areas in relocation. With such information, regional staffs can deal with these problems in their early stages. By pointing out these issues to local public agencies and indicating the HHFA's policy relative to them, our regional people have been able to achieve local cooperation in improving the relocation process.

Cities are no longer able to get approval of urban renewal projects unless they can substantiate assurances that they will follow federal requirements for relocation. This means that such local agencies must provide, in their applications for urban renewal projects, reliable surveys of site residents while projects are in the planning stage, and specific information on the location, number, and cost of new housing proposed to be built to meet displacement needs. In addition, complete information on the relocation program must be made available to the public before final approval by the local governing body.

By word, deed, and regulation HHFA has, in recent months, indicated clearly that the quality of relocation had to be improved. In some instances, where results were not forthcoming, execution of projects was delayed until relocation was upgraded. Occasionally programs were stopped in execution, and coordination of the provision of relocation accommodations with further demolition was required.

These reforms were facilitated by two circumstances. The first was a looser housing market with a more normal vacancy rate. This was not of our doing, save as it reflected the Agency's contribution to raising the volume of housing starts as set forth in Chapter V. The second, new HHFA programs, was decidedly of our making, reflecting the planning of the Kennedy Administration to meet the issue.

As far as the latter is concerned (and no elaboration is required to demonstrate that relocation is facilitated by availability of a larger number of vacant dwellings), several programs were involved. Some have been set forth above and include provision of more low- and medium-income housing at the same time that there was emphasis upon rehabilitation and conservation and a de-emphasis upon the bulldozer approach exclusively. However, such a statement of intent means little unless there is machinery to effect it. Consequently, we tackled the difficult problem of rehabilitation. Our first efforts, providing a new program of mortgage insurance under FHA, proved unequal to the task, but we kept at the problem.

Activities in this area were facilitated by an earlier move; my attempt to get greater cooperation between the constituent agencies in HHFA. By June, 1963, we seemed to be on the way. FHA and URA had worked closely together, commingling staffs in seeking solutions in several cities. New Minimum Property Standards for Urban Rehabilitation were developed by the two constituents of HHFA. They represented a potential breakthrough in this most difficult and frustrating area. They provide, we believe, for the first time a practical and realistic basis for establishing levels of property rehabilitation which can be reconciled with the objectives of an urban renewal plan and the requirements for FHA loan insurance. Also, there are provisions for facilitating a flexibility which will be responsive to local variations and requirements. The July, 1963, issue of *House and Home* reported that "the new standards *do* provide rehabilitators with the first really concrete set of standards to help rehabilitation fulfill its promise."

The agreement does more. It outlines methods for gearing FHA programs and skills into the services the local public agencies must provide property owners in assisting them to plan and finance their rehabilitation. At the same time the Office of Program Policy in HHFA is formulating a companion program for accelerating rehabilitation in tenant-occupied areas and structures.

Yet another approach to rehabilitation seemed to be developing. Under the new moderate-income program authorized in the Housing Act of 1961, a novel activity has been initiated by a non-profit foundation in Chicago. Apartments in various parts of the city, which were structurally sound, but in need of repairs, were presented to the FHA. A first building was approved for rehabilitation in July, 1963, and the presentation indicated that minimal increases in rents and no enforced dislocation of tenants would be involved. The sponsor had some 1200 units before the HHFA for similar action, and it contemplated rehabilitating 100 buildings averaging 45 dwelling units.

In contrast to earlier efforts in the field of rehabilitation, the Chicago experiment gathered momentum quickly. By mid-August, 1963, FHA commitments had been issued on three buildings containing 180 dwelling units averaging slightly less than 4.5 rooms. On the basis of this initial group, which was said to be typical of many buildings already identified in Chicago, it was possible to delineate the program more fully.

The structures selected required improvements, which, for the most part, involved work to correct deferred maintenance and replace deteriorated equipment. No structural changes were needed, thereby facilitating rehabilitation while present tenants remained in occupancy. Estimated costs indicated that it was possible either to limit rent increases to a nominal amount or even reduce rents because of the financing under the moderate-income housing program provided for in Section 221(d)(3) of the Housing Act as amended in 1961. The purchase price as well as the costs of rehabilitation are included in the FHA commitment. Thus, with thirty-year loans at below the market interest costs, it seemed possible to keep rents within the moderate-income range. In August, 1963, FHA was processing forty cases of rehabilitation under Section 221(d)(3) in the Chicago area.[3]

FHA's revisions of standards to reflect a realistic attitude toward the structures and the neighborhood in which they are situated, and its insurance of mortgages for the purchase and rehabilitation of existing structures, may enable us to provide a sizable amount of decent housing for existing tenants at rentals they can afford. Involved are realistic housing standards in both efforts and refinancing at low interest rates in the latter. What was under way in Chicago could, and should, be duplicated in many large cities of the Nation.

The emphasis we have placed upon rehabilitation yielded results in the fiscal year 1963, even before the new techniques described above had become operative. By June 30, 1963, some 45,500 structures containing about 107,000 dwelling units were identified for rehabilitation under urban renewal. In the six months immediately preceding the end of the fiscal year, the rate of rehabilitation had been accelerated by over 25 per cent. Thus in that short period, 5500 of the 25,505 dwelling units for which rehabilitation had been completed were added to the inventory. The Public Housing Administration was also encouraging and assisting the upgrading of existing housing for low-income family

[3] By December 1, 1963, some 740 units of rehabilitation had been approved in Chicago under Section 221(d)(3). Five rental and one cooperative developments were involved. There was $1,832,000 of rehabilitation on dwellings valued at $2,628,000 before repairs. Of the rental developments, one had the same rentals after as before rehabilitation, two had rental increases of less than $5.00 per month, and the other two had $1.00 and $1.50 rental increases. In the cooperative, where the cost of rehabilitation was three times the value of the building before repairs, monthly carrying costs increased from $73.21 to $109.16 per month.

occupancy so that by June 30, 1963, more than 1600 rehabilitated dwelling units had been completed under that program. Concurrently, the low-income demonstration program, described in the next chapter, had been experimenting with new techniques to facilitate rehabilitation.

Encouraging beginnings had been made in this difficult, but vital, aspect of urban renewal and housing. The newer approaches are expected to accelerate results at a much more rapid rate. This will serve many purposes. It will provide more efficient utilization of the existing supply of housing, upgrade the gray areas of our urban communities, and augment the supply of standard low- and medium-income housing. Such action will also reduce displacement and the volume of relocation. It will not, of course, eliminate relocation as a problem in urban renewal. But it will combine with the recent expansion of FHA insurance of moderate-income housing mortgages (detailed in Chapter V), the expansion of Section 221(d)(3) housing, and the increase in the volume of low-income housing to facilitate the process.

As of the summer of 1963, reports were available on the housing conditions of over 86 per cent of those relocated incident to urban renewal. Less than 8 per cent, according to statements from local public agencies, were in substandard accommodations and the whereabouts of only 5 per cent were unknown. This is not, of course, perfection; nor does it reflect satisfaction on our part with what has been achieved or with the quality of local statistics. It does reflect, however, the Agency's concern for this vital phase of urban renewal and local agencies' increasing recognition of the crucial importance of upgrading performance in relocation. In this connection, it must be noted that the statistical maximum as far as the percentage of families relocated in standard housing is concerned has been approached. The proportion—from 6 to 7 per cent—of families which move out of a city during relocation re-mains fairly stable, and many of those who go into sub-standard housing do so by choice.

There are, nonetheless, many ways in which reloca-tion can and should be improved. An initial reform in-volves upgrading the quality of local reporting in this field. We have not known, also, how much the new ac-commodations cost, to what degree this cost represents a reasonable increase as related to incomes, and the total impact of the movement upon the city. We are now seeking the answers. Thus, the Urban Renewal Administration is developing a procedure to obtain in-formation on the relation between incomes and housing costs among those displaced. At the same time, the Office of Program Policy in the Office of the Admin-istrator of HHFA is carrying out a research project de-signed to provide more accurate processes to estimate the volume of dislocation in urban areas.

There is another phase of relocation which is still not adequately taken into account by the program. It relates to the criteria established for the selection of sites to be demolished. There remains a tendency to place too great dependency upon evidences of physical blight and ignore the social attributes. This reflects a failure to differentiate between an area of low-rent housing and a slum. Thus, until recently, little atten-tion has been paid to the incidence of home ownership. We still do not probe sufficiently into the cohesiveness of neighborhoods, even when they evidence physical decline. As we come to grips with these issues, the hu-man costs of relocation will be greatly reduced.

Even if we should achieve the maximum possible in the way of upgrading those who are dislocated, in terms of their personal choices and economic capacities, and should we avoid demolition of cohesive neighborhoods, we would not have met the challenge of urban renewal. This was what I had in mind when, addressing the

Eighth Annual Forum of the National Conference on Social Welfare at Minneapolis on May 17, 1961, I said:

> . . . it is just at the moment that a family has been uprooted, has been provided through relocation assistance with the means of establishing a new home, and has been brought into contact—some for the first time and many for reacquaintance—with the social agencies of the community, that miracles can be accomplished.

A proposal to do just this has been developed by the New York City Housing and Redevelopment Board incident to the West Side Renewal Project, described earlier. Its execution will be in three stages and an effort will be made to minimize dislocation by relocating present residents in vacancies in on-site locations, in public housing now under construction in this area, and in moderate-income accommodations to be built in the area.

Present occupants will be studied so as to identify their needs and provide and evaluate the impact of a range of services required to relocate them permanently. The residents will be divided into three groups: (1) stable households able to relocate readily; (2) households of low- and medium-incomes desirous of remaining in the area but facing obstacles (as revealed in their social history) to qualify or adjust readily to the new environment; (3) households with severe or complex disabilities.

According to the description of the proposal, financed by a Section 314 Urban Renewal Grant:

> The study will include an appraisal of the needs of this population which will give direction to a program of action for social as well as physical community rebirth, and to offer services which will ameliorate the problems of families who must be relocated. In so doing, it will yield knowledge about how such action programs might be devised for similar purposes in other renewal areas.

Thus, a rare opportunity exists to stimulate a true rebirth of a community and to provide a model which will contribute to other renewal projects throughout the country. Information from the proposed study will also provide some basis for demonstrating that urban renewal projects take into account the human implications of renewal for the families directly affected and for the community institutions and services as well as physical change and improvement.

Carrying out this proposal will apply another innovation of the present HHFA administration: the development of programs which involve the cooperative efforts of several federal departments and agencies. Already, we have jointly sponsored and financed programs for dealing with social problems in public housing programs. In this instance the Health, Education, and Welfare Department is cooperating with HHFA. The West Side Urban Renewal proposal outlined above will, too, involve a cooperative effort between HEW and HHFA as well as the participation of several agencies of local government.

The original concept of urban renewal did not face up to these problems. It was conceived primarily in terms of land values, tax revenues, and slum clearance. As the program matured, it disclosed a complex of social problems. Thus, without design, urban renewal became a catalyst in highlighting problems that most Americans had either not known or preferred to ignore. Today urban renewal must deal with human renewal as well as physical renewal. HHFA is now attempting to define federal responsibility in this area and develop effective programs for meeting the issue.

In the quest for workable approaches to the human problems in urban renewal, HHFA will be assisted by many local activities under way and by the experiments in this field of the Ford Foundation. The latter organization has for several years been working with school systems in our larger cities in an effort to make the education process more effective and meaningful for newcomers. It has, in four urban areas, experimental programs designed to coordinate local resources in an effort to meet the human problems of the gray areas.

Concern for the human aspects of urban renewal, preliminary analyses of the economic costs of relocation to those affected, and recent emphasis upon rehabilitation indicate the need for new and expanded approaches to moderate- and low-income housing. Thus we are preparing legislative proposals in this area. We propose:

(1) Permissive admission to federally assisted low-income housing of low-income single persons under sixty-two years of age displaced by any form of public activity.

(2) Programs for utilizing, through purchase and leasing, existing housing for occupancy of low-income families.

(3) Supplementary housing payments over a period of two years to assist low- and moderate-income families and individuals displaced by urban renewal and public housing to acquire housing without increasing significantly the ratio of their monthly payments for shelter to their incomes.

In addition, we shall propose use of Section 221(d) (3) for rehabilitation of one-unit and duplex houses owned by low- and moderate-income senior citizen families in rehabilitation and conservation areas, with deferred principal payments. There will also be a proposal for an expansion of the present public housing program and additional subsidy payments to facilitate greater utilization of existing housing for low-income families under the public housing program. The volume of low-rent public housing would be almost doubled.

The first four of these proposals, if authorized, would not only ease relocation and reduce its economic burden for poor people, but they would also augment the quantity and improve the quality of housing available to low- and moderate-income households and individuals. Expansion and extension of the existing public housing program would augment the amount of standard low-income housing.[4] Combined with the other proposals, it would increase the number and categories of low-income households in areas subject to demolition and rehabilitation (and elsewhere) eligible for federal assistance.

Economic Considerations

When urban renewal was proposed and seeking support, like most new proposals it was often oversold by its champions. One aspect of this involved the assertion that it would, by providing fully taxpaying, high-priced housing, commercial, and industrial reuse, make a major contribution toward local tax problems.[5] Implicit

[4] Of all the myths about urban renewal, none is more persistent and misleading than the notion that only a few of those offered public housing as a relocation resource accept it. Actually, only 55 per cent of the families (and none of the single persons under sixty-two) are eligible, on the basis of income, for public housing. Second, among those who meet income requirements, many are ineligible because of family composition. Finally, public housing and urban renewal are both long-time programs most difficult to schedule precisely in advance. Thus, even when public housing is designed and planned to be a relocation resource, it may come on the market too soon or too late to make the maximum relocation contribution.

[5] Of course, urban renewal almost universally does make such a contribution, but it is not the financial panacea it was first expected to be. Where there is a market for higher-priced housing, industrial, or commercial reuse, the results are dramatic. But when the demand for such reuse is doubtful or delayed, similar consequences do not readily occur.

An excellent example of the former situation is provided by Southwest Redevelopment in Washington, D.C. Here redevelopment—already definitely successful—is expected to produce some 4.8 million dollars annually in taxes as contrasted to slightly less than $600,000 prior to redevelopment. The other side of the coin is represented by those urban renewal projects

in this promise was the assumption that there was, and would continue to be, a large and expanding demand for high-priced shelter or commercial and industrial reuse in the central cities of the United States. In addition, of course, such promotion failed to anticipate, realistically, the opposition from site occupants and liberals to a program of public grants which was instrumental in replacing the poor or the small-business man with the rich or large-scale commercial or industrial enterprise.

Actually, the demand for high-priced housing in central cities was limited at the outset of the program, except in places like Los Angeles, New York, San Francisco, Chicago, Washington, and a few others. Everywhere, the demand that existed at the beginning of the program was often satisfied by private construction on other sites during the long period initially required to plan and execute an urban renewal project. Of course, the situation is not static; and urban renewal, defying our currently accepted economic theory, may yet support, to a limited degree, Say's law that supply creates demand. This suggests that as time goes on the creation of a new environment through urban renewal serves to condition more people to want the type of living it provides and to support downtown commercial and industrial facilities. Already this trend is apparent in many cities.

Thus, both political and economic problems, incident to the high rentals and sales prices in urban renewal developments, faced the Kennedy Administration. To meet these problems, and to assist in relocation and recognize a forgotten income group in the

where there are no redevelopers ready, willing, or able to undertake high-rent residential, industrial, or commercial reuse. Now, as is indicated below, it is often possible to redevelop such sites for moderate-income housing. In this event, there will also be significant increase in local tax revenue, but, of course, it will be less than that flowing from more expensive construction.

housing market, we developed the first national moderate-income housing program. It is identified as Section 221(d)(3) housing and has been described in the preceding chapter. In the context of this analysis one need only note that it has proven to be an outstanding success. Among new programs in FHA, it has moved with the greatest speed.[6] It provides a tool for housing moderate-income families in urban renewal areas (as well as elsewhere), thereby facilitating greater economic diversification in our urban communities.

The new moderate-income program had been used, as of October, 1963, to refinance five urban renewal developments which were in economic trouble due to a paucity of demand on the part of higher-income tenants. Most important, it has provided a vehicle for immediate construction on sites which could not have been successfully undertaken for higher-priced housing. A good example of this is the program of St. Louis, where an urban renewal site had been cleared but where the market did not support rapid or extensive redevelopment. One of the redevelopers had, in the summer of 1963, completed a fairly high-rent project of some 125 units, and subsequently started a 600-unit moderate-income project on the site. The latter supplements the former while assuring economic diversification and more rapid utilization of the cleared land.

In Paterson, New Jersey, 188 units of a 752-unit moderate-income cooperative, constructed on an urban renewal site, were in occupancy by October, 1963. Neighboring Newark was in the process of developing over 370 units of moderate-income housing immediately and an undisclosed number of additional units on ur-

---

[6] For a favorable response from homebuilders, see "221 d 3 May Be the Answer," *Practical Builder*, February, 1963, pp. 84–86; "Low Rents—Good Living in 221 d 3 Pilot Project," *Ibid.*, June, 1963, pp. 90–93; and "221(d)(3) It's the Greatest Program We Have Today," *Ibid.*, November, 1963, pp. 95–97.

ban renewal sites which had been cleared for some time. Three moderate-income projects, composed of over five hundred town houses, had been announced in urban renewal areas of Michigan. Elsewhere, scores of commitments were issued, allocation of funds set aside, or construction started on similar developments.

The potentialities of Section 221(d)(3) in urban renewal had been demonstrated by the fall of 1963. In Brookline, Massachusetts, the local redevelopment authority took its responsibilities for relocation seriously. In connection with its first project, initial construction was designed to meet relocation needs. There were 206 families and 85 individuals in the area prior to demolition. The local agency had completed 100 relocation units of low-rent public housing and had developed plans for 116 units of Section 221(d)(3) housing. Both of these resources, located on the site, are to be used primarily for the relocation of families displaced by the redevelopment. The third phase of the program proposed to construct some 750 units of high-rent apartments. The final result will be a socially integrated development containing public, moderate-priced, and high-priced housing.

The local redevelopment agency of White Plains, New York, is redeveloping a core area, composed of slums and outmoded commercial buildings largely occupied by non-whites. Originally it had been planned for commercial, public, and low-rent reuse. The final proposal is much more desirable. It involves ultimate construction of a complex of public buildings, commercial facilities, and, possibly, high-priced apartments. The first aim will be to provide for those relocated from the slums. Consequently, the initial construction will be for housing designed to accomplish this purpose.

There were 400 medium-income and 350 low-income families on the site. The redevelopment and associated activities will provide an equal number of dwelling units in each of these income ranges. First there will be a 150-unit Section 221(d)(3) development and a 50-unit low-rent project in areas near, but not in, the redevelopment site. Subsequently, 250 Section 221(d) (3) units will be constructed in the urban renewal area. One hundred additional low-rental units will be built in another urban renewal site. The redevelopment and its environs, therefore, will have a mixture of multi-income housing, constructed in four or five clusters rather than one larger concentration of low-rent housing as was originally proposed. This will not only provide better planning and economic diversification but will also minimize the impact of relocation.

As of September 30, 1963, the Federal National Mortgage Association had purchased or made commitments on mortgages to finance some 12,000 units of moderate-income housing. Of these some 8000 units were under construction. FNMA funds had been allocated for over 39,000 units involving $465,000,000, and we expect to make allocations for an additional 33,000 units in the remainder of the fiscal year of 1964. This seemed a realistic goal in light of the fact that in the first two weeks of August, 1963, allocations for 25 projects involving 2060 dwelling units were made under the 221(d)(3) program. All of these, of course, are not in urban renewal areas, but many are.

Between July, 1961, and September, 1963, allocation of funds, commitments insured, or indorsements have occurred for Section 221(d)(3) developments in some 44 urban renewal areas in 38 communities. They will provide moderate-income housing for over 9200 families. The number will be augmented significantly by the Mitchell-Lama and other middle-income units provided under financial assistance from the State and City of New York. Applications had also been approved for moderate-income senior citizen housing which will provide over a thousand dwelling units in seven urban renewal sites.

The development of moderate-priced housing in urban renewal areas will be accelerated by other changes in the policy and procedures of the Housing and Home Finance Agency. In May, 1963, URA announced that local public agencies would be permitted to include architectural and other consulting services for the preparation of illustrative plans to help determine the feasibility of providing moderate-income housing in urban renewal areas. Subsequently, FHA and URA developed a coordinated approach, involving local public agencies, to facilitate and accelerate moderate-income housing in urban renewal areas.

The 1961 Housing Act had authorized sale price of land in urban renewal projects in terms of its value for the provision of housing for occupancy by families of moderate-income rather than for the highest level of use in accordance with the Urban Renewal Plan. The new procedure further assists moderate-income housing by enabling the local public agency to (1) test and establish the suitability of using Section 221(d) (3) to finance residential redevelopment in a project; (2) identify in general terms the physical character, cost, required rents, and market for such a project; and (3) provide assistance and advice to an eligible sponsor in obtaining an FHA-insured loan to finance the development. Among other things, it calls attention to the possibility of utilizing local tax abatement to achieve desired rents.[7]

There remained, however, a disinclination on the part of some local redevelopment agencies to abandon their original commitments to high-priced shelter. In part, this was a reflection of earlier representations of the economic magic in urban renewal. In part, it reflected optimism born of unrealistic assumptions. Of course, it followed from the fact that prior to the Housing Act

[7] In the fall of 1963, URA sent a letter to local public agencies setting forth techniques by which they can accelerate use of urban renewal sites for low-rent public housing.

of 1961, local public agencies outside of New York State had no choice. There was no effective financial instrument for moderate-income housing in urban renewal areas. But the current volume of multi-family luxury housing starts elsewhere in our cities is requiring increasing realism, and the new Section 221(d)(3) program provides a tool for giving expression to this realism. This is reflected in the increasing amount of land in urban renewal areas available for moderate-income housing. Incomplete reports indicated that there would be a demand for some 8000 dwelling units in this price range during the calendar year 1963, and a much larger number in the following year.

Significantly, many of the larger cities were making available a sizable proportion of urban renewal acreage for moderate-income housing. New York City, which from the start of its redevelopment, enjoyed the advantage of a moderate-income program and during the Harriman Administration first benefited from the new Mitchell-Lama Law which greatly extended the efficacy of such a program, led the way. Indeed, its action, as no doubt similar action in other large cities, reflected response to political pressures opposing concentration of benefits for the affluent on sites formerly occupied by the poor through a program that involves public grants. By the spring of 1963, San Francisco contemplated urban renewal sites for 2500 medium-income housing units in 1963 and 1964; Oakland, California, 900 units; Chicago, 2000; Buffalo, 1300; Boston, 900; and Stamford, Connecticut, 1500. Smaller cities, too, had sizable programs in sight: Danville and Norfolk, Virginia, 600 and 625 units respectively.

The economic considerations that necessitated a moderate-income housing program also demanded better market analysis data. The deficiencies in this area had many roots. In the first place, prior to 1961, there were no agency-wide economic market studies. Each of the constituents either did its own studies or none at all.

Then, too, the local public agencies frequently tested out the market at the time of project planning and assumed that findings of that period would be sound years later, when execution took place.

To aid in meeting this situation, HHFA has provided, in its pending budget, for the establishment of regional teams of economists to carry out market analyses, and we have already initiated pilot comprehensive studies of the market. We are in the process of adapting market analysis to urban renewal requirements, because in the latter program it is necessary not only to project the demand into the future but also to estimate the part which may be met by construction incident to urban renewal. Thus HHFA and its constituents are gathering economic data which reflect more realistically the feasibility of additional high-priced housing in many urban renewal programs. Of course, Section 221(d)(3) provides local agencies greater flexibility in redevelopment. Should, at the time of construction, the market analyses indicate a thin demand for high-rental or high-priced sales housing, the moderate-income program can be substituted.

Digestibility and Design

Closely related to market analysis is the matter of the "digestibility" of urban renewal. This refers to the volume of activity that can successfully be carried on in any city at a given time. First, of course, is the question of how much new housing, additional industrial sites, or new office space the market will absorb. Second is the practical issue of how many displaced persons the community can digest. This involves not only the problem of providing physical relocation resources, and the machinery for carrying out relocation, but also the community receptivity to the disruptive impact of demolition and dislocation. Finally, there are a host of associated issues; the political impact, the strains upon public facilities and services, and the like.

As long as there were year-to-year or patently inadequate authorizations of federal funds for urban renewal, built-in pressures motivated local authorities to program far beyond capacity to perform. This existed throughout the latter part of the 1950s, when many of the more aggressive local authorities sought maximum federal allocations of what appeared to be shrinking available resources. The Housing Act of 1961 re-established the original 1949 institutional framework appropriate to a program having a long lead-time. As observed above, it provided for the authorization of two billion dollars to be committed over three years. As a consequence, there was no necessity for a locality to seek greater annual allocations in the early 1960s in order to be sure that its program might have continuity. Rather, it could think and act in terms of a three-year period. While, of course, this circumstance did not, in itself, assure realistic programming at the local level, it did re-establish a financial milieu favorable to such results.

In July, 1962, URA initiated a procedure for reviewing each application from a local public agency for additional capital grant allocations. Evaluations were based upon past performance and current work load, and they were designed to make sure that additional funds can be used effectively. The basic criteria are previous performance and evidence that there are staff, potential redevelopers, relocation resources, and community acceptance. This is a programming operation as distinct from the fund rationing procedures of the Eisenhower Administration. Special attention is also given to the quality of the relocation operation.

Insofar as dislocation is reduced and relocation improved, capacity for "digestibility" is increased. A similar consequence flows from success in rehabilitation and expansion of the low- and moderate-income housing programs. Related, too, is the long time lag between the announcement of an urban renewal project and execution. In the past an element of delay resulted when the FHA's appraisal of land in an urban renewal area for mortgage insurance purposes disappointed the expectations of the private residential redeveloper who had paid a higher price for that land. To meet this issue, in the late summer of 1963, URA and FHA established a procedure under which a minimum acceptable disposal price agreeable to both of them and to the local public agency would determine the value for FHA mortgage insurance purposes, with this fact being made known to the private redeveloper. Under this procedure, the reasonable expectations of the redeveloper are not disappointed if he chooses to make a higher bid in order to obtain the land. With all these easements, however, "digestibility" is a real and abiding problem, and we are continuing to develop additional criteria for our guidance and that of local public agencies in this regard. One of the instruments used in this connection is the Community Renewal Program which, as was indicated previously, provides a city-wide approach to urban renewal.

The nature of such planning has been set forth, but it should be observed here that it is designed to facilitate a community-wide concept of urban renewal in which each project and associated activity would take its place as a contributing factor in achieving city-wide objectives and plans. Community Renewal Programs are concerned with the scheduling of urban renewal in a manner consistent with a city's resources and other capacities. In this frame of reference, each project is developed as a part of a whole which has been envisioned. This enables a city to analyze its needs for urban renewal and then program its activities in this field along with its scheduling for capital improvement.[8] Some notion of what is involved can be derived from summarizing a few cities' programs.

[8] For a comprehensive analysis of CRP, see David A. Grossman, "The Community Renewal Program: Policy Development, Progress, and Problems," *Journal of the American In-*

Philadelphia, in its comprehensive analysis of urban renewal needs and potentials, is undertaking (1) a review of past renewal programs to glean the best experience for future application; (2) an examination of the social characteristics of each of the city's neighborhoods to provide more understanding in selection of projects; and (3) an appraisal of all city programs with urban renewal significance to see where coordination is needed.

Chicago is working on a detailed study of the renewal needs of its industrial areas and is also making an interesting survey of the relationship between street improvements and urban renewal areas so that these city expenditures can be related. Providence, Rhode Island, is developing through its Community Renewal Program a proposal for streamlining the city's renewal machinery.

Until 1961, only seven cities had Community Renewal Programs in execution. Since then almost one hundred have been approved, and most large cities, as well as many smaller ones, are now taking a comprehensive approach to urban renewal. We are on the way to meeting the issue of "projectitis" through this and associated activities, and in the process we shall not

---

stitute of Planners, November, 1963, pp. 259–269. The following quotes from this article are pertinent, reflecting the new policy on CRP recently developed in URA: "As between the concept of the CRP as a research tool and the CRP as a guide for decision-making and urban renewal action, URA's policy is clear. In the face of many unknowns, there is a great temptation to engage in research (often badly needed) and to avoid action. The ties of the CRP to the action process of urban renewal are vital, however, and must be given first priority. . . .

"One of the most crucial aims of every CRP is to open channels of communication between technicians and policy-makers, and between renewal administrators and the general public, to ensure that the CRP's recommendations will be conscientiously considered. This is perhaps the greatest single challenge facing everyone concerned with the CRP, whether in federal or local government" (p. 268).

only improve the program but also forge instruments for dealing more effectively with some of the human problems which have been ignored and avoided.

One of the indices of digestibility in urban renewal is the rate of land disposition. It is perhaps the most significant initial indicator of the economic soundness of the activity. Consequently, there is much discussion about the intensity of demand for urban renewal sites. As was indicated in the previous chapter, during the earlier years of the program, urban renewal sites frequently remained cleared and unused for long periods of time. This gave rise to the notion that there was little effective demand for land made available through urban renewal. As all early defects of the program, this one has become a part of "conventional wisdom" and is constantly repeated.

The fact is, however, that well planned and well located urban renewal sites are very much in demand. As we perfect the changes outlined above and initiate additional ones, more of the sites involved will fall in the category described above. Already results are apparent. For example, the total area which local public agencies conveyed to redevelopers in the last two fiscal years exceeds the entire area which had been transferred to redevelopers in the whole of the preceding period from the beginning of the program in 1949. Of course, a part of this is inevitable in that the final land disposition in a long-term expanding program is sure to increase if the undertaking is at all successful. Much of the acceleration in this aspect of the program, however, is due to the efforts recently directed toward "digestibility."

At the end of June, 1963, about 22,000 acres had been acquired by local public agencies. Of that ready for disposition (16,000 acres), redevelopers had been selected for 80 per cent. In addition, during fiscal year 1963 the pace of redevelopment was significantly stepped up as evidenced by an increase of 37 per cent during the year in the acreage for which redevelopers had been chosen. About three-quarters of all land disposed of, exclusive of streets and alleys, had been purchased by private persons or organizations. Most of it will be used for residential purposes; the remainder will be devoted to commercial, industrial, or institutional use.

There is also another pressing issue, the matter of design in urban renewal areas. This involves taste, and it is sure to inspire and occasion heated controversies. HHFA has devoted much effort to emphasizing the importance of aesthetics in the development of our cities during the past three years. In doing this, of course, we were reflecting the Kennedy Administration's concern for these matters. Witness the address of August Heckscher, then the President's Special Consultant on the Arts, before the First Conference on Aesthetic Responsibility, and White House Assistant Arthur Schlesinger's statement before the American Federation of Arts.[9]

In addition, the HHFA has encouraged the substitution of good design for maximum land prices as the major criterion for selecting redevelopers. In the spring of 1963, URA issued a new policy stating that "reuse appraisals should be based on controls and design objectives in the Plan and such approved design criteria as are intended to effectuate the use control in the Plan." This rescinded an earlier instruction to the field stating that appraisers were to disregard any design objectives of criteria not contained in the original Plan. This change permits local public agencies to experiment and allows URA wide latitude for approval.

[9] For a more comprehensive treatment of the Administration's concern for aesthetics in building, see "Architectural Policy in Washington," *Architectural Forum*, July, 1962, p. 5; also "A Hunger in the Land," *Ibid.*, December, 1962, p. 73. For a brief statement on URA's position on design and a series of illustrations of buildings constructed on urban renewal sites, see "Design in Urban Renewal," *Urban Renewal Notes*, July–August 1963, 15 pp.

Of course, we have encountered some state and local laws and court decisions which have thwarted us, but, on the whole, there has been acceptance of the point of view we have articulated. Our position is categorical. The Federal Government cannot, and should not, establish standards of taste, but it does have a responsibility to encourage local communities to be concerned with design. This we have attempted to do. As a consequence, increasingly, urban renewal projects involve architectural competitions.[10] These not only usually result in better designs but they also involve the people of our cities in discussions—and controversies—over aesthetic values.

Three of the most dramatic of these contests occurred in Boston, New York, and San Francisco. In Boston the result was a striking, and controversial, design of the new city hall now under construction. In

[10] For an analysis of the present efforts in the direction of better design and results to date, see "Urban Renewal: A New Face on the American City," *Architectural Forum*, August, 1963, pp. 80–85.

FHA, too, is fostering better design. In 1963 that agency announced that it would give honor awards for residential design. And the new Commissioner of the Public Housing Administration has stressed upgrading the quality of design in public housing. Under the leadership of Albert Mayer, an outstanding architect who has long been concerned with low-income housing, PHA recently sponsored jointly with the American Institute of Architects and the National Association of Housing and Redevelopment Officials six regional design seminars. In addition to encouraging improved design, these meetings have afforded URA an opportunity to outline for public housing officials its Community Renewal Program with special emphasis upon comprehensive and total planning to achieve more livable communities. Also, PHA commissioned Elizabeth Coit, an architect with long experience in a local housing authority and a consultant to PHA, to undertake a study of methods to make public housing developments more livable. Commissioner Marie McGuire of PHA has set forth her objectives in this field. They include melding public housing into the community and development of more imaginative planning. (" 'Livable' Housing Sought in Study," *New York Times*, Oct. 15, 1963, p. 17.)

San Francisco, the Golden Gate Redevelopment was involved. The design that resulted is generally regarded as inspired. In New York the competition was for an urban renewal area in which middle-income housing is to be built. The winning proposal tapped technological developments and aesthetic effects. In all three instances, fresh and imaginative ideas evolved, and in Boston and New York the winners of the competition were new to the type of work or the geographic area involved.

The Washington activities of the Housing and Home Finance Agency are currently scattered in some eighteen buildings in the Nation's capital. Thus, it was inevitable that thought would have been given to consolidating them. The Kennedy Administration recognized the importance of this and took effective action. The Agency received authorization for a new building in 1962 and appropriation for its initiation in the spring of 1963.

As the agency of the government responsible for urban renewal, HHFA felt that its new building should be identified with this program. Consequently, a site for the proposed 29 million-dollar structure was secured in Washington's Southwest Redevelopment Area. Also, the Agency wanted the new HHFA building to symbolize the high standards of design it was encouraging. Through the cooperation of the General Services Administration, two firms were secured as architects: Marcel Breuer, and Nolen, Swinburne and Associates. Of this move the *New York Times* in its August 9, 1963, edition observed:

> The selection of the Breuer firm as co-designers of this major structure has aroused more than routine interest in architectural circles. Professional observers consider it the first visible spark struck from the recent heated controversies about the pedestrian dullness of office buildings in most American cities, including the nation's capital. It is also the first large commission awarded under the G.S.A.'s new Assistant Commissioner for Design and

Construction, Karel Yasko, in response to the President's directive on the pursuit of excellence in government architecture.

Impact upon Minorities

All that has been done to minimize dislocation, emphasize rehabilitation, provide moderate-income housing, improve the process of relocation, and strengthen the Workable Program reduces the adverse impact of urban renewal upon minorities. In addition, some of these efforts have a positive consequence. The most significant in this regard is the new program of housing for moderate-income families. Not only does it meet a shelter need at economic levels where there is a great concentration of non-whites, but it also provides a new and important potential for integrated patterns of living.

Urban renewal, even in its earlier phases, resulted in significant demonstrations that white and non-white families of comparable economic and social backgrounds can and will live together in well-designed, attractive developments. The potentialities of the moderate-income program are even greater. Witness Park Town in Cincinnati where, in a predominantly Negro neighborhood, a Section 221(d)(3) conversion involving 322 dwellings was providing integrated housing in this border city. Equally significant is one of the earliest developments completed under Section 221(d)(3), the St. Francis Square Project in Western Addition, a renewal area in San Francisco. In mid-August, 1963, when 270 of the 300 apartments then completed had been sold, the racial breakdown of applicants was 50 per cent white, 35 per cent Negro, and 15 per cent other non-whites. This distribution was being achieved by an aggressive sales campaign among whites and it seemed likely to persist, provided the school problem was solved.

The Commissioner of Urban Renewal stated in June, 1963, that the objective of urban renewal is "not only the physical renaissance of the city but also the dignity and well-being of the city's people." Thus, free access to housing for all families, regardless of race, creed, or national origin, has been announced as a goal in this program.

In the spirit of President Kennedy's Executive Order on Equal Opportunity in Housing, HHFA revised its regulations to make equal opportunity a central factor in the development of communities engaged in such programs. Cities undertaking Community Renewal Programs were required to include:

(a) an anaylsis of existing racial residential patterns;

(b) projection of the housing needs of minorities;

(c) development of affirmative programs to increase the quantity, improve the quality, and eliminate the barriers to housing for Negro and other minority families.

In addition, URA revised its regulations to prohibit the listing of relocation housing accommodations which are not available to all families regardless of race, creed, or national origin.

As the Kennedy Administration attempted to improve the direction of urban renewal, inject consideration for the human elements involved, and secure more citizen participation, non-whites shared in the benefits derived. One of the dividends which accrued was a trend toward less concentration of colored people among those displaced. Of course, as long as slums and blighted areas are torn down, non-whites will be disproportionately involved, but results indicate that the degree of this involvement is being reduced.

In 1957, among those for whom color was indicated, some 53 per cent of those displaced by urban renewal were non-whites.[11] As of December, 1961, the percent-

[11] In 1957, some 30 per cent of those who were displaced were not identified by color, reflecting, in large measure, families displaced in Puerto Rico and New York City. By December, 1961, the figure was 22 per cent, but rose to 28.7 per cent by March, 1963. The latter increase was attributable primarily to the large urban renewal programs in Puerto Rico.

age was 51.5. In March, 1963, it was 46.1 per cent. The proportion of whites in this category increased during this period. In 1957 it was 16.6 per cent; at the end of 1961 it was 26.5 per cent; and in March, 1963, it was 25.2 per cent.

Urban renewal has frequently been described as "Negro removal." As most catching phrases, this one overstates the case, reflecting the tendency to judge the program by its past deficiencies. It ignores the potential for integration and better housing for minorities which *could* be in urban renewal. As delineated above, we are moving toward a realization of these potentialities, through Administration policies, new programs authorized by the Housing Act of 1961, and more effective realization of the long-existing protections contained in the law. While the full impact of our activities is not yet apparent, there are data indicating how the urban renewal program has affected non-whites.

The results to date are inconclusive. While it is undeniable that at least twice as many non-whites as whites were displaced by demolition incident to urban renewal and the proportion of whites rehoused in urban residential redevelopment sites was at least double that for non-whites, urban renewal has established many areas of bi-racial living, most of which should remain stable. In addition, there are a score of redevelopment areas of token bi-racial character. Most of these are predominantly white and should also remain bi-racial in the future. As was indicated earlier, almost all relocated families upgraded the quality of their shelter, but relocation frequently contributed to the creation or the extension, of existing ghettos. In large part this was a consequence of attempts to relocate families in an extremely tight housing market. On the other hand, where there is an effective program of relocation and a growing supply of low- and moderate-income housing, the relocation process can not only upgrade the quality of shelter for the vast majority of those displaced but can also provide non-whites greater access to the total housing market.

As in all discussions of non-white housing trends, it is difficult to identify the degree to which non-white displacement incident to urban renewal was due to racial or economic factors. There is evidence to suggest that the former was frequently responsible, at the same time that redevelopment provided a significant degree of segregated new housing for non-whites in the South. Thus, as of June 30, 1963, in that region three times as many redevelopment areas were for completely non-white occupancy as for all-white occupancy. Four redevelopments in the region had token occupancy by a second racial group, and four were mixed racially.[12]

Everywhere both race and economics were involved, and one finds it perplexing to identify the impact of each. However, in a situation such as the Waverly project in Baltimore it appears that while the cost of redevelopment housing might have eliminated most non-whites, rental levels alone cannot account for the absence of non-whites in the redevelopment. An equally, if not more, expensive project in the city's Broadway redevelopment, where the sponsor announced open occupancy, had token non-white participation. On the other hand, in the Flake Hill redevelopment in Eufaula, Alabama, urban renewal resulted in the demolition of a Negro area and the redevelopment of a 100 per cent white neighborhood.

In most instances, however, where there was complete displacement of non-whites under the program, the reuse was non-residential. But the impact of this was greater for whites than non-whites since a larger number of areas so affected had whites rather than non-whites as their original occupants. Where formerly

[12] A redevelopment area is considered racially mixed if it has 10 per cent or more of a second racial group. For large projects, involving 400 or more dwelling units, 50 or more families of a second racial group is the criterion.

whites and non-whites had lived in urban renewal areas, incomplete data indicate that some 30 per cent were in mixed occupancy after renewal, slightly over 7 per cent became all-white, about 8.5 per cent became all non-white, and over half were redeveloped for non-residential use.

Regional differences in racial patterns are interesting. Of the 46 racially mixed redevelopments as of June 30, 1963, 37 were in the North and West, 5 in border cities, and 4 in the South (of which 3 were rehabilitation projects). There were 20 redevelopments with token bi-racial patterns;[13] 14 were in the North and West, 2 in border cities, and 4 in the South. In addition to the 24 completely non-white redevelopments in the South, there were 4 in border cities and 14 in the North and West. On the other hand, only 10 projects in the South had all-white occupancy, 1 in a border city was in this category, and 12 in the North and West (for the most part in cities with small non-white populations or predominantly low-income non-white populations) were in this group.

The greatest degree of bi-racial housing in urban renewal areas is in the larger cities. New York City, as of June 30, 1963, had 15 projects in occupancy. Of the total, 9 were of mixed racial occupancy. Two in Harlem had token white participation; 3 high-rental redevelopments in Manhattan and 1 in Rockaway had token non-white participation. Except for redevelopments in, or contiguous to, centers of non-white concentration, non-white occupancy generally varied inversely with the cost of the new housing. The total program of the city had some 19,250 units occupied; of these, about 13,500 housed whites (or those for whom color was not identified); and 5725, non-whites.

In Chicago, where there were five urban redevelop-

---

[13] Projects where there were some of a second racial group but a lesser proportion or number than in the criteria set forth on p. 133 n as the basis for identifying mixed occupancy.

ment projects in occupancy, all were racially mixed.[14]
Actually, of the 4867 units in occupancy, 2099 housed
non-whites. In Philadelphia the 9 redevelopment areas
in advanced occupancy had a significant degree of non-
white residents. Five of these were mixed; 2 had token
white or non-white participation, and 2 were all-non-
white. Of the 2000 odd dwelling units involved, 80
per cent were occupied by non-whites. Reference has
been made above to Detroit, where the one redevelopment area in a significant degree of occupancy had 10
per cent non-whites. In Minneapolis, the one urban
renewal development in occupancy had some 20 per
cent non-whites. In Washington, D.C., the redevelopment projects established a new pattern of racial
occupancy in upper-income housing. As of October,
1963, there were 2172 dwelling units completed in the
relatively high-cost Southwest redevelopments. Of
these, 92.5 per cent had either been rented or (in the
case of cooperatives) sold. Among the rental units,
90.2 per cent were in occupancy, and all of the 518
cooperative units had been purchased. Of those living
in the area, 9.4 per cent were non-white. The latter's
participation was larger in the cooperative than in rental
accommodations; for 13.7 per cent of the cooperators
were non-white.

Urban renewal is providing, for the first time, a sizable supply of new racially integrated housing in a
growing number of our cities. Some 92 per cent—over
17,500 dwelling units—of the housing in racially mixed

[14] It is significant that Hyde Park redevelopment was at-
tacked in an article (Elinor Richey, "Keeping the Outsiders
Out," *Saturday Review*, October 19, 1963, pp. 22–24). This
created a great amount of criticism, including a letter from
C. Sumner Stone, Jr., the racially militant editor of the *Chicago Defender*. The editor of *Saturday Review* admitted that
he and his associates had "been caught off base." This incident
reflects the tendency to repeat old criticisms of urban renewal
and to avoid seeking current facts which reflect new directions
in the program.

areas (of which some 7000 were occupied by non-whites) were privately financed. In the urban redevelopment areas with token racial mixture, slightly over 72 per cent of the dwelling units were privately financed. The remainder in each category was public housing.[15] This is significant because it indicates that urban renewal is slowly affording non-whites (most of whom are middle-income) a chance to move out of racial ghettos into what, for the most part, seem to be stable ethnically integrated neighborhoods. Non-white families involved—far too few to date—are thereby able at long last to begin to emulate the residential mobility of earlier migrants to urban centers.

Among middle-income non-whites there has long been a paucity of desirable shelter to meet their aspirations and ability to pay. Insofar as urban redevelopment provides such facilities it is a boon to the middle-class non-whites. Where there is a limited number of minority group occupants, or the site is favorably located and well-served with public facilities, the stability of integrated neighborhoods is greatest. At the same time, however, if the area involved was formerly all non-white or racially mixed with a significant number of non-white residents, the price of a probably stable racially mixed redevelopment is usually large-scale non-white displacement.

[15] As of June 30, 1963, there were in urban renewal areas 4056 occupied units of public housing. Of these 2830 were occupied by non-whites. The greatest concentration of this public housing was in Pennsylvania, where there were 1796 units of which 1375 were occupied by non-whites (93 per cent of this public housing in the state was concentrated in Philadelphia). In Minnesota the units were predominantly in white occupancy (436 of the total, 528 units). Connecticut, Massachusetts, and Michigan had a small amount of public housing, but it was largely in white occupancy. The limited amount of public housing in one urban renewal area in New Jersey was largely occupied by non-whites. In the South, there were 1441 units of public housing in urban renewal areas; all but 168 units were occupied by non-whites.

Urban renewal, therefore, can safely (from a point of view of avoiding generating class antagonism or occasioning undue economic hardship among non-whites as a whole) make a contribution to the establishment of stable racially integrated neighborhoods only if the supply of housing available to low- and moderate-income non-whites is concurrently augmented significantly. The bi-racial patterns which have emerged in urban redevelopment reflect, primarily, a limited degree of benefits for middle-income non-whites in a program which has displaced poor people and generally provided rehousing for the more affluent. Urban renewal, if it is to achieve sufficient popular support for its continuation, must assure that displaced families, both white and non-white, have an opportunity to upgrade their housing without experiencing unreasonable economic costs. Our efforts to improve the relocation process are designed to deal with these requirements for a sound program, and the new legislation we shall propose will, if enacted, accelerate the process while also easing the economic burden involved.

With these still unmet needs in mind, it is possible to set forth the benefits which have accrued to non-whites under urban renewal to date. By and large, it has served to upgrade the quality of housing available to minorities. More important, it has established in *new*, predominantly privately-financed housing, racially integrated patterns in Richmond, San Francisco, and Seaside, California; New Haven; Washington, D.C.; Chicago; Detroit; Minneapolis; St. Louis; Jersey City, Newark, and Paterson, New Jersey; New York; Rochester; Cincinnati; Philadelphia, Easton, Farrel, and Harrisburg, Pennsylvania; and Johnson City, Tennessee. Token integration exists in Sacramento, California; Louisville; Baltimore; Brookline and North Adams, Massachusetts; St. Paul; and York, Pennsylvania.

As of June 30, 1963, over 48,000 dwelling units had been completed on urban renewal sites; some 44,000

were privately financed and slightly over 4200 were public housing accommodations. Exclusive of Puerto Rico
(where there is no color identification of occupants)
about 44,000 units were occupied, and some 36 per
cent, or about 15,500 units, were occupied by non-
whites. Of these, 12,635 were privately financed and
the remainder were public housing. The majority of
the non-whites were living in racially mixed redevelopment areas.

Data for mid-1963 cannot, of course, reflect more
than a suggestion of the impact of the new moderate-
income program of Section 221(d)(3) or the Executive Order for Equal Opportunity in Housing. It is already apparent, however, that the former will facilitate
greater quantitative participation of non-whites in urban renewal residential projects at the same time that
the latter will result in a larger volume and proportion
of racially mixed housing in the program and elsewhere.
This will be assured by the fact that between November 20, 1962, and September 30, 1963, some 265 URA
Survey and Planning applications were approved and
92 Loan and Grant contracts authorized. Thus, as of
June 30, 1963, one-half of the grant reservations and
the areas involved in the urban renewal program were
covered by the non-discrimination prohibitions of the
Executive Order. In proportion as more redevelopment
housing is designed to meet the needs of moderate-
income families, the Executive Order for Equal Opportunity in Housing will become more meaningful to non-
whites. Already urban renewal, once identified as "Negro removal," has in many localities become an effective
instrument for facilitating non-segregated patterns of
living in newly created desirable neighborhoods.

To realize urban renewal's full potential in this regard, local agencies and the Federal Government will
have to be more sensitive to site selection and its implications for racial residential patterns. It must be
recognized, however, that urban renewal will not, and

probably cannot, always create bi-racial patterns of living. While this matter was discussed in some detail in Chapter II, it should be observed at this point that certain areas now in completely non-white neighborhoods will, and should, be redeveloped. This will occur because these sites are well-located and desirable for residential use. Often they will be occupied, after redevelopment, primarily or exclusively by non-whites; and this will happen, as it did in Cleveland, even when there is an aggressive policy of open occupancy. In other instances, high-rent redevelopment projects, primarily on economic grounds, will attract few or no non-white occupants, but there are bases for expecting a lesser number and proportion of high-cost residences in urban redevelopment sites in the future.

There can, of course, be no urban renewal without some demolition, displacement, and relocation. As has been repeatedly indicated above, we are well on the way to reducing the volume of these disruptive activities where residential reuse is contemplated. At the same time, however, the shift toward non-residential redevelopment will somewhat offset our successes in this regard, although the volume of human displacement is usually small in such areas. Subsequent discussion of racial patterns among low-income non-whites in Chapter VI will set forth the limitations of effective immediate action for establishing lasting bi-racial patterns in much of the relocation affecting this group. In accordance with the analysis in Section Three of Chapter II, both class and color are involved, and if we are to preserve our dedication to maximum freedom of choice in selecting a place to live, progress in this phase of ethnic residential patterns will be slow. We are speeding progress, and we shall continue to accelerate it as fast as possible. Meanwhile we are upgrading and shall continue to upgrade significantly the quality of housing and to augment the choices available to all low-income families in the Nation.

The past three years have afforded the present Administration an opportunity to evaluate and, to a degree, redirect the urban renewal program. As has been noted, in the process minorities have gained greater participation in the program at the same time that they have been subjected to a lesser amount of dislocation. Those displaced, white and non-white alike, have received greater assistance, and the relocation program has been significantly improved. The approaches, programs, and emphases that have emerged give promise of more positive results in the future.

Just as this was written, a local public agency announced a project in San Francisco that was controversial and, at the same time, exciting. This redevelopment is adjacent to the Western Addition Area I, where there are high-rent units and the racially integrated moderate-income St. Francis Redevelopment. The proposed new urban renewal project in the neighborhood is much larger and more significant than the first. It involves some 14,500 residents, composed of 2720 families and close to 5000 single persons. In addition, there are almost 900 businesses in the area. As in most sites currently designated for urban renewal, there has been a high degree of mobility; 41 per cent of the households had resided in the area less than a year. About 70 per cent of the families and 40 per cent of the single persons in the area are non-white.

By utilizing all of the tools now available to urban renewal, the local public agency expects to provide, under redevelopment, some 4500 dwelling units for families, and accommodations for 1450 single persons. By utilizing Section 221(d)(3) (of which there will be 1400 new units), rehabilitation of a large proportion of the better 2200 existing dwelling units and 650 existing hotel units in the area, erection of 200 units of scattered public housing and 800 units of senior citizen housing, and construction of over 500 additional dwelling units, it is expected to rehouse as many as 45 per cent of the families presently in the redeveloped area. In addition, 1760 single resident individuals will be able to find accommodations in the redevelopment. This means that almost one-half of the families now in the area will be able to stay in their present accommodations or move into new or rehabilitated dwelling units. A third of the single individuals will have a similar opportunity. For the remainder, there are or will be sufficient existing accommodations to facilitate relocation in standard units at rents they can afford elsewhere in the city.

The new community, like St. Francis Redevelopment, will be a stable racially integrated neighborhood, if the announced plans are successfully carried out. But it will have an additional feature; it will be composed of low- as well as moderate-income occupants, and, perhaps, a few higher-income households and individuals. There will be an almost equal number of rehabilitated and newly constructed dwelling units in the redevelopment. Here is an example of what can be done to minimize dislocation, provide a stable pattern of bi-racial living, and achieve a degree of economic diversification under urban renewal. In this respect it is similar to the West Side Urban Renewal of New York City. These two proposed redevelopments represent a prototype of the potential of urban renewal to make a positive contribution toward the establishment of democratic housing patterns. They present a challenge to the program and to the cities of the Nation.

IV   URBAN PLANNING AND
RESEARCH

Metropolitan Planning

The Kennedy Administration placed increasing emphasis upon metropolitan planning, particularly in the administration of new and existing programs of federal aid to localities for urban improvement. The Housing Act of 1961 not only extended and amplified existing programs in housing, urban renewal, and public facilities, but broke new ground in providing for federal grants or loans to localities for open space and mass transportation. Significantly, aids under these new programs are available only to localities or groups of localities in metropolitan areas which are engaging in planning. At the same time, the Federal Government is now authorized to extend increased financial assistance to metropolitan areas and smaller communities for the preparation of comprehensive plans.

Thus, planning is no longer an esoteric concept of interest only to academicians. Planning is now part of the vocabulary of elected officials at the federal, state, and local levels of government in the United States. It is a recognized governmental function in most of the larger localities and many smaller communities, and it will become increasingly important in the years ahead.

Planning means different things to different people; it is well to define our terms at the outset. City or community planning, as practiced in this country, is a responsibility of the state or locality, not of the National Government. Typically, the planning is done by technicians who serve under officially appointed citizen boards or in some cases under the chief executive of the local government—a mayor or city manager.

Planning entails a systematic effort to lay out a suitable physical framework for the community by the designation of major land use districts, principal routes of circulation, and basic public improvements. City planning, which started as a reform movement, has always been concerned to some degree with social and economic problems and prospects, housing needs, parks and open space, employment patterns, and investment opportunities. In essence, then, planning is a process by which a community perceives the future, articulates its objectives, and considers its alternatives. In the United States, community planning is now regarded as a continuous process because advancing technology and changing citizen and consumer preferences are continuously altering the opportunities for community development.

In many communities experience with planning as a governmental function covers a period of two to three decades or longer. But it is an experience largely confined to the individual locality. Planning on a metropolitan-wide basis has been conducted in some areas for particular functions, such as water and sewerage facilities, park systems, and more recently, transportation systems. Comprehensive planning for entire metropolitan areas is still in its infancy in this country. The most obvious reason is the absence of general governmental jurisdiction embracing metropolitan areas. Indeed, in 1962 there were 18,442 political or administrative jurisdictions in the 212 metropolitan areas of the Nation. Behind this lies the existence of numerous power centers in each metropolitan area whose interests are difficult to reconcile. But there are also unifying forces which support the need for area-wide planning within the metropolis. It will be useful, therefore, to summarize the evolution of the metropolis in the United States.

Virtually all economic and population growth in the Nation is now occurring in metropolitan areas. The overwhelmingly economic advantages of metropolitan concentration in an advanced industrial society have been amply documented. As was stated in Chapter I, these turn on tremendous external economies when the market is sufficiently large to permit high specialization of skills, massive overhead investments in transportation and other public facilities, and the grouping of cultural and educational institutions. Such concentrations also give rise to significant problems, however, such as the contamination of air and water, traffic congestion, and social frictions. Nevertheless, our metropolitan areas are here to stay and to grow.

The spatial pattern of metropolitan growth is particularly significant. We have already observed that the gridiron plan was the dominant pattern for laying out the early cities. It made for a quick, measurable division of large land holdings and facilitated the development and sale of land for speculative profit. Thus, older cities in the United States continue to live with a layout which is wasteful of land and inefficient for circulation, and a legacy of high expectations about land values.

The industrial city of the nineteenth century required dense concentrations of activities. Efficient utilization of steam power demanded that factories be located close by the power generating source. For lack of mass transportation facilities, workers had to find living quarters within walking distances of the factories and shops. Overcrowding of industrial and residential districts was the basis for rising land values in the central zones of many growing cities.

In this framework of rising central city land values, the introduction of the elevator and steel frame construction at the turn of the twentieth century led to vertical expansion. Increasingly higher buildings were constructed for offices, lofts, department stores, and some housing. But growth of industry and population also created expansionary pressures for outward movement of residential and commercial districts. Horse-drawn mass transportation facilities were organized in many cities but were soon replaced by electric traction trolley systems. In some cities underground subways and overhead rail transportation also were introduced. These local transit developments aided in the contiguous expansion of the city and the development of some outlying suburbs. The bulk of the new development, however, tended to be clustered close to the transit lines.

The disintegration of the massed city and the swift diffusion of industry and population into the peripheral zones is a familiar phenomenon. Each successive wave of suburban and exurban development takes place at a lower density. This new form of human settlement reflects the coincidence of the auto, truck, and the private passenger car; electrification of the countryside; horizontal-line processing in many sectors of manufacturing; rising family income; and not least, the apparent readiness of the urban population—in the absence of real alternatives—to accept the increased mobility implied by residential densities of two to five homes per net acre.

Let it be noted, however, that not all segments of the population are equally mobile. Newcomers to the city are generally unskilled and semi-skilled and thus frequently lack the income to purchase mobility. Moreover, many of them are members of ethnic and racial minorities and share with older minority residents the artificial limitations and disabilities that are only beginning to yield to our public ethic of equality of opportunity.

The American metropolis today is a large and productive complex but also a fragmented and costly organization. Seventy out of 257 central cities actually lost population during the last decade. Commercial property values, which provide a significant part of the central city tax base, have declined. Maintenance and repair of residential buildings in many older neighborhoods has been neglected with the consequent spread of blight. Meanwhile, the cost of city services has risen.

In the independent suburbs, on the other hand, there are heavy demands for public investments in schools, water systems and sewage disposal plants, fire stations, streets, and utility lines to accommodate the rapidly expanding populations. The provision of these community facilities by individual suburban governments has proved a costly business. Not only are costs of financing higher than those available to larger, consolidated districts, but the facilities themselves are commonly too small to achieve full economies of scale.

Our patterns of metropolitan growth leave much to be desired. More than one million acres of land at the metropolitan fringe are being taken up each year for new development without conscious choice of the metropolitan public with respect to density, pattern, or functional relationships. Permanent park and open space requirements of the metropolitan populations for today and tomorrow have been neglected. Nor are there yet effective public measures to set aside land needed for later development as industrial parks, sites for moderate- and low-priced housing, rights-of-way for future highways, or other public improvements. A high rate of metropolitan growth thus presents a formidable challenge to metropolitan planning in this Nation.

There has been a significant surge in metropolitan planning activity in the postwar years. Some of this planning is unofficial, that is, carried out by private groups such as the Regional Plan Association of New York. Most of it is advisory only, there being no governmental entity empowered to program or zone for the planning area. Indeed, there are only two large metropolitan areas that are served by a single governmental unit: Dade County, Florida, and Davidson County, Tennessee, which cover the metropolitan areas of Miami and Nashville respectively. Impressive planning programs are found in certain functional authorities such as the Metropolitan District Commission in the Boston area, and the Port of New York Authority. But these are, by definition, concerned with only one or several functions, and planning by such bodies cannot view the whole spectrum of metropolitan community problems and objectives.

Metropolitan planning, in the sense used here, is generally carried on by a board or commission authorized by state law and made up of representatives of at least the more important governmental units in the area. It recruits a staff or retains consulting firms to do its technical work. Unlike a city planning board, it does not report to a single executive or legislative body but the plans that it develops are available to the officials of all of the political units in the area.

While the metropolitan planning board itself is a purely advisory body, it may be delegated limited powers to approve the street and lot layout of suburban housing schemes or to review changes in zoning codes. *But for the most part, it merely recommends.* Its recommendations may be accepted or rejected by any or all of the political units in its planning area. Success in seeing its plans adopted depends not on legal authority but on inherent merit and persuasive presentation.

Plans prepared by advisory planning bodies are useless without the support of the various private and public interests whose decisions will govern the future development of the metropolitan area. If the representatives of the private utility companies, the railroads, the leading industries, labor, and the city and local government officials in a metropolitan area can be brought into the planning process at an early stage, there may develop a concert of agreement and understanding of the desired over-all physical development of the area.

A form of organization which draws together representatives of the public and private interests in the metropolitan planning and development process has begun to take shape. One organization of this type has been operative in the Penn-Jersey Transportation Study. The scope of this study transcends transportation since future travel is being calculated as a function or result of future metropolitan development patterns, rather than being derived from trends in highway and transit usage alone. The future distributions of homes and jobs that will evolve in response to demographic and economic forces and to the particular transportation systems under consideration are the major factors being evaluated.

The area under study includes the cities of Philadelphia, Camden, and Trenton, and involves a nine-county region with a population of nearly five million people. The study has been financed largely by funds from the highway departments of the States of Pennsylvania and New Jersey and from federal highway research funds provided through the United States Bureau of Public Roads. The nine counties in the area and the City of Philadelphia also have contributed to the support of the study. Each of these agencies and political jurisdictions has been represented on the policy committee for the study. There have been, in addition, a technical advisory committee and a civic advisory committee containing representatives of private industry and commerce, homebuilders, labor, professional groups, and citizens' groups who are consulted on the various phases of the study. Thus, varying points of view are heard, and area-wide participation is secured for the planning, hopefully, as the basis for its subsequent implementation.

A related innovation is the establishment of a regional conference of elected officials. Among other

duties, they serve as an official audience for the metropolitan planning board and permit continuing communication between the elected officials and the planners. Often there is also an unofficial citizens' planning
association which helps to publicize the work of the
planning board and offers constructive criticism. These
efforts represent a groping of public officials and civic
leaders toward agreements about metropolitan development through voluntary associations. The emergence of
these conferences reflects both a recognition of common
problems for the many jurisdictions that make up a
metropolitan area and a reluctance to surrender power
to a federated or consolidated government. It is hoped
that such voluntary groupings will prove effective in
implementing metropolitan planning.

Because metropolitan planning involves cooperation
between different jurisdictions, often between urban
and rural or suburban units with different outlooks,
it is much more difficult to organize a metropolitan
program than one for a single unit such as a city. It is
partly for that reason that federal funds have been
available, since the Housing Act of 1954, to help finance such programs.

As of June, 1963, in the 212 Standard Metropolitan
Statistical Areas in the United States, planning work in
100 had been financed in part with federal funds and
applications from one other was pending. These funds
have been used to assist comprehensive metropolitan
planning programs which included elements such as
metropolitan park and transportation systems.

Major aspects of metropolitan area planning also can
be financed in large part with Highway Planning
Survey funds from the United States Bureau of Public
Roads through the state highway departments, as in the
Penn-Jersey Transportation Study. The United States
Department of Commerce, which administers the high-
way program, and the Housing and Home Finance
Agency, which administers the Urban Planning Assist-

ance Program, have been encouraging the joint use of these federal monies to assist in developing truly comprehensive area-wide planning. As of June, 1963, 37 jointly assisted planning programs were under way and 23 more were being considered. Many other areas throughout the country are actively considering the initiation of comprehensive area-wide planning to be financed in large part by the joint use of these federal funds.

It should not be assumed that metropolitan planning is undertaken only in response to the offer of federal funds. Major metropolitan areas carried on planning work for years before federal assistance was available. Also, private citizen organizations, not eligible for federal aid, have performed and are continuing to perform a valuable service in this field. Nevertheless, federal grants are likely to be increasingly important in inducing metropolitan planning in the years immediately ahead.

In addition to direct assistance for metropolitan planning, the requirements of two new federal programs, enacted in the Housing Act of 1961, offer powerful stimulus to such efforts. The program of partial grants for acquisition of land for permanent open space requires that the applicant be actively carrying on a program of comprehensive planning for the urban area, and the proposed use of the land to be acquired must be shown to be important to the execution of such plan. Where the operating unit covers a single jurisdiction, the federal grant is 20 per cent of the land acquisition cost; where it exercises or participates in open space responsibilities for an entire area, the grant increases to 30 per cent. By September, 1963, these planning requirements were paying off. They seemed to be facilitating a new level of formal intergovernmental cooperation on a regional basis. Incident to the open space program, twenty intergovernmental agreements had been completed or were in the process of development. Six of the ten largest metropolitan centers of the country were involved. Collectively, these six agreements represented arrangements for unified open space land planning and action programs in urban regions containing some 30 per cent of the Nation's population. In most cases, the agreements provide for a coordinating body, usually a regional planning agency, to review all land acquisition proposals for conformance with regional plans, or in light of open space requirements, objectives, and standards.

Likewise, with certain emergency exceptions, loans for mass transportation facilities and equipment may be made only where there is being actively developed, or has been developed, for the whole urban area being served by the applicant, a program for the development of a comprehensive and coordinated mass transportation system. Whether or not a mass transportation program will be considered acceptable as a basis for a loan will depend upon its relation to planning for the total transportation system and other major elements of comprehensive planning for the whole metropolitan area. Similar planning requirements apply to the transportation grant program proposed by the Kennedy Administration and provided for in the Urban Transportation Act passed by the Senate early in 1963.

The 1962 Federal-Aid Highway Act established the requirement that all urban highway projects must be, beginning July 1, 1965, based on "continuing comprehensive transportation planning process" in metropolitan areas. Under law, plans must be "formulated with due consideration to their probable effect on the future development of urban areas of more than fifty-thousand population."

Regulations promulgated by the Bureau of Public Roads carry out the intent of this provision by setting forth requirements for an acceptable transportation planning process. These criteria cover economic factors, population, land use, effect on social and community-value factors, and other elements of urban development in such a way as to make the transportation planning process virtually synonymous with comprehensive metropolitan planning. In operation, the highway planning process has been closely related to HHFA's Section 701 urban planning assistance program. In many cases BPR and HHFA finance joint metropolitan planning programs to give the fullest effect to the highway act requirement.

The Public Works Acceleration Act specifies that a project must conform to a locality's comprehensive plan, if one exists. Under the water pollution control bill passed by the Senate, a waste treatment grant may be increased by 10 per cent (from 30 per cent to 40 per cent) for a project that is in conformity with the comprehensive plan developed or in process of development for the metropolitan area.

As proposed by the House Commerce Committee, the Federal Airport Act would be amended by including a requirement that planning and project applications be not inconsistent with development plans for the area in which the airport is located. Thus, the day may not be far ahead when all federal grant programs affecting the urban environment and metropolitan development will be linked to metropolitan planning.

The hallmark of a democratic society is the opportunity of the population to exercise choice among alternatives. The role of metropolitan planning is to present in a systematic way the choices that the population can make in guiding the development of the metropolis. Metropolitan planning will not, any more than metropolitan government, solve all our problems. Rather, it can help clarify the public needs and objectives of the community and suggest ways to meet them.

What is the community with which metropolitan planning is concerned? It is all the people who rely upon a transportation system that laces together hundreds of residential neighborhoods and scores of work centers; it is all the people who make use of the beaches and parks; all who send their waste waters into a single drainage basin; all who live within a common sootfall district. For these area-wide needs, autonomous planning and programming by dozens of local governments are bound to be wasteful or ineffectual. For such functions, metropolitan planning is most obviously required, and indeed is gaining increasing acceptance.

But what about the location of housing, shopping centers, and industrial plants? These are frequently viewed as vital interests over which each city and suburb seeks to retain unilateral control. For these presumably determine the status of one's neighborhood, the value of property, the local tax base. These issues of necessity are within the purview of metropolitan planning. If we are serious about eliminating overcrowded slum quarters in the central city, we may have to build moderate- and low-income housing on outlying vacant land. If public funds are to be expended to revitalize downtown, it is folly to ignore the potential competition of peripheral shopping centers. If an official economic development agency is to promote industrial growth, suitable plant sites must be set aside somewhere in the metropolitan area. Metropolitan planning should be expected not to resolve these questions, but to raise and examine them in a systematic way so that responsible officials and private leaders can make informed decisions.

Thus metropolitan planning will require far more extensive research and data-gathering than is now carried on. What is needed are studies of population migration, adaptation of migrants to community life, household mobility, intra-area flows of goods, journey-to-work patterns, municipal service requirements and fiscal capacity. This is but a partial list. Studies of this type have already been initiated in a number of metropolitan areas both by private and public groups, and more should be encouraged.

Metropolitan planning will grow increasingly important in the United States as more and more of our people concentrate in metropolitan areas. It will produce no authoritarian design but a set of alternative developmental paths for the metropolis. It will carry the stamp of voluntary association which Max Weber placed at the heart of a democratic society. Its progress will be measured by the growth of a sense of metropolitan community.

The Role of the Federal Government

Because of their significance to the welfare of our people, to the vitality of our economy, and to the defense capabilities of our Nation, the problems of metropolitan areas are of universal concern. The Federal Government has a direct stake in the effective social and economic development of metropolitan areas. This, in addition to the physical and economic elements delineated previously, requires a socially and physically healthy urban population, provided with facilities and opportunities permitting each person to make a maximum contribution to society and the economy.

In recognition of the needs of urban areas and their populations, the Congress has established a number of programs that directly or indirectly affect metropolitan development. These programs cover assistance for a variety of local activities, such as urban transportation, housing, urban renewal, water, sewerage, and other facilities; health, education, and recreation facilities; and many others. Some of these federal programs are provided primarily to assist metropolitan development, while others do so as a secondary function, at the same time that they meet other national objectives.

The total impact of these programs is, of course, tremendous. Expenditures, for these activities, are in the nature of twenty billion dollars annually. Considering secondary effect, the significance of these activities of metropolitan areas is even greater.

To provide an example of how this impact relates to a specific single metropolitan area, consider a typical one, Atlanta, Georgia. More than 117.6 million dollars in public and private expenditures were put into circulation in Atlanta during 1962 by programs of twelve major federal agencies. This total covered direct grants and matching funds for such projects as road construction, airports, and so forth, in the amount of $35,841,-400; authorization of $2,296,400 for expenditures on Federal Government projects; direct loans for housing, small business, public works planning, etc., of $594,-000; and various types of insuring programs for housing and construction amounting to $78,965,800.

There is no question that the Federal Government plays a major financial role in metropolitan areas. Its programs have had varying effects. Some have tended to accentuate the forces operating to expand metropolitan regions and reinforce characteristics of diffusion; others have been directed toward opposite ends. Some federal programs have supported and reinforced traditional operations of local governments, while others have given rise to new institutions on the local level. At times, activities or projects of one agency have been in direct conflict or at variance with projects or activities under another program.

It was the policy of the Kennedy Administration to bring together, as far as possible, these conflicting forces and to direct them toward mutual, rather than divergent or unrelated, objectives. The purpose was primarily to utilize limited resources, to maximize over-all benefit, and to eliminate waste and inefficiency.

A prime example of program coordination and the relating of activities to metropolitan needs has been the agreement between the Department of Commerce and the Housing and Home Finance Agency for the joint use of highway and urban planning funds in areas where local and state bodies are required to establish coordinated planning. The main emphasis so far has been placed on coordinating the urban renewal and highway programs of the two agencies and achieving an effective planning program. Other instances, mentioned in the preceding chapter, involve programs addressed to social problems in public housing and attempts to plan and provide for better relocation services for those displaced in the urban renewal process.

Conflicts between urban renewal projects and highway construction have been resolved through the institution of a procedure for clearance of urban renewal proposals with the Bureau of Public Roads in the Department of Commerce, prior to allocation of renewal funds. Specifically, preliminary urban renewal applications and urban renewal plans are reviewed by the Bureau of Public Roads to assure that highway and renewal programs relate to one another in a sensible way. In case conflicts arise, they are resolved through mutual action.

Effective comprehensive metropolitan area planning is thus being achieved through joint use of urban planning assistance funds provided by HHFA to states and localities, and highway planning funds, administered by the Bureau of Public Roads. As a matter of standard procedure, whenever either Federal Agency receives a request to finance a planning or transportation study in a region, the possibilities of a common undertaking are investigated.

We have similarly been working with other agencies, exploring, for example, with the Federal Aviation Agency procedures for cooperation in airport and metropolitan and state planning. As an initial result, information on the respective planning programs is being exchanged. Airport planning program information is being relayed to our regional offices and the FAA is informing its regional and airport district offices about the Housing and Home Finance Agency's planning assistance activities.

Joint discussions have also been held regarding problems of land use and housing around airports. We believe that a working relationship can be achieved with FAA similar to those already established with the Bureau of Public Roads.

The beginnings of consultation have been held between the Housing Agency and the Department of Health, Education, and Welfare. Several meetings have been held to discuss problems of air pollution in urban areas, although formal arrangements have not as yet been worked out. An agreement was reached between the Area Redevelopment Administration of the Department of Commerce and the HHFA on the use of urban planning assistance funds administered by the latter agency for the preparation of over-all economic development programs, required to be submitted by localities under the Area Redevelopment Program. All of these efforts are directed toward carrying out more effectively federal responsibilities toward metropolitan development and more effective use of federal aids.

This program-by-program coordinative effort is a major advance over the years when each program went its own way. It is, however, not enough. Concern with metropolitan areas and their development cannot effectively be carried out on an *ad hoc* basis. It requires continuing concern and the fixing of responsibility. It is this need, in part, which led the Kennedy Administration to recommend and support strongly the establishment of a new Department of Urban Affairs and Housing.

President Kennedy and others who have advocated the creation of the United States Department of Urban Affairs and Housing have viewed it as an essential vehicle for assisting in the coordinated discharge of federal responsibilities in metropolitan and other urban areas. The proposed department would be responsible for seeing to it, on a systematic basis, that the necessary planning and programming activities of the Federal Government in and for metropolitan and other urban areas are carried out most effectively and efficiently, benefiting both the people in those areas and the country as a whole.

We have, in the meantime, been gearing our efforts, insofar as possible in this field, toward meeting the needs of metropolitan areas. HHFA recently established an Office of Metropolitan Development. This office is designed specifically to assist in coordinating and furthering agency programs and activities related to the planning and development of urban regions. In addition to serving as a focal point for metropolitan program coordination within the agency, the new office will help implement HHFA's interest in federal interagency collaboration toward establishment of common approaches to metropolitan area planning and development.

The Agency's emphasis on the comprehensive metropolitan approach is also reflected in its assistance to over-all Community Renewal Programs, referred to above. In recognition of the interrelation of conditions in metropolitan areas, we have oriented this operation in such a way that the programming of activities in individual communities will be related to area-wide considerations, when and where there is effective governmental machinery to carry out the function.

Making adequate planning a prerequisite to federal assistance, as we are increasingly doing, does more than help implement local objectives. It actually can produce a frame of reference for federal activities within a given area. This country is too vast and its conditions too diverse to be able to coordinate programs and projects affecting specific metropolitan areas in Washington, D.C., even if this were otherwise desirable. However, airports, highways, sewage treatment plants, mass transit, open space, and other programs must, if federal funds are not to be wasted, be related to each other and to local development. The comprehensive plan for each metropolitan area can provide the most effective means of relating such programs and projects to each other within the framework of federal criteria and local decision-making.

The application of federal criteria gives rise to controversy. Performance standards, procedures, and other requirements are frequently inserted in laws and regulations to assure that national objectives will be met whenever federal aids are provided. Of course, a recipient of federal aid may seek to avoid such requirements. Usually, the issue will revolve around the reasonableness of requirements and the manner or degree of enforcement. In cases such as these, we take the position that a community knows best what it needs, provided that national standards prescribed or indicated by the Congress are met.

When we deal with metropolitan planning, the question of standards can become quite pertinent, particularly those having to do with organizational structure. We are often faced with the questions, "Who should do metropolitan planning?" "Who can speak for the metropolitan area and its people?" These questions go to the very basis of metropolitan planning and metropolitan governmental structure.

We certainly do not deem it appropriate for us to specify to any metropolitan area what type of governmental forms it should have for the performance of planning and other local functions. At the same time, it is important that a federal grant go to a representative metropolitan planning group that will make an appropriate contribution to metropolitan area development. This is a problem with which we are still struggling. The complexity of the large metropolitan area is such that planning will be meaningful only if related to decision-makers and decision-making processes. If political leaders of the localities are not represented or consulted in the planning process, it is not likely that their communities will take planning very seriously. A proper balance must, therefore, be maintained between a completely standoffish process as to community organization, and the establishment of requirements for a responsible and responsive metropolitan structure.

To help achieve an appropriate balance, where feasible, we are working more directly with individual metropolitan areas. We give them as much technical assistance as possible. We are assisting but we are also still learning, as we go about helping metropolitan areas with their planning and organizational problems. While it is not likely that we will find any formula that will meet the needs of all areas, our experience will provide a framework for broader and better technical assistance.

We believe that this cooperative approach to metropolitan area development will, in the end, bring the greatest results. We see our general role in the development process as one of providing assistance where assistance is needed, and requested, by states and localities. And we always try to provide it in such a manner as will assure that both local goals and national purposes will be achieved.

Urban Growth and Research

During the past decade, the meshing of central cities and surrounding counties into an integrated economic metropolis has become a recognized pattern in the United States. There has also been a growing awareness of the declining fiscal base of the city. We realize that the revenue-short, expanding suburbs and their common transportation woes are related to physical and economic development of the entire area. Clearly, research and analysis are essential to help plan a more rational regional development.

As a first step there is a need to measure the impact

of demographic trends upon the growth of different regions and parts of regions. This requires not only measures of the natural increases of population, but also judgments as to the nature of the future migration and mobility in a country where one-fifth of the people change residences every year. These changes in population location and density bring with them problems of social adjustment, physical accommodations, and economic development. These problems require identification in quantitative and qualitative terms, if we are to cope with them intelligently.

It will also be necessary to anticipate, as far as possible, where the people of our changing metropolitan regions will live, and where they will work, play, go to school, and do their shopping. If such prognostication is to be within a rational framework, we have to learn more about the economic functions of different types of communities and districts within a region. What are the appropriate regional functions of the central city, and what is the role of specific large cities within the economy of the Nation? What should be the internal structure of the city with respect to the location of its industries and a balanced supply of housing for its various income groups? Research is also needed on the public and private cultural, commercial, and health services that the city must provide for the residents of its region.

How should satellite communities be shaped? What should be their size, location, and function in relation to the central city? We have to amplify and organize our knowledge about the relative advantage of having certain productive activities carried on in more spacious suburban areas, as compared with the central city and its cluster of activities that make special economies possible for many producers. Similarly, data on economies of size for the provision of various public services have to be compiled and expanded, to serve as a guide for coordinated and efficient public services in an entire area.

Then, there are the clearly mutual interests of the central city and the rest of a metropolitan region which have to be identified and studied to develop more satisfactory methods of handling them. These common interests include the preservation of open space for recreational and scenic purposes, the development of an adequate regional transportation system, and the fiscal resources to provide the necessary public capital improvements for the future development of the region. To treat these regional problems effectively, new forms of local intergovernmental arrangements and organizations have to be developed, and this, in itself, is a major area for study.

In recent years a number of regional studies have been executed which attempted a simultaneous attack on a number of variables shaping the growth of a region in the United States. The most extensive of these studies was the *New York Metropolitan Regional Study*, previously cited, which resulted in the publication of ten volumes on the economic, demographic, and sociological trends in a twenty-two-county region that extends into New Jersey and Connecticut, and embraces sixteen million people. The study was under the supervision of the Harvard University Graduate School of Public Administration, which assembled a task force of experienced analysts to perform the compilation and analysis of relevant data. The New York regional study stirred some healthy controversy as to whether a continuation of present trends leading to a decline of older parts of the central city are inevitable, or whether we can bestir ourselves and restore the vitality of declining districts.

Currently, there is under way an extensive program of economic study of the Upper Midwest region of the United States. The geographic coverage of this regional study program is indicated by the participating agencies, headed by the University of Minnesota and the Upper Midwest Research and Development Council, and the cooperating agencies which are the state universities and colleges of Montana, North Dakota, and South Dakota, and the Federal Reserve Bank of Minneapolis. The studies will cover a wide range of demographic and economic developments in the region, including urban migration, urban fringe areas, the labor force, personal income, recreation resources, and the agricultural economy of the region.

The Pittsburgh Regional Planning Association has been conducting a study of that area's metropolitan region. A co-sponsor of the Pittsburgh study is the Pittsburgh Regional Industrial Development Corporation, a not uncommon type of private, non-profit local organization that has been formed to attract industry to a region and further its economic development. Official agencies, too, are participating in regional studies. In the spring of 1963, six counties joined to form the Southwestern Pennsylvania Regional Planning Commission. The communities in Wayne County, Michigan, took a similar step a few weeks later, and in mid-May, a transportation and land use program for the seven counties in northeastern Ohio was announced.

In contrast with the large regional studies there are numerous so-called economic base studies of smaller urban areas. These analyses may be for moderate-sized cities or for an entire county. They frequently involve population projections, land use needs, public facility requirements, and housing needs. Such studies are typically done by the business and economic research bureaus of large universities, particularly the state universities, such as Wisconsin, Texas, Maryland, and others.

The economic base studies made by consultants for a community will frequently be in connection with a development plan that is required as part of a Workable Program for Community Improvement which, in turn, is a prerequisite for federal assistance for urban renewal, moderate-income housing, or public housing. The planning itself may be aided with a federal grant, under the urban planning assistance program of the Housing and Home Finance Agency.

As a result of experience with the urban planning assistance program, which goes back to 1954, there has been a crystallization of thought as to the function of the planning process and the research findings that result. If planning is to serve its purpose, it must be a process which provides current data to help public and private decision-makers arrive at rational decisions, as to capital improvements, that will affect the growth of their urban area.

There are many ancillary problems for which solutions must be found if our urban research and planning is to be effective. They require research on the economic impacts of alternative ways in which the component physical factors that enter into the make-up of an urban area are provided, utilized, and controlled.

A basic urban problem in the United States has been the land use pattern that has evolved as a consequence of the concentration of population growth in metropolitan areas, with a concurrent diffusion of development within the metropolitan areas. The result is popularly known as urban sprawl. To cope with this phenomenon we have to identify the factors leading to the present pattern of land use, measure their impact, and analyze remedial control methods.

Some broad studies of the demographic trends that lead to our present urban land use pattern have been supported by large foundations, such as the Twentieth Century Fund study on Megalopolis, mentioned above, or a Ford Foundation-supported study of Migration and Urbanization in the United States that is in process at the University of Pennsylvania Population Research Center. The basic data for such studies are generally available from decennial population statistics for geographic areas and are published by the United States Bureau of the Census.

The explosive growth of the urban population in the United States over the last two decades has been accompanied by a marked uptrend in urban land prices. In response to the long-term rise in urban land prices and their effect upon land uses, there are current research programs concerned with special aspects of this problem.

The Urban Land Institute, a private non-profit organization supported largely by companies in the real estate, building, and mortgage lending businesses, has a current program of studies on Changing Urban Land Uses as Affected by Taxation. The individual studies would include analyses of the impact upon land uses of property taxes, alternative forms of taxation, and tax abatement or exemption.

The Department of Agriculture has made staff studies of alternative forms of local taxes that may be levied upon land in agricultural use in the metropolitan fringe areas. These studies have explored the effect of taxes based upon urban land values, upon ownership, use, and prices, compared with the effects of preferential assessments of land in agricultural use, tax deferrals, or taxes on capital gains.

The relationship between land values and distance from the center of a city and from major thoroughfares has been studied by the University of Kansas in the Topeka, Kansas, area. If we had more information on this subject we could develop more rational policies to guide the use of land for different purposes in an urban area. This brings to mind another facet of research related to urban land policy, namely, methods of public control of land use for planned development and related specific uses. Thus, at Michigan State University a project has been undertaken to determine appropriate zoning and other land use regulations for urban fringe areas.

As another example of a special study related to land use control, the University of Pennsylvania Institute of Legal Research recently made an analysis of legal problems in the preservation of open space in metropolitan areas without public land acquisition. This study was part of the Pennsylvania-Delaware-New Jersey Metropolitan Project, a tri-state regional research project covering a region from Trenton, New Jersey, to Wilmington, Delaware.

The responsibilities of the Housing and Home Finance Agency cause it to have a special concern with the pervasive upward trend of urban land prices. To examine the root causes of land inflation, under its Urban Studies and Housing Research Program, the Agency is currently sponsoring two studies in depth of institutional and economic factors which underlie the price increases. The University of Pennsylvania in Philadelphia and the University of California at Los Angeles will each examine the ownership patterns and demographic and public improvement patterns which have affected land prices in developing areas of their metropolises.

Within cities, land uses are constantly changing as redevelopment takes place. One recalls a series of land use maps of London at fifty-year intervals which illustrated how that city had been substantially rebuilt every half-century over a few hundred years. These changes are in response to changing technology, such as reinforced steel construction, automatic elevators, and automobile transportation. With the increased pace of technological innovation, cities will change at a more rapid rate and we must have the bases for well-planned redevelopment.

HHFA also is concerned with the development of new and more effective urban renewal techniques which will have general applicability in many communities.

To help develop such techniques we have an urban renewal demonstration program, identified as Section 314 Demonstration Grants. Under this program, a federal grant is made to cover two-thirds of the cost of a demonstration project, while the state or local public body sponsoring the undertaking must contribute the other third. The public sponsor may assign its own staff to do the work, recruit staff especially for the project, or contract with consultants or public or private institutions.

Generally, demonstrations directly concerned with urban renewal, such as on methods and techniques for easing relocation and rehousing families and single-person households, upgrading citizen participation, experimentation in relocation, code upgrading and enforcement, conservation planning and execution, preservation and restoration of historical areas, and the like, have been done by local redevelopment agencies. There have also been projects by state bodies, as, for example, one on establishment of a method of combating blight through conservation and rehabilitation, by the Temporary State Housing Rent Commission of New York. University groups have done demonstration studies under contract on such subjects as "Economic Aspects of Urban Renewal" and methods for coordinating and integrating urban university development programs with urban renewal efforts. And, as set forth in detail in the preceding chapter, the demonstration program has recently been used as a key element in an approach to the human problems in relocation.

One of the objectives to be sought in our future urban growth is a pattern of locational relationships within a region which will minimize the frictions of transportation and communication. Toward this end, we need a balanced supply of housing in the city and in the suburbs where lower-income people may be employed in commercial establishments and increasingly in industrial establishments. To formulate policies that will bring about a balanced supply of housing, we have to know, first, the pattern of effective demand, and how it is affected by different government programs and different types of financing.

Studies concerning special segments of the market have been carried on by university research groups. For example, at Temple University, a study has been under way on financial programs for lower-middle income housing. Two other studies are on The Housing Market and Urban Renewal, at the University of Pennsylvania Institute for Urban Studies; and on Housing Needs for the Aged, at Cornell University Center for Housing and Environmental Studies. The Housing and Home Finance Agency has contracted for special tabulations on the characteristics of our senior citizens gathered in the 1960 Census, thereby facilitating the collection of a wealth of information on the needs of the aged.

To have a balanced housing supply for different income groups in different parts of the metropolis, we need to have, in addition to prices, rents, and financing that are commensurate with incomes of the groups to be served, freedom of choice in residential location. Through zoning or less formal devices, low-income workers and minority groups are excluded from certain areas. This has been extensively documented by the United States Commission on Civil Rights, a Presidentially appointed agency; and by the Commission on Race and Housing, a private, non-profit commission of distinguished citizens.

Studies of the Commission on Race and Housing resulted in the most comprehensive analysis available in the field. One of these studies on property values and race helped dispel the myth that the entry of minority groups into a neighborhood inevitably causes a decline of property values. Other studies investigated housing demands in racially mixed areas, to determine what circumstances facilitate a stable balance of an integrated neighborhood, and a host of other related matters.

In less than a dozen metropolitan areas, there are private residential research groups that publish periodic reports containing market information. These reports by local real estate, mortgage lending, and homebuilding industries may be prepared with the collaboration of a local university research bureau. The reports carry metropolitan area information on homebuilding volume, vacancies, and pride trends.

The Federal Government, through the Bureau of the Census, has been providing two broad indications of national housing market conditions. These are a monthly series on housing starts and a quarterly series on housing vacancies. In 1962, under contract for the Housing and Home Finance Agency, the Bureau of the Census initiated a new monthly series of current housing market data. The resulting data were highly praised by homebuilders, mortgage finance people, and other user groups.

This series provides monthly information for the country as a whole and for three major geographic regions on the number and price distribution of new one-family homes sold, of new one-family homes under construction but unsold, and of new one-family homes completed but unsold. There is also some information, published quarterly, on the types of financing. Other information, published annually, pertains to certain basic physical characteristics of the new homes sold in different price classes.

The types and densities of housing located in different parts of a metropolitan region will affect the need for transit facilities and highways in the area, and the provision of highways, of course, shapes the residential development and density of a metropolitan area. Whatever the casual relationships, we have developed highly uneconomic modes of transportation for our necessary everyday journeys to work, to shop, to visit, and so forth. The predominant mode of passenger transportation by private automobile brings to the fore such problems as traffic congestion and regulation, the need for parking facilities, and increased air pollution.

Research on the effects of highway construction upon land uses and values has often been done by university bureaus of community planning and economic research, by geography departments of universities and by state highway departments. Recently, the focus of urban transportation research has been broadened to include studies of all types of urban transportation and their relation to land use planning, studies of rail commuter services, and regional transportation studies analyzing all possible transportation modes. Research of this type has been undertaken by the Joint Center for Urban Studies of Massachusetts Institute of Technology and Harvard University, by the Institute of Public Administration in New York, and by metropolitan regional transportation authorities or study groups that have been organized in some of our metropolitan areas.

Studies on public administration, or "the science of muddling through," as one writer phrased it, have generally been made by scholars who have surveyed the problem broadly in books or articles that have been published. In the current research program of the Housing and Home Finance Agency we have completed a project to provide information on the most promising methods that have been employed by political jurisdictions in an urban area to prepare and implement joint plans for capital improvements and services. The results have proved to be so significant that the study has been published.[1]

With respect to one aspect of urban research, namely, technological research on building materials and methods and the related subject of building codes, much remains to be done. In the spring of 1963, the Department of Commerce requested an appropriation of funds to operate a program of grants to universities and

[1] Roscoe C. Martin, *Metropolis in Transition* (Washington: Housing and Home Finance Agency, 1963), 159 pp.

foundations for basic research into construction methods and construction materials. However, the Appropriations Committee indicated that the research funds made available to the Department were not to be used for this purpose. According to the June, 1963, issue of *House and Home,* the program of research was opposed by the trustees of the Research Institute of the National Association of Home Builders and the United States Chamber of Commerce.

In conjunction with its mortgage insurance operations, the Federal Housing Administration has long conducted a contract research program for the analysis of materials and construction methods, soil conditions, architectural developments, and other technical matters related to residential construction. These studies also seek to find solutions to specific problems, such as basement moisture-condensation and poor insulation qualities of interior partitions. The Public Housing Administration is involved in similar activity. It has investigated, for example, such problems as the improvement of incinerators for multi-family houses. Some of the FHA projects are carried out by the Building Research Advisory Board, an arm of the National Academy of Sciences. The Building Research Advisory Board may have field investigations made by its own staff or employ special task forces for the studies. Some of the FHA technological research projects are also carried out under contract at universities which have the necessary staff and facilities. Work is also done under the FHA program by other federal agencies, such as the Public Health Service and the Forest Products Laboratory.

A demonstration grant program, to help develop new and improved methods for the provision of housing low-income families, is administered by the Office of Program Policy in HHFA. This program, which has $5,000,000 for grants, was referred to in Chapter III. The grants may cover all or part of the demonstration,

but contributions by local public or non-profit sponsors
are encouraged. The sponsors may make third-party
contracts with a university or other organizations to do
all or part of the development work and reports on projects. Among many types of demonstrations approved,
those which involve utilization of the existing supply of
housing have received special attention. In addition,
there are projects which experiment with new design,
materials, and building methods. Some are concerned
with preparing apparently economically mobile, low-
income families for home ownership. Others experiment with the provision of adequate shelter for residents of skid row who will be displaced by urban renewal. One challenges the traditional concept that
families which have spotty credit reports must be undesirable candidates for home ownership.[2]

The Housing and Home Finance Agency also administers the Urban Studies and Housing Research
Program, which has been mentioned. There is at present
a total authorization of $2,500,000 for such research in
the housing law, but our annual expenditures are limited to funds appropriated by the Congress for specific
studies. For the fiscal years 1962 and 1963 we have
had appropriations of $375,000 annually. For fiscal year
1964 we requested $2,500,000 for this research and
received $387,400.

A noteworthy method of supporting urban research
is that used in connection with the Residential Research Program carried on at the numerous state universities and colleges in California. Funds for this
program are derived from a portion of the real estate
transfer taxes which the state law requires shall be used
for the program. There are also a variety of state and
local agencies that provide funds for urban research.
Some of these are state economic development commissions or housing and commerce departments of state

[2] Appendix A lists and presents a brief description of these
projects.

governments. Local housing and redevelopment agencies have contributed to or sponsored research. Then, there are large special authorities, such as the Port of New York Authority, which carry on regional research as well as the planning activities discussed above.

In discussing the types of organizations engaged in urban and regional research, reference has been made to various institutes of urban studies at universities. These centers for urban studies are fairly new and have been nurtured by millions of dollars of private foundation grants plus some research funds that were made available through federal programs concerned with urban development. A principal source of support has been the Ford Foundation, which has contributed generously to a number of large regional and other urban studies. Additional private organizations, such as the Rockefeller Brothers Fund, the Kellogg Foundation, the Eugene and Agnes Meyer Foundation, Action, Inc., and others, have provided funds for research by the university centers for urban studies.

Over the next decade, there will be hundreds of billions of dollars invested in housing, local public facilities, private utilities, and private commercial and industrial enterprises in this country. To the extent that urban and regional research can provide a basis for rational decisions as to the location, size, and type of public and private facilities to be built, the benefits will far outrun the costs to our society.

Yet there continues to be great opposition in the Congress to basic research in housing and community development. What seem to be practical, demonstration projects secure federal appropriations. But if philosophy and concepts are involved the proposals are considered esoteric and unworthy of public financial support.

There is need in this Nation for data and analyses which afford a logical and informed basis for public and private decision-makers. The subjects involved include future population movements and economic and financial trends. The functional relationships between different elements of community development, such as residence, transportation, and employment, must be analyzed. Then, too, we need to know more about the housing requirements and resources for the economically, physically, and socially disadvantaged and the revenue resources needed to support such amenities. Also, as in all the research which is inevitable relative to this and other subjects in the Nation, there has to be concern for sound and improved methodology. And, of course, the United States, typified by a reverence for technological advancement, would be expected to develop a body of knowledge responsive to technical operating problems in connection with homebuilding, land use, transportation, communication, provision of water and sewer facilities, and related activities.

Regardless of how much we do to solve immediate and describable, practical problems, we shall fail to appreciate and maximize the potential of public action and expenditure in the field of community development and housing unless we raise our horizons of thinking. The public—and rightly so—expects HHFA to assume a leadership role in such matters as building and housing standards and performance standards for codes. But this is one of many areas where effective action is dependent upon a scientific body of technical knowledge. For example, it has become popular to assert that building codes are primarily responsible for the high cost of housing. I am convinced that, at best, this is a half-truth, and at worst it fails to face up to the fact that few of the "new technological breakthroughs" have met the economic test of feasibility. We shall never achieve the reforms in this field that are desirable (and I believe that they are most productive in prefabricated housing and in the fabrication of components) until we have the facts.

Perhaps the best summary of this discussion rests in

the statement of the Housing Sub-Panel on Civilian
Technology as set forth in its report *Better Housing for
America*. It observes that there has been a lack of adequate criteria for measuring performance of new materials and methods in homebuilding. I submit that in
this technological field, no less than in economic, planning, and social areas, we need criteria. And the
Federal Government, involved as it is in financing so
much of the related activities, has a responsibility for
developing them.

In a society which has great respect for technology
and research and which in its private sector glorifies and
generously supports these activities, it is difficult to
understand why there is so much opposition to similar
activities in the public sector. Yet such is the situation.
As one who has been nurtured in these value concepts,
I cannot do other than point out our shortsightedness
in this regard.

Operations Research

Operations Research has had only a short history. Yet,
within the brief span of ten to fifteen years it has become almost a legend. It has acquired an aura of om-
niscience, and through mathematical formulations it is
presumed to be able to make things fall into their
proper places so that order may appear where chaos
existed before. Whether Operations Research actually
can accomplish all that is implied by the powers attributed to it remains to be seen.

The enthusiasm with which this relatively new development in research techniques has been received,
however, indicates the existence of a great demand for
methods which would enable the researcher, planner,
or decision-maker to deal effectively with the extremely
complex problems in our ever evolving and rapidly
changing social economy. At the heart of the changes
in this dynamic social economy is urban growth, for

which improved research methods are needed. Those who are concerned with the urban complex are asking, "Can the methods of Operations Research be applied to urban planning?"

When an industrial enterprise commissions an Operations Research team to solve a problem, the problem usually involves measurable physical inputs and a productive process. Both the inputs and the productions process can be subjected to controlled experimentation and the results usually can be measured. The goal generally would be to arrive at an optimum production situation where costs would be minimized or profits maximized. There is a well-defined goal—either the minimization of costs or the maximization of profits —to be achieved via alternative production processes through varying the kinds and amounts of physical inputs and controlled experimentation.

In urban planning and development, the problems involve the relationship of numerous variables for an integrated development to achieve a plurality of goals that are simultaneously operative in a metropolitan area. Thus, the goal of efficiency in many productive economic activities requires that they be clustered so as to reduce the costs on transportation of goods, afford easy communication, and permit external economies through joint use of specialized business services and professional specialties.

Such a concentration of activity, facilitated by high rise office buildings, complicates the achievements of another goal—the minimization of transportation requirements in daily commutation to work. The average journey from residence to work tends to lengthen as more people have to assemble in a central area each day. This phenomenon is reinforced by economic factors; as the land in the central city and immediate environs assumes a high use value, moderate-priced housing should be built on cheaper land in the outlying suburbs. Another alternative, high rise housing, increases density of use, impedes circulation, and increases the time and cost of movement within the city.

Now, if moderate-priced housing could be built in the suburbs and made available to various income and minority groups employed in industries that are moving to the suburbs, it would facilitate the minimization of transportation needs at the same time that it promoted another goal, freedom of opportunity in housing location. But housing for low-income and minority families is greatly restricted in most suburbs. Consequently, many blue-collar and domestic workers, who live in the gray areas and slums, commute "out" while many middle-class white-collar workers commute "in" every morning. In the evening the process is reversed. This creates a need for mass transit facilities at price and service levels that will attract customers and reduce the motor traffic load and the requirements for added highways.

The exclusion of low-priced housing from the suburbs is motivated, in part, by social prejudices and, in part, by a mistaken approach to another goal of urban planning and development, namely, the minimization of public service charges to residents, in the form of user charges and ad valorem property taxes. Widespread credence has been given to the assertion that low-priced homes do not provide sufficient tax revenue to pay their proportionate share of costs for educational and other public service. Consequently, it is believed that should suburban areas be open to low-income families, the middle-class owners of somewhat higher-priced homes would have to pay unduly high taxes. This belief is based on an average cost, instead of a marginal cost analysis. There is a need to know the dimensions of increasing returns to size in many public service operations and to incorporate them into urban developments if the goal of minimization of public service charges is to be met.

The public service charges to the householder can also be reduced if the fiscal base of the community includes commercial and industrial properties. This goal—of providing the suburbs with a broad property tax base, including commercial and industrial property —may, however, run counter to the central city's goal of conserving its fiscal base through renewal and redevelopment by retaining and enlarging commercial and industrial activities in the city. It will certainly collide with what has by now become a traditional sales appeal for suburban living, the concept of an exclusively residential community.

The land use pattern will affect more than the economic goals outlined above. The amount, shape, and uses of land that is left in open space will influence the chances of carrying out the recreational goals of the communities. The uses of redeveloped central city areas, with choices ranging from a Lincoln Center to a warehouse or parking lot, will affect the fulfillment of cultural goals. The extent to which redevelopment should help universities expand their facilities is dependent upon the priority given to our educational goals. Our health goals must also be considered in planning the allocation of resources for sewage and water treatment plants or air pollution treatment facilities.

Clearly, in planning for urban development many goals are operative at the same time. Some of these are fairly straightforward and unambiguous, others are quite general. Simultaneously, a multiplicity of changeable variables, subject to consumer choice, such as residential location and mode of transportation, are involved and one cannot vary certain elements while keeping others constant. Not only the consumer choice, but the freedom of consumer choice varies. In this situation, goals are frequently not clearly defined and changing variables cannot be controlled.

The complexity of urban planning is increased because it has to be concerned not only with the numerous and intricate facets of existing community life but, in dealing with the human element, it also has to be sensitive to the changing attitudes and activities of people residing in urban places.

The effect of changing attitudes and a changing legal framework in eroding the racial barriers to freedom of choice in housing must be judged in estimating the housing and various public service requirements in different parts of a metropolitan area. Expected increases in family income and leisure time would tend to increase the desire of families to exercise choice in acquiring housing accommodations; to participate more fully in cultural activities and consequently increase the use of cultural facilities; to make greater demand on public services and facilities, such as schools, water and sewer lines, hospitals, and transportation facilities; to increase the desire for recreational facilities; in short to improve the standard of living, both quantitatively and qualitatively.

The difficulty is that we do not have adequate knowledge about consumer preferences for the goods and services under varying circumstances. For example, we do not know how people would choose their housing accommodations under varying price and financing conditions; what the choice of transportation would be if different types of transportation were available; to what extent some consumers would prefer to live in the less densely populated suburban communities and face the ordeals of congested transportation and others to sacrifice living space for reduced transportation friction. The reason for our uncertainty is that social and economic phenomena do not exist in a vacuum but are constantly subjected to interactions; and we cannot be sure which force would exercise the stronger pull. We have learned that people themselves are limited in anticipating choices until and unless they have related experiences. Yet, urban planning has to take these things into consideration.

Then, there are the external influences which have an impact on the internal structure of a community.

For instance, technological innovations may affect the employment opportunities in an area. And technology is constantly changing as is also the demand for certain commodities. It is difficult enough to quantify existing relationships. How much more difficult it is to quantify relationships in such manner as to incorporate changes which would take place in the future. Yet, this is what has to be done if the urban plan, evolved through Operations Research or any other technique, is to serve as a basis for cohesive economic development of the area in the future.

In view of the many goals to be considered and the numerous changing variables to be encompassed, alternative dynamic models have to be presented to public officials who must make decisions. They will have to know how certain allocations of resources will further one goal at the expense of another, by assuming the projected behavior of variables in the models. What is implied here is a cost-benefit analysis. This does not mean a cost-revenue analysis which has at times been used in justification of planned urban renewal projects.

There are costs suffered by some who receive no compensation and, therefore, there is no chargeable project cost involved.[3] On the other hand, there are benefits derived by some which cannot be identified with revenues accruing to any public or private organization. Nathaniel Lichfield of England has led in the conceptual development of cost-benefit analysis in city planning, and Julius Margolis in this country has worked on cost-benefit analysis techniques related to urban economics. Recently urban economists and planners have begun to look for guidance in the systems analysis adopted from Hitch and McKean in analyzing the effectiveness of costs and benefits of military defense expenditures. Cost-benefit analytic techniques have

[3] Such costs underlie the discussion of relocation incident to urban renewal presented above in Chapters II and III.

been used to a lesser extent by practitioners than other frameworks for analysis of urban areas.

There has been a significant ferment in adapting national economics concepts and developing new frameworks for analysis of metropolitan and regional urban areas in the last decade. This subject was well covered by John Meyer in an article on "Regional Economics" in the March, 1963, issue of the *American Economic Review*. He pointed to the practical utility of the modern modifications of location theory developed by E. M. Hoover and Walter Isard and the adaptation of the multiplier concept and the input-output analysis for regional area analysis.

Meyer also described what he terms "the most ambitious effort to date in the use of linear programming techniques in a regional project—the Penn-Jersey study's household location model." In attempting to find the association of families of different income and family composition with housing selections involving different land usages, the Penn-Jersey model had to expand a few times to bring in such factors as size and amenities of the house, and the costs for each housing type and location for such related items as transportation. This simply illustrates the need to know a great deal more about the behavior of the inputs that are incorporated in models that can be used in urban planning.

In two metropolitan regional studies, that of New York, directed by Vernon, and that of Pittsburgh, directed by Hoover, behavioral trends were projected, and in Pittsburgh simulation models were developed.

Exposure to problems of analyzing and projecting the behavior of households, homebuilders, mortgage lenders, and commuters in metropolitan areas creates sympathy for John Meyer's observation "that at the moment regional analysis tends to be somewhat stronger in the formulation of analytical frameworks than in fundamental understanding of any behavioral regularities at work shaping regional and metropolitan growth patterns." Meyer concluded that there might be "less relative effort on income accounting and interregional trade flow coefficient estimation and more attention to developing and testing hypotheses . . . about the behavior and role of financial organizations, market structures, entrepreneurship, private and public investment decisions, taxes, fiscal policies, and all the other subjects normally encompassed in economics."

There is one evolving tool for decision-making which needs more precise formulation and design. It is the metropolitan data bank. The purpose of the data bank would be to establish regular collections of data for a metropolitan area that would be useful in urban development planning and in making public investment decisions, to put such data on computer tape, publish the data periodically, and have them available for special analyses, as required for guidance of policy decision-makers.

Before these purposes can be met by metropolitan data banks, it will be necessary to identify clearly the users of the data bank products, their statistical and analytical needs, the present availability of data to meet the needs and additional data that may have to be developed, the methods to be employed in processing the data, and the staff requirements. With such a format, a good deal of expensive trial and error will be avoided.

In the broader context of applying Operations Research techniques to the problems of urban planning and development, there are two avenues which should be pursued. The testing of hypotheses about the behavior of pertinent economic, social, and psychological determinants of metropolitan growth patterns is needed to provide a better understanding of the variables which must be dealt with under different conditions. An example is the testing of the hypotheses that fare reductions and/or service improvements of given amounts and types can significantly alter the proportion of peak-hour commuters who will choose mass transit means as against a private auto, or the quantitative effect of lower fares and more frequent and better service on the system's off-hour commuter volume.[4]

Then, there is the challenge of arriving at alternative models of relationships of the variables, to allow the decision-makers a choice as to the optimum combination for achieving the plurality of goals that are the aim of the urban planning and development process. For example, two basic alternative planning models might be developed for a metropolitan region. One would have successive contiguous rings of high-density residential suburbs surrounding the central city; the other would have satellite communities with industry and commerce located at some distance from the central city. Which of these two models would more closely approach the optimum in terms of the goals of efficiency in productive economic activities, minimization of transportation requirements, minimization of public service costs, provision of adequate open space, opportunity of choice in residential location, and adequate cultural and education facilities?

The challenge to Operations Research is greater in the area of urban planning and development than in other areas beset by fewer complexities. There is a real need to promote greater understanding of the intricacies involved in our urban growth problems and to attempt to apply Operations Research methodology toward their solution.

At the same time, those who function in the field of urban development and housing should avoid premature abdication to Operations Research. Of course, facts are basic. The way these facts are related and analyzed is important. But in all that is done, value judgments are involved. What data are selected, the

[4] The demonstration program in mass transit has several projects which are devoted to these matters. Appendix B lists these projects and provides brief descriptions of them.

modes of analysis employed, the very problems chosen for study—all involve such values. These values must be recognized and identified. Indeed, I am old-fashioned enough to agree with the late C. Wright Mills in believing that "social research of any kind is advanced by ideas; it is only disciplined by fact."

So, it seems to me, that Operations Research, in addition to providing specific breakthroughs in knowledge and understanding, can make an even greater contribution in constantly challenging definitive conclusions based upon inadequate analysis of data. Concurrently, those who are not a part of Operations Research can, and should, question its methodology when, and if, on the basis of factual analysis it fails to set forth its value judgments. Together, in the best tradition of constructive criticism, the practitioner and the researcher can close the gap of ignorance in this most difficult field where people are the most important ingredient.

V ECONOMIC CONSIDERATIONS

Federal Policy

It is Congress, of course, that determines our national policies, and this is true of housing and urban development as much as it is of other public affairs. When the Housing Act of 1949 was enacted, with bipartisan sponsorship and bipartisan support, it included a "Declaration of National Housing Policy" that still sets the context for these federal activities. Congress, in that enactment, declared that the general welfare and security of the Nation, and the health and living standards of its people, require:

(1) housing production and related community development sufficient to remedy the serious housing shortage,

(2) the elimination of substandard and other inadequate housing through the clearance of slums and blighted areas,

(3) the realization as soon as feasible (and this has been repeated a thousand times) of the goal of "a decent home and a suitable living environment for *every* American family."

In accomplishing these objectives Congress has said ". . . private enterprise shall be encouraged to serve as large a part of the total need as it can." These are our guidelines, and they reflect as nearly as any legislative enactment can a consensus of what the American people believe. Within that framework there can be, and inevitably are, many differences of opinion.

Soon after he was inaugurated, President Kennedy

sent to Congress a message on housing and community development. In that statement he set forth the policies his Administration intended to pursue.

The objectives, he said, would be as follows:

"First, to renew our cities and assure sound growth of our rapidly expanding metropolitan areas.

"Second, to provide decent housing for *all* of our people.

"Third, to encourage a prosperous and efficient construction industry as an essential component of general economic prosperity and growth."

When the new Administration took office the country was at the depth of a recession. Nearly 7 per cent of the labor force was unemployed. Almost a fifth of our manufacturing capacity lay idle. Non-farm private housing starts were down, and the recordings of non-farm mortgages of $20,000 or less were at the lowest point since early 1958.

A significant part of the economic slowdown could be attributed to a 32 per cent decline in the annual rate of housing starts between December, 1959, and December, 1960. One of the Kennedy Administration's highest priorities, therefore, was to facilitate restoration of the homebuilding industry to a prosperous condition.

By the end of the first year of the Kennedy Administration, results were apparent. In 1961 there were over 55,000 more private non-farm housing starts than in 1960. This upward trend continued throughout 1962, and in May, 1963, the seasonally adjusted rate of non-farm housing starts rose to 1,663,000, the highest figure since August, 1950. Building permits in May, 1963, were 12 per cent above the figure for the previous month. According to the F. W. Dodge Corporation, the dollar volume of new construction in May, 1963, was the largest dollar volume on record for any month.

This revival in our economy, as represented by developments in the real estate market, did not happen by accident. It occurred, in large part, because there was in Washington an Administration dedicated to using the power of government to encourage homebuilding and to complement the forces of free enterprise where they were not effective.

The steps we took to revive the homebuilding industry were incorporated in the Housing Act of 1961 and supported by administrative actions. The approaches that we pursued reflected the Kennedy Administration's basic philosophy. Our convictions were as follows: Where the government can enlarge the housing market by credit programs, as it does through the Federal Housing Administration, it has an obligation to do so. Where the government can enlarge that market through a combination of credit and fiscal programs and policies, as it does through the Federal National Mortgage Association, it also has an obligation to do so.

The Federal Housing Administration was created at the depth of a depression to induce lenders to make mortgage loans in cases that might otherwise have been excluded from the market. Its purpose was to insure loans to those whose credit was not as good as that then demanded by conventional lenders, on terms more generous than such lenders would consider. If this were not true there would be no purpose for an insurance system; for insurance is always related to risk.

The Housing Act of 1961 enlarged the area in which mortgage loans could be insured so as to bring into the housing market as many additional persons as possible, without jeopardizing the security of existing insurance funds. It did so at a time, however, when the pockets of moneylenders were overflowing. With mortgage funds amply available, and federal credit policy utilized to assure that interest rates reflected this situation, lenders were willing to make uninsured loans they would never before have considered. The loan that yesterday was marginal, and could not have been placed without FHA insurance, had become readily acceptable. As a result, the share of the mortgage market insured by the

FHA diminished, and it probably will continue to diminish as long as the funds available for conventional mortgages increase more rapidly than the demand for such funds.

In the development of monetary and credit policies of the Kennedy Administration, discussed in detail at a later point, there has been recognition of the peculiar requirements of mortgage financing and residential construction in the total economy. This has been a principal factor in the current low-interest rates and ample supply of funds for home mortgages which have contributed so much toward sustaining housing starts, facilitating real property turnover, and preserving a healthy homebuilding industry, even in the face of a leveling off in the formation of new households.

The role of the Federal Government does not end with these credit and fiscal devices, however. There are still many persons whose incomes are such that they can neither buy nor rent adequate housing in the private market. For them some form of subsidy is necessary, and the form which has provided the greatest assistance for this group is public low-rent housing. We are, of course, well aware of the shortcomings of public housing. But we are equally cognizant of its many successes and its unique contribution toward providing good shelter for a half-million American families.[1] We propose to continue the public housing program at the same time that it is supplemented by new approaches which will utilize to the maximum degree the existing housing which can be adapted to occupancy by low-income families. Some possible new departures were summarized in Chapter III.

[1] Actually public housing has many successes to its credit. In a score of cities—especially smaller ones—it has set high standards of design. But more important, most of the half-million families that live in it are pleased with their accommodations. For a critical evaluation, see Alvin L. Schoor, *Slums and Social Insecurity* (Washington: U. S. Department of Health, Education, and Welfare, 1963), pp. 114–116.

There is one additional way in which the Federal Government can, and will, act to enlarge the housing market and make it more responsive to the needs of our people. That is in combating the racial, religious, and ethnic discrimination that excludes certain minority groups from moving freely in the market. Obviously, limitations upon freedom of participation in the housing market restrict the effective demand for housing. It is difficult to understand how proponents of free enterprise and those who champion the operation of a free market can oppose a step designed to widen the market and make more universal the promises of a free enterprise system. But they do.

A characteristic of the depressed housing activity in 1961 was the inability of prospective home-buyers to qualify for mortgage loans. For many of these potential buyers, mortgage money had priced itself out of their market. The interest rate for conventional mortgages ranged between 6 and 7.2 per cent. The FHA rate of 5.75 per cent meant an effective rate for the buyer of 6.25 per cent when the insurance premium was added. Even conventionally financed homebuilding volume, which had withstood more moderate interest rate increases since the War, showed a sharp decline in activity under the credit situation that prevailed during this period.

These conditions persisted through the latter part of 1960 and into 1961, even though the inflow of institutional savings had begun to pick up. There was gradual improvement in secondary market prices for FHA and VA mortgages and some slight decline in conventional mortgage rates. Yet mortgage interest charges generally clung near their peak levels and institutions made no substantial increase in outstanding mortgage commitments.

Instead, investors began turning to the purchase of existing mortgages from the Federal National Mortgage

Association. Purchase reservations from FNMA, which had been negligible in the first three quarters of 1960, rose to 10,000 mortgages in a month in the last quarter. In the first two months of 1961 they averaged 40,000 a month. Sales reservations reached 100 million dollars in a week in January and 150 million dollars a week in February. The amount of FNMA mortgages reserved for future sale rose to more than 500 million dollars, and actual sales jumped to 26 million dollars in January and 71 million dollars in February, compared to 1 million dollars in October, 1960.

Many investors apparently preferred seasoned 5.75 per cent FNMA mortgages at par—rather than investing their funds in new mortgages on the market even though the average price was 98 per cent of par. It did not seem in the public interest for the FNMA to continue to absorb large amounts of mortgage funds that were critically needed to revive home construction and to help the economy out of its recession. Accordingly, the FNMA Board of Directors raised FNMA mortgage sales prices in February, 1961, bringing the sales price for the 5.75 per cent FHA mortgage to 103.

The enthusiasm for mortgage purchases from FNMA disappeared. Subsequent months showed substantial increases in institutional mortage loan commitments. Conventional mortgage interest rates began to decline, and there were more funds for FHA-insured loans, even at the lower interest rate set in February, and for VA-guaranteed loans. In addition to this change in FNMA sales prices, we also reduced the FNMA stock subscription requirement in February from 2 to 1 per cent of the amount of the mortgages sold to FNMA. The statute requires, in fact, that conditions in the mortgage market and the general economy be considered in determining this stock requirement. In the light of these factors, the reduction seemed already overdue.

The February, 1961, FNMA actions were all taken in coordination with FHA's announced reduction of the maximum FHA home mortgage interest rate from 5.75 to 5.5 per cent. These actions seemed a logical move in view of the increased inflow of savings, and decreased mortgage and non-housing capital demands. The FHA action also had the support of government monetary policies. The Federal Reserve System had been supporting the lending power of the banks all year, and had broadened its open market purchases to include some intermediate and long-term bonds. The record also shows that government agencies and the Treasury-administered trust funds significantly increased their holdings of longer-term marketable government securities during the first half of the year. Judged by results, these policies were effective.

Under the money market conditions that prevailed following the FHA February action, homebuilding and financing activity under the FHA program began to advance. Between January and May, 1961, FHA existing home applications increased substantially, and new home applications showed a smaller rise. Their combined effect helped to stimulate total homebuilding activity.

Another spur to homebuilding activity was the increase in VA-guaranteed 5.25 per cent mortgages. VA appraisal requests showed a sharp increase after February, 1961, for both new and existing homes, reflecting a more favorable money market climate and higher savings inflow. By the end of May the mortgage market had improved to the point where FHA 5.5 per cent mortgages commanded the same price on the secondary market that had been paid for 5.75 per cent mortgages four months earlier. Under these circumstances, on May 29, 1961, FHA again reduced the FHA maximum interest rate from 5.5 to 5.25 per cent.

Events substantiated this judgment. FHA new home applications rose steadily from an adjusted annual monthly rate of 227,000 in May to 258,000 in August. Although there was a decline in September, the rate for

October rose. On the record, therefore, there was immediate substantial progress in restoring a prosperous level to the homebuilding industry as a component of economic prosperity and growth, within the framework of our private market processes with governmental credit support.

The provision of decent housing for all the people is not only needed to sustain a prosperous economy, it is also essential to provide for the sound growth of the Nation's rapidly expanding urban areas. Our programs and policies with respect both to housing and urban programs must be closely interrelated. Unless we can achieve a balanced supply of decent housing for the whole range of income groups and needs in the city and its suburbs, we will continue to face overcrowding, blight, and slums in the city, an exodus of middle-income people to the suburbs, the deterioration of central city property values and its fiscal base, and an aggravation of our serious commuting transportation problem.

It is ironic that illegal overcrowding of slum properties makes them more valuable, in terms of capitalized income. It also increases the cost of acquiring them for rehabilitation or clearance. Federal urban renewal grants can take care of only a small portion of the clearance problem, and our federally aided public low-rent housing can meet the housing needs of only a fraction of the people whose incomes preclude them from obtaining decent housing in the private market.

We do not have pat answers to these problems. The public interest, however, demands that we experiment with new methods of solving our slum problems and of serving the untended needs of many of our low- and moderate-income families. Provisions of the Housing Act of 1961 are responsive to these demands. The demonstration grant program to develop new methods of meeting the housing needs of low-income families, described in Chapter IV, provides a machinery for probing more deeply into this problem. The 1961 Housing

Act sets up a new long-term FHA-administered rehabilitation loan program. We are hopeful that this program coordinated with, and supplemented by, 221 (d)(3) activities in rehabilitation, will stimulate major upgrading of our existing housing supply and retard the formation of more slums. The FNMA will buy, under its special assistance program, rehabilitation loans in urban renewal areas, specifically provided for under Section 220(h). The FNMA will buy, under its secondary market operation, rehabilitation loans outside urban renewal areas, under Section 203(k). And FNMA also purchases Section 213(j) supplementary cooperative loans in both its secondary market operations and special assistance functions.

To expand the housing supply for low- and moderate-income families, the Housing Act of 1961 provided more liberal types of mortgage insurance for sales-type housing, under Section 221(d)(2). Previously Section 221 housing had been closely tied in with relocation needs of local communities, requiring a Workable Program, a community's formal request for this housing, HHFA certification of need, and the holding of such properties for sixty days so as to make them available, if possible, to displaced persons. The Housing Act of 1961 expanded and liberalized the program, removing all of the requirements set forth above. Cost limitations upon the structures eligible were raised and mortgage terms were extended from 30 to 40 years for displaced families (who still have preference but no sixty-day waiting period in which to exercise it) and from 30 to 35 years for other purchasers. The latter 35-year term can be extended up to 40 years if the owner-occupant mortgagor cannot meet the payments on a shorter-term mortgage. Also, these mortgages may now be purchased by FNMA through its regular secondary market; where displaced families are involved, FNMA special assistance continues to be available.

The impact of the legislative changes in Section

221(d)(2) of the Housing Act of 1961 was dramatic. During the fiscal year 1960, applications were received for some 10,500 dwelling units under this program; for the next fiscal year, ending June 30, 1961, the figure was 8137. The new legislative provisions became effective at the start of fiscal year 1962, and the volume of dwelling units covered by applications under Section 221(d)(2) increased to over 33,500. In the fiscal year 1963, the figure was 42,000. Not only was there a much higher volume of participation under the programs but the resulting developments were of greater economic feasibility since the market they served was, from the start, of greater magnitude.

Through this program we have already brought home ownership within the reach of scores of thousands of families who could not before have afforded homes. The numbers will continue to increase at an accelerated rate. Other provisions of the Housing Act of 1961 and the credit policies of the Kennedy Administration have made it possible for much larger numbers of families to buy a better house than they could previously have afforded.

Fiscal Policies

The responsible use of public credit is as essential as sound private credit to meet our national growth requirements and preserve a stable, sound economy. Public and private credit, effectively used, are not mutually exclusive, nor are they inimical one to the other. On the contrary, they are interdependent. The failure of one can have serious unbalancing effects on the other, as we have seen in the continued recurrence of cyclical recessions and the nagging persistence of unemployment and underproduction in important parts of our economic life.

It would be convenient if we could rely on the textbook theory that private capital automatically flows where it is needed from time to time. The fact is that capital does not rush in to buy up and clear slums; it rushes away from them, despite the heavy loss they impose on community and property investments. Neither does capital move in to create jobs and retrain workers in areas left stranded by economic change and technological advance.

Furthermore, when mortgage or municipal borrowers are squeezed out of the market, non-transferable resources become unemployed and make for economic instability. Responsible use of government assistance and public credit can correct many of these situations, and re-establish them as healthy parts of the normal economy where private capital and investment can again serve their needs.

Public resources at our disposal should be used not negatively and inadequately. They should be used positively and effectively to carry out the public purposes they are intended to serve, and they must do so within the limits set by Congress. The use of public credit, whether through guarantees, loans, or subsidies, to meet needs that repel rather than attract private investment is desirable and necessary. Such credit is essential to our national growth and welfare and to the rebuilding and creation of greater opportunities for private financing of our needs. This is demonstrably true in the case of writing off the incurred cost of urban slums and blight in order that private capital can be soundly invested in our urban future. It is equally true with respect to many of the low- and moderate-income housing needs that the private market is unable to serve, and of many of the public facility requirements that our smaller communities are finding it difficult to meet.

In magnitude, the largest federal housing program is the mortgage insurance system of the Federal Housing Administration. It consists of underwriting private risk in housing investment through a mortgage insurance operation. This does not necessarily involve public

money, although it can do so since the credit of the
Federal Government underpins the system. Companion
to this is the Federal National Mortgage Association
which buys and sells FHA- and VA-underwritten mortgages. The larger part of the operation is to provide a
secondary market outlet for such mortgages. These activities are financed primarily through private capital,
by the sale of debentures, or of short-term discount
notes. Its special assistance functions, however, are financed with funds borrowed from the Treasury.

The public housing program, which initially was
financed by government loans, was converted to private
long-term financing during the Roosevelt and Truman
Administrations. Virtually all of the permanent investment in these projects, as well as a large part of the
short-term construction money on new projects, is privately held. The same is true of short-term loans incident to the urban renewal program. The 3.3 billion
dollars of public funds that have thus far been committed for more than 1400 urban renewal projects will
generate some 20 billion dollars of private investment
made possible by opening these areas for redevelopment.

Federal subsidies are necessary to make both public
housing and urban renewal projects possible—subsidies
that are far less than the heavy cost in human and
property values that the spread of slums and blight in
our cities entails. It is because of these subsidies, in
fact, that many of these needs can now be met on a
basis of sound private investment in their future. In
dollar terms of appropriations, these are the programs
that constitute the bulk of Housing and Home Finance
Agency's activities—and they all open up large opportunities for private investment that would not have
been otherwise available.

There are special programs in which government financing plays a more direct role. One of these is the
special assistance function of the Federal National

Mortgage Association. While this is the lesser part of FNMA's operations, it is an important and sizable one, and depends on government resources for its support. Under this program the FNMA has bought special types of FHA-insured mortgages—particularly housing loans in urban renewal areas, cooperative housing mortgages, military housing mortgages, and loans for housing for the elderly. These mortgages bear the regular rates and terms, and carry the basic protections of FHA-insured loans. They differ from other FHA mortgages chiefly in the special terms and conditions applicable to the special purposes involved.

In addition, FNMA provides other services which have significance from a public service point of view and for the economy. It provides financial assistance for victims of major disasters such as hurricanes and floods. It provided a major part of the financing needed for the development of housing in Alaska prior to the recent development of a secondary market for government-backed mortgages in that area as well as financial assistance for housing in Guam where private capital thus far has not been attracted. It pioneered a market for FHA-insured and VA-guaranteed mortgages in Puerto Rico and Hawaii and, through its secondary market operations, made a market for mortgages on housing in the Virgin Islands. A much larger program, that involving low- and moderate-priced housing mortgages of $13,500 or less authorized on April 1, 1958, was a principal factor in sparking recovery from the 1957–1958 recession.

When FNMA buys these mortgages, it does so because they are willingly offered by private lenders who do not wish to hold them in their portfolios. We would be very glad to have them hold and service as many of these as possible, as some lenders are doing. Early in 1962, FNMA amended its requirements on multi-family mortgages in order to encourage the placement of permanent mortgages of this type with private lenders. By June 30, 1963, some 250 million dollars in such commitments had been canceled as a result of this action. The FNMA special assistance program in these areas simply provides the developer with a guaranteed takeout for these mortgages in the event that private investors cannot be found to finance the permanent loan. In a similar vein, FHA announced a policy of encouraging private financing for sales of FHA-acquired home properties. Prior to the summer of 1963, these sales had been financed with purchase money mortgages taken by FHA. Under our new policy, FHA will insure mortgage loans by private lenders.

In one new program, however, private investors admittedly cannot be expected to participate as investors. This is FHA's new 221(d)(3) program of insured loans primarily to non-profit, limited dividend, and co-operative sponsors for rental and cooperative housing for moderate-income families, as enacted in the Housing Act of 1961. This is an experimental program and one in which the use of public credit to serve a pressing need is well justified. Public credit in this field becomes a matter of public interest and necessity. It represents an important economic as well as a social need. In this neglected market for moderate-income housing, we can find a source for housing production which will assist in maintaining our volume of housing starts and thereby help sustain our economy at the present time. This is a non-competitive area for it represents the use of government credit where there had previously been no credit at all. In addition, the moderate-income housing program under Section 221(d)(3) has administrative requirements for maximum income limitations for families at the time of initial occupancy, thereby avoiding competition with other new housing.

The HHFA is also involved in direct lending at low rates in the field of college housing. In the past ten years it has approved more than 1.5 billion dollars in loans for college housing for students and faculty, and for related facilities. The interest rate, under the formula set by law, was 3.5 per cent until June 30, 1963, when it was increased to 3.625 per cent. This again is a program of national urgency. Without it, many of our institutions of higher education would have been unable to keep up with the housing demand resulting from increased enrollments. This would have meant serious restriction on admissions, and would have forced many students to forego advanced education because of limited facilities. Education must not be considered solely as a dollar commodity.

It has, however, been our policy to offer these loans to private lenders, and to assist private investment to absorb as much of this financing as it can. We require applicant institutions to offer their financing on the private market, prior to applying to us, in blocks covering the first ten years of maturity, and in five-year blocks subsequent to that period. We have found, when money is available, that private interest rates on the first ten to twenty years of maturity are often lower than the federal rate which applies to the whole issue. As a result of this policy, private investors financed about 50 million dollars' worth of these loans in the fiscal year ending June, 1961, compared to about 211 million dollars in bonds bought by the Community Facilities Administration which administers this program. During fiscal year 1962, private investors financed loans for which applications had been approved by CFA in the amount of $97,550,000, and CFA bought $245,850,300 of these bonds. During the first nine months of fiscal year 1963, private investors financed $141,520,000 and Community Facilities Administration bought $229,-872,350 of these bonds.

Thus, this has not only been a matter of extending federal credit. As was indicated above, private lenders have frequently been involved in a part of these loans from the time of their inception. In response to the favorable bond market of 1963 we turned to that market for additional participation. In the spring of that year we announced an initial offering of college housing bonds totaling over 41 million dollars, and 16 million dollars' worth of these bonds were sold at an aggregate premium of over $39,000. The acceptance of these investments by the public was immediate, and plans were under way for additional offerings by CFA to bond houses. This was the first time in the history of the program that such an offering had been made. Significantly, HHFA will not accept a bid less than at par.

A third major financial program is our direct loans for public works—sewer and water systems largely, but also public buildings and other community facilities. These loans are confined by law to localities under 50,000 population, or under 150,000 if they are in an economically distressed redevelopment area. Like college housing loans, this program is administered by the Community Facilities Administration, one of the HHFA constituents. It is not a large activity. Less than 226 million dollars in such loans have been approved since 1954, and they represent only a tiny fraction of the total investment in public works and facilities in our towns and cities. These, too, are financed in part by private investments. In June, 1963, for example, $170,000 out of $680,000 approved for a Public Facility Loan for Wyandotte, Michigan, and $30,000 out of a $120,000 approval for Caro, Michigan, were financed by private sales of bonds. In the Guy Island Levee Drainage District in Illinois all of a $1,270,000 loan was similarly financed.

The CFA, furthermore, administers a program of interest-free advances for the planning of public works that is widely used by communities of varying size throughout the country. These advances make it possible for the communities to plan their public works undertakings ahead of time. Their actual construction, however, is financed largely from local and private sources, with only a small number of these using CFA's direct loans.

Under the provision of the Housing Act of 1961, the current top interest rate on long-term public facility loans is 3.875 per cent, with 3.625 per cent authorized in economically distressed redevelopment areas. The Congress established this low rate on the principle that the public interest requires that our smaller towns, hard pressed to meet their growth problems, should be able to obtain credit for their public works expansion on terms more nearly equal to those of larger places. Prevailing market rates, the Congress said, "discriminate against worthwhile projects undertaken by small towns compared to the rates available to larger communities."

It is our policy in this program, as in others, to give private investors opportunity to participate in the financing of these projects. To do this we have determined that a private bid .25 per cent higher than the federal rate is still consistent with the principle of equity set forth by the Congress, and takes precedence over a federal loan. Many towns, as a result, have been able to obtain their financing on the private market for these facilities. About 15 per cent of these issues, in fact, are sold privately.

There are two things about our financing policies that are basic. First, where we have the responsibility to serve a public interest, we consider it our duty to use public credit effectively and fully. Secondly, where private investors can and will enter these markets on terms consistent with the program's objectives, we open the door as widely as possible for them to do so.

Public credit and private credit are both essential instruments of the national economy. Without private credit our housing and urban programs could not function. But without public credit, applied in the necessary places, private investment could not play its full role in the development of housing, urban areas, and our economic growth.

Federal Housing Administration

Since the Kennedy Administration assumed office, there has been much discussion of its housing policies and practices. None has been more enduring than that which relates to the role of the Federal Housing Administration.

There are those who feel that FHA is designed to serve only the building and mortgage industries or certain segments or affiliates of these industries. Therefore, they would separate FHA from the Housing and Home Finance Agency and restrict it to the support of long-established programs. National organizations of mortgage bankers and real estate boards have proposed placing control of FHA in the hands of an "independent" board which would be industry-oriented. Our position is that FHA is a governmental agency designed to serve the public as well as the building and mortgage industries and their affiliates. We feel that FHA can best do this as a part of HHFA and by administering programs which are needed to promote a healthy housing industry and urban development.

Instances of fruitful cooperation between FHA and URA, cited in Chapter III, illustrate the benefits which accrue from such cooperation. Only through close administrative identification are these possible. Also, as we plan for more effective utilization of land in the impending boom in suburban homebuilding, it is unthinkable to separate mortgage-insurance functions from those concerned with planning (now in URA and the Office of the Administrator of HHFA) and those involving provision of public facilities (in CFA).

The most persistent criticism of FHA and the way it is currently operated is that it has departed from its traditional role. It is alleged that FHA today is involved in social programs rather than strictly business activities. As a matter of fact, FHA is engaged in both activities, and this is precisely what the Congress intended that it should do. In this period of relatively plentiful mortgage funds, it would be unwise and uneconomic for FHA to do anything else.

In a word, the current activities of FHA—to continue to process and insure its traditional and established programs and to develop similar activities in its newer ones—is no accident. When the Housing Act of 1961 was being formulated, two new activities were decided upon early. The first was the below-the-market-interest-rate program for moderate-income families, and the second was relatively long-run insurance of rehabilitation loans.

Immediately a basic issue arose. How were the two new programs to be administered? It seemed fairly clear that the latter, that of mortgage insurance for rehabilitation, should be assigned to the mortgage insurance agency, FHA. But the moderate-income family housing program was more complex. It could have been a direct loan program, assigned to the Community Facilities Administration (as was the direct loan program for housing for moderate-income senior citizens), or it could have been assigned to the Public Housing Administration.

It was soon clear that the latter alternative (which was never seriously in the thinking of the Administration) would not be acceptable to the Congress. That left unsolved the method of financing this new program. After careful consideration, it was decided to select the Federal Housing Administration–Federal National Mortgage Association formula. There were several reasons for this, and they are as follows:

(1) It was a successful method of introducing other new programs—cooperative housing, urban renewal housing, and the like.

(2) It avoided establishing a new bureaucracy.

(3) It would facilitate better coordination of middle-income and high-income construction.

(4) It would further involve a risk-taking agency, FHA, in risk-taking.

The implications of this line of thinking soon became apparent. During the Congressional hearings on the Housing Act of 1961, there were repeated suggestions that the rate of insurance premium charged by FHA be reduced from .5 to .25 per cent. I stated at that time that there were sound economic grounds for FHA to insure greater risks. The shift from a sellers' to a buyers' market in housing, with consequent reversal of inflationary forces, and the general economic climate of the early 1960s occasioned a rise in FHA and VA foreclosures. The reserves accumulated by the premium charges proved adequate to meet the need during the early 1960s and indicated that our earlier resistance to reductions had been wise. In retrospect, it is now evident that it would have been improvident to have reduced insurance reserves at a time when we were entering a period of greatly expanded demands upon these reserves.

It was, and is, my position that there is no justification for an insurance system unless it takes risks. Of course, the risks of different types of mortgage insurance programs are covered under separate insurance funds. Thus the reserves of the Mutual Mortgage Insurance Fund (Section 203) or the Housing Insurance Fund (Sections 207, 213, 231, and 232) will not be affected by risks taken under the 220 and 221 programs.

At the depth of the depression, when FHA was created, there were very few people with money to lend, and they were not inclined to risk it in financing new homes. There were far too many vacant houses and houses with foreclosure notices tacked to their doors to make the construction of new homes attractive investments. Yet new construction was essential if the country was to pull itself out of the wreckage of a depressed economy. That was a social as well as an economic purpose. And that was why Congress created the FHA—

to take the risks, by insuring mortgages, so investors would be willing to come back to the financing of construction for new homes, and the country could start its recovery.

The FHA did that job, and did it magnificently. In the eight years before the FHA was established, non-farm housing starts had plummeted from a high of 937,000 to a depression-low of 93,000. In the eight years after the FHA was created they climbed back to 619,-000. In that latter year, when the bombs at Pearl Harbor plunged us into World War II, the FHA insured mortgages on over 35 per cent of the private non-farm housing starts in the country. Without those FHA-insured starts new home construction would still have been drifting in the depression doldrums.

During World War II, the FHA became an even more important factor in the Nation's construction economy. And during those years it assumed a new role of helping to finance the massive construction required to house the country's war workers. That, too, was a social as well as an economic purpose, and certainly consistent with the original purposes of the FHA.

Congress created new mortgage insurance programs in those years specifically for the financing of war housing. Between 1941 and 1954, while those programs were in operation, they insured mortgages on more than a million housing units. In the peak year of 1943 they boosted the FHA share of total non-farm housing starts to almost 80 per cent.

After World War II and years of devoting all its energies to military construction, this country was starved for housing. Again the FHA had a social purpose role to play, and once again it was a risk-taking role, stimulating the highest volume of housing construction in the history of our Nation. In four years the FHA helped to lift housing construction from the 1945 wartime level of 208,000 private non-farm starts to a record of 989,000 units in 1949.

As homebuilders began to catch up with the pent-up demand from the war years, however, they began looking for new markets to conquer. At the same time the FHA was called upon to move toward a new social and economic purpose role, of attracting builders to sectors of the market that had been neglected during the years of depression, war, and postwar boom. The first direction in which Congress chose to move was toward encouraging the construction of cooperative housing, and in doing so, it established a new criterion for the FHA in insuring loans, the criterion of "acceptable risk."

Under earlier FHA programs Congress had required a finding of "economic soundness" which in practice limited the amount of mortgage insurance to what a judicious private investor would lend. This ignored the reluctance of any investor to venture his capital in new fields, such as cooperative housing, until they had been proven sound. Congress recognized this in 1950, when it authorized mortgage insurance for cooperative housing. For it dropped the requirement of "economic soundness," and substituted a new concept of "acceptable risk" in view of the purposes of the program. This was not an invitation to irresponsibility. It was an instruction to the FHA to ask itself not what the private market *would* allow, but what it *should* allow if it were to assess an investment objectively.

The same principle was extended by Congress to the two FHA programs which it established in 1954 in connection with the redevelopment of cities. The first of these authorized mortgage insurance for housing in urban renewal areas. The other authorized such housing for those who had been displaced by urban renewal or other government action. In 1959 Congress extended the principle again, to the insurance of mortgages on proprietary nursing homes and mortgages on rental housing for the elderly.

Since 1938 there has always been standing behind

the FHA the powerful financial resources of the Federal National Mortgage Association. Whenever private investors have been slow or reluctant to accept mortgages insured by the FHA, Fannie Mae (as the FNMA is frequently called) has been ready to step in and demonstrate their soundness.

Not many people remember it now, but when Fannie Mae began it was authorized to make direct loans, secured by FHA mortgages, to help get the first rental housing program off the ground. The direct loan program was terminated on July 1, 1948. Today the FHA-insured rental program, which struggled for a while to win investor acceptance, is the most popular of all the FHA multi-family programs.

The first special assistance program directly authorized by Congress after it reorganized Fannie Mae in 1954 was for cooperative housing. Over the years Congress has increased the funds available for this special assistance to 225 million dollars. Long before that money was used, however, mortgages on cooperative housing had proven their soundness, and become readily acceptable to private investors.

The experience of the FHA with mortgages for cooperative housing has demonstrated how, working together with Fannie Mae, it can serve to introduce new types of mortgages and investment opportunities to the private market. Somewhat the same process is now taking place in regard to FHA-insured mortgages in urban renewal areas. These mortgages, also, are increasingly going to private investors rather than being purchased under the special assistance function of Fannie Mae.[2]

In the current period of more than ample mortgage

[2] The Johnson Administration's proposals for land are basically an extension of this approach. Today the cost of money for land improvement is frequently excessive. FHA-insurance for this purpose would attract reluctant funds and decrease the cost of credit for this purpose. FNMA special assistance (for new communities) would assure a supply of mortgage money, thereby facilitating a reasonable interest rate.

funds, Fannie Mae has responded to the market situation, substituting private funds for mortgages previously financed by it. During the fiscal year of 1963 its sales of mortgages topped one billion dollars. This was almost double its previously high year of sales, 1954. While most of the 1963 sales were made from the secondary market operations portfolio, some 300 million dollars of sales involved mortgages originally financed with public monies. Of this amount, 294 million dollars' worth of mortgages came from the special assistance function portfolio.

Under the Kennedy Administration the FHA extended its risk-taking role in two areas; rehabilitation of housing and housing for moderate-income families. These programs not only serve an unmet social need, but they also facilitate a high level of housing activity. They are economically desirable in this period of less-than-full employment and a plateau in the rate of new household formation, so that expansion in the special housing areas is not inflationary. From a point of view of economics, this is the most propitious time to encourage them.

It is against these programs, and those concerned with housing for the elderly, that recent attacks against the FHA have been directed. Under the guise of sounding an alarm against reckless insuring practices, a charge that has never been substantiated, these attacks seek to paralyze the FHA and restrict its operations to areas where it is today less needed.

Senator Sparkman, the Chairman of the Housing Subcommittee of the Banking and Currency Committee of the Senate, took note of these attacks in a speech he made recently before the annual convention of the National Housing Conference, and he declared in that speech:

"I want to point out that, rather than moving away from mortgage risks, we should move toward taking more risks but to do it with our eyes open and with the proper reserves to meet expected contingencies."

This was the policy of the FHA long before the Kennedy Administration. It continues to be the policy of the FHA. We shall meet, to the maximum degree, the housing needs of as wide a sector of the American people as possible. In doing this, we shall utilize to the fullest extent the know-how and organizational resources of all the constituents of the Housing and Home Finance Agency.

FHA will, of course, continue to have a major role. Our real problem is to make it flexible enough to meet the changing requirements of the housing market. We need more, not less, effective participation of FHA in the new programs assigned to it.

The Economic Consequences of Open Occupancy

At the time this manuscript was prepared, we had experienced less than a year's application of President Kennedy's Executive Order on Equal Opportunity in Housing. The most controversial aspects of this Order were the provisions which banned racial discrimination in FHA-insured and VA-guaranteed housing committed on or after November 20, 1962.

The building and real estate industries asserted at the time of, and subsequent to, the issuance of the Executive Order that it would seriously reduce the volume of housing starts. In this prophecy, they were joined by many trade publications of the industries. The Administration and the HHFA took decided exception to this opinion.

Although it is too early to evaluate definitely the effect of the Order, events subsequent to November 20, 1962, have clearly disproved the assertions of the builders and real estate operators. Actually, subsequent to the issuance of the Executive Order, the volume of housing starts increased. The annual seasonally adjusted rate of non-farm housing starts for May, 1963, was the highest for any month since August, 1950. This rate was 4 per cent above that for April, 1963, and 8 per cent above that for May, 1962. And although the proportion of FHA-insured loans in the total was 14 per cent, or 3 per cent less than in May, 1962, the volume was 4 per cent higher than in April, 1963.

As a matter of fact, in the first nine months of 1963, non-farm housing starts totaled 1,209,000, a gain of 8 per cent over the like period in 1962. There was, at that time, every reason to expect the annual figure for 1963 to top the 1,500,000 mark.[3] On the basis of these data, it was generally conceded that the President's Order would not result in a downturn of housing starts during 1963, but would be followed by a significant acceleration of homebuilding. An article in the Real Estate Section of the October 6, 1963, *New York Times* significantly had the following headline and subheadline: "Bias-Order Fears Seem Unjustified" and "Signs Indicate Best Year in Housing Since 1955."

What the future trends in housing starts will be or what factors will influence them can only be determined later. Thus there will be no attempt to discuss these developments in this book. Instead, an analysis of the effect of a state law in New York which had similar coverage of home construction is presented here.[4]

This analysis is pertinent because it was written at the time the New York law was enacted and prior to its enforcement. It presents a theoretical treatment of the subject. And, interestingly, subsequent events sup-

[3] The figure for 1963 was almost 1,600,000.

[4] Of course the proportion of FHA and VA involvement in the housing market declined between 1955 and 1962. In the former year 51 per cent of housing starts were supported by these two agencies; in 1962 it had fallen to 23 per cent. This was offset by the wider and more diversified coverage of President Kennedy's Order.

ported its conclusions, indicating that, if anything, the paper overstated the adverse impact of the state law.

This section is an abridgement of an article written by me and published in the November, 1955, issue of *Land Economics* under the title, "The Effect of Anti-Discrimination Legislation upon the FHA- and VA-Insured Housing Market in New York State." I have, however, changed the tense of verbs to reflect current situations and identify descriptions which applied to 1955. Also there is a postscript reflecting the degree of acceptance of the President's Executive Order on Equal Opportunity in Housing.

New York State passed the Metcalf-Baker Law banning racial discrimination in FHA- and VA-insured construction where multiple dwelling units or projects of ten or more units are involved in 1955. This extension of non-discrimination legislation was significant both regionally and nationally. It aroused serious forebodings on the part of builders and other segments of the real estate industry. Many, if not most, assumed that it would be a catastrophe. Since, however, any and all proposed changes in racial patterns seem to inspire similar fears and forebodings, it may be useful to inquire into the dimensions and nature of the problem which the Metcalf-Baker Law created.

Until the turn of the century, the presence of a few Negro families in any particular neighborhood was accepted without comment in many American cities. Little thought was given to adverse effects upon property values. When the rapid influx of large numbers of low-income families of varied ethnic backgrounds into urban areas occurred at the same time that the supply of low-cost housing failed to grow commensurately, the resulting slums, blight, and social decay were associated with the newcomer and identified with him when he was of a darker hue. Equally important, but not unrelated, was the rise of the suburbs and their newly created sales-point of exclusiveness.

In the development of recent attitudes toward non-white neighbors there were and are two basic factors: rapid introduction of large numbers of minority-group families and the possibility of escape from minorities through the purchase of a new home in a "restricted neighborhood." Restriction of this type was made respectable and desirable by well-organized and carefully-nurtured sales promotion; until a few years ago it had the official stamp of approval since FHA accepted and furthered industry's approach to the matter. In our democratic society where there is general belief in the existence of widespread social and economic mobility, exclusiveness in residential areas found ready acceptance. Few families on the way up could afford to go against the current. Then, too, respected and widely disseminated real estate economics coupled racial (and often income) homogeneity with stability of values about the same time that racially mixed areas became associated with slums and low-cost housing. There was every reason for the average white family to consider Negroes and other non-whites undesirable neighbors; the real estate industry, in all its branches, had made them forbidden neighbors.

Given this institutional setting, the basic fears of the building industry are understandable. Indeed, it would be unrealistic to expect an industry which had grown for two generations on the basis of championing and expanding residential segregation to greet a proposal for its partial eradication with anything less than apprehension and resistance; and it could cite supporting evidence.

"Open occupancy" and "interracial" housing in New York and elsewhere had usually been *de facto* non-white housing. When an occasional FHA-insured project of this type had been announced and constructed, the Negro demand had been so great as to fill the project or indicate the probability of large-scale colored occupancy. In the latter situation, whites preferred to buy elsewhere and the project had "gone Negro." If the non-white market was significant, as in the New York City area, the developer suffered no financial loss and often made a larger than normal profit due to the possibilities of charging higher prices than the more competitive white market would absorb. Where the non-white market was more restricted, as in parts of upstate, failure of whites to enter the project might mean vacancies and losses to developers.

As long as most new construction is closed to the non-white purchaser, there is always the possibility that he and others similarly discriminated against will gravitate to the few projects (or neighborhoods) which will accept him. At the same time, the doubtful white purchaser is being wooed by many other developers who are emphasizing, urging, and offering racial exclusiveness. Such a setting creates a concentrated non-white demand at the occasional open occupancy project and accentuates avoidance of open occupancy developments on the part of white families.

The Metcalf-Baker Law recognized and was designed to meet these difficulties which plague the individual developer of open occupancy housing. Because it affected all builders who enjoyed certain governmental assistance, enforcement of this legislation was expected to accomplish two important objectives: (1) disperse non-white demand over *all* developments of the prescribed type, and (2) eliminate the possibility of escape from one such development by finding racial exclusiveness in others of the same category. The tight mortgage market of 1955 contributed to the law's efficacy since there were relatively few alternative sources of finance available to FHA and VA builders.

The fear of widespread inundation of FHA- and VA-underwritten projects seemed unwarranted *unless* the building industry materially reduced the volume of such construction, or scared away white purchasers by establishing early patterns of all-colored occupancy. Although some suggested that the new law would sound the death knell of construction financed by government-insured loans, sober reflection cast serious doubts on such an eventuality. As *House and Home* observed in the April, 1955, issue, "the industry's ability to sell the million-plus new homes a year that means prosperity hinges on the low downpayments made possible by FHA and VA. Abandoning them is so unthinkable it is not even discussed."

In the final analysis the effect of this new legislation upon the FHA and VA housing market was determined by the extent of immediate effective demand of non-whites for this type of construction, the distribution of this demand among projects affected by the law, and the reactions of white neighbors to non-white residents in such volume and occupancy patterns as might result.

Fortunately, there were fairly reliable income data for non-whites in the State of New York. In addition, it was possible to estimate roughly how large a proportion of the families financially able to move into new FHA and VA developments were ready to do so. Since the basic non-discrimination legislation covering publicly assisted housing (the Wicks-Austin Act) had been in effect for five years, there was a body of experience indicating how non-whites would probably distribute themselves as a result of the Metcalf-Baker Law and the extent of litigation resulting from non-discrimination legislation governing publicly assisted housing.[5] Finally, there was available material indicating various reactions to, and results of, the movements of non-whites into neighborhoods of varying economic ranges.

In 1950, there were 210,000 non-white households in New York State; estimates for July, 1955, put the number at 236,000. Since 90 per cent of these were in the New York City metropolitan area and another 5 per cent in the Buffalo metropolitan area, it is obvious that the demand of non-whites for FHA- and VA-insured

[5] The latter was negligible.

housing was largely concentrated in and about these two urban communities.

On the basis of estimated 1953–1954 family incomes made by the New York State Housing Rent Commissioner, only 18.6 per cent of non-white families in New York City had annual incomes of $5000 or more after federal income taxes were deducted. Applying the FHA definition of effective income, which excluded about 90 per cent of all secondary incomes (usually in the form of earnings of a second wage earner), the proportion fell to 8.3 per cent. Only 13.1 per cent of the non-white families in Buffalo had incomes of $5000 or over in 1955.

In order to estimate ability to pay for housing expenses, the experience of the FHA was drawn upon and its standards applied in computing the potential rent-paying and home-buying capacity of non-white families. The maximum number of non-white families able to pay for FHA- and VA-insured housing carrying a mortgage of $9600 or more in the New York metropolitan area was about 14,230, on the basis of estimated 1955 population distribution. For the Buffalo metropolitan area, the maximum would be about 550 families. In the New York City metropolitan area, about 12.5 per cent of the non-white families could afford a gross monthly rental of $100 and over. This would involve some 26,550 families; the comparable figure for the Buffalo metropolitan area was about 1132 families.

Because of several circumstances, the number of non-white families in New York theoretically able to pay for new housing was much greater than the immediate effective demand. The following factors are significant in this regard:

(1) Most of the higher-income non-white families were professional and business people. Some of them, for political or business reasons, could not and did not want to move to the suburbs.

(2) Some of the higher-income non-white families

were already living in suburban areas where they were well housed; others owned attractive homes in Manhattan, Brooklyn, Queens, and the Bronx. Most of these households did not contemplate moving.

(3) A large segment of non-white families able to pay for FHA and VA rental housing were either living in existing standard housing or planning to move to new developments under way in Harlem or other localities within the city limits. In this connection, it must be recalled that there was *some* good and desirable housing in Negro-occupied areas and more was planned or under construction.

(4) Most non-white families able to afford FHA and VA housing were currently paying much less for rent than the minimum requirements of new construction. Many so housed had commitments and budget patterns which were adjusted to their then present level of spending for shelter. While they and others were potential purchasers or renters of new FHA- and VA-insured housing, a large proportion would not, for economic reasons, be immediately in the market.

Although it is impossible to make an estimate of the immediate effective demand of non-whites for new construction, one can safely assert that it would involve but a fraction of those whose incomes nominally would permit them to purchase or rent such housing.[6] Since the latter number was small, it is conceivable that the total number of non-whites actively and effectively in this market in 1955 could, if spread out over a large volume of construction, have been absorbed without involving appreciable numbers in any one project. This was equally true of most urban areas in the Nation.

[6] The situation will, of course, change in time. As new patterns are established and more opportunities for participation develop, a larger number of non-whites will enter FHA- and VA-insured housing. For this to come to pass there must be rather radical changes in spending habits, widespread realization of new opportunities for housing, and the concomitant passage of time.

The fact that so-called open occupancy, FHA- and VA-insured projects had, in the past, been inundated by non-whites was not a valid basis for assuming a similar eventuality under the Metcalf-Baker Law. Formerly, the non-white homeseeker had no choice in the matter since most FHA and VA construction was not available to him. After 1955 all would be open. How non-whites would respond to the new situation was best demonstrated by their distribution in that segment of publicly assisted housing in which racial discrimination has long been banned. Because of rentals and income limitations, non-whites have participated widely in public housing projects in all New York cities where they reside. In spite of non-whites' widespread occupancy and the existence of non-discriminatory legislation for over a decade, projects far removed from established Negro neighborhoods had only sparse non-white occupancy.

Even in New York City, where the demand of non-whites for housing was so large and where over a third of those in public housing were Negroes, the greatest concentration of Negroes was in projects built on sites within established non-white ghettos; the next highest concentration was in sites contiguous to established ghettos; and the lowest concentration was in projects farthest removed from established centers of non-white residences. Since most of the vacant sites are located in outlying areas, there was a similar correlation between vacant sites and low concentration of Negro occupancy.

In addition to subsidized public housing which has counterparts in all sections of the Nation, the New York City Housing Authority operated a no-cash subsidy program where apartment rents averaged about $71 per month and maximum income of families at time of admission was $5400. There were in 1955, twenty completed projects of this type offering accommodations to about 22,000 families. One, Colonial Park Houses, is situated in upper Harlem and almost all its

tenants were colored. More than half the tenants of a
second Manhattan development on the fringe of Harlem were Negro. The two remaining projects in Manhattan had about 25 per cent Negro occupancy. Of the
no-cash subsidy developments outside Manhattan, five
had Negro occupancy of less than 10 per cent; six had
from 10 to 15 per cent; and five had from 15 to 20 per
cent.

In limited dividend housing under the supervision
of the State Division of Housing, the degree of non-
white participation was negligible. This was due in part
to the fact that, in contrast to the public housing program, past enforcement of non-discriminatory legislation had been diffident. It was due chiefly, however, to
two circumstances. The extent of non-white effective
demand for such housing had been far less than for
public housing and, more significantly, these projects
had been developed on vacant sites, none of which
was close to existing concentrations of non-whites.

Similarly, in Queensview, a cooperative housing development just across the Triborough Bridge from
Manhattan's Harlem, there was only a handful of Negro
occupants in 1955. This was a project of 726 units requiring $600-per-room downpayment and costing $17
per room per month at that time. Despite a genuine
desire on the part of its sponsors to recruit Negro occupants, only fifteen or twenty colored families moved
in around 1950 when it was opened. Five years later
about the same number resided there. Yet the widely
publicized announcement of a non-discriminatory policy
did not complicate filling the project and maintaining
a large waiting list of white applicants.

These experiences, when considered in light of the
growing volume of middle-income housing which was
available to non-whites in Manhattan subsequent to
1955, led to the inescapable conclusion that there
would be no general inundation of FHA- and VA-insured projects covered by the Metcalf-Baker Law. Much

of the pent-up effective demand for this price shelter was absorbed in Manhattan and inlying areas in other boroughs. As the incipient trend toward development of moderate- and medium-rental housing in Harlem continued, and more Title I housing open to non-whites was produced in Manhattan and surrounding areas, the immediate effective demand of non-whites for FHA and VA construction elsewhere was proportionately reduced.

It has been noted above that the Metcalf-Baker Law removed the assured "escape" from minority-group families which had been a trademark of new FHA- and VA-insured housing. Realization of this fact, in itself, rendered futile the selection of any one development of this type as a means of entering an assured lily-white neighborhood. It also meant that racial exclusiveness as a sales appeal was both illegal and dishonest. These facts alone had a marked effect upon the attitude of whites to the presence of a few Negro neighbors.

There are, however, additional developments which have pertinence. First, we are learning that the building industry has often overestimated the opposition of whites to a few non-white neighbors of similar economic and social backgrounds. Second, there were successful examples of racial integration in New York and other states which suggested that neighborhood reaction to colored occupants was either changing or different from what had been assumed. Third, whites were beginning to resist appeals for panic sales at the advent of the first colored purchaser and, finally, research was documenting the fact that there is no one universal relationship between race and property values.

Builders, financial institutions, and real estate dealers are generally convinced of the color consciousness in their market. Yet there was some evidence which challenged their conclusions. Levittown in Long Island had been a symbol of suburbia's racial exclusiveness; nevertheless it had by 1955 absorbed a few Negro owners without confusion. In the early 1950's no other single issue aroused so much guilt and dissension among its residents as racial discrimination against Negroes. Although those living in Levittown hadn't created the pattern of exclusion, they sustained it. Most of them agreed, however, that had Negroes been in the project from the first, there would have been no problem. As one put it, "I'll admit that it wouldn't have made a damn bit of difference to me originally." Apparently, it doesn't make too much, if any, difference to the neighbors who continue to live next door to the small number of colored owners now in Levittown.

There were desirable, middle-class neighborhoods throughout the State of New York and elsewhere which would have been surprised to learn that Negro occupancy is supposed to depress property values. In these residential communities a few Negroes had been and were accepted without comment. So stable are these neighborhoods that they have not even become the subject of social scientists' research.

In the last few years, . . . new factors have entered the situation which are changing . . . [the] pattern of "invasion and succession." One factor is the change in attitude toward living near members of a minority group. Partly as a result of an organized effort to reduce prejudice and discrimination, and partly as a result of the housing shortage, more people are "willing" to live next door to members of minorities than was formerly the case. The second new factor is a Supreme Court decision of 1948 which removed the legally enforceable basis of the restrictive covenant, which has hitherto been the most powerful legal device used to prevent members of the minority groups from buying or renting in majority group areas. Since 1948, in most Northern cities and some Southern cities as well, Negroes have been moving into many white neighborhoods which under the old system would have taken them decades to penetrate, if ever they could have gotten in at all. There are now a large number of otherwise white neighborhoods into which one or two Negro families have moved. Mixed housing seems to be becoming the dominant pattern in at least the northern cities.[7]

By 1955, a growing, though still small, number of areas were working toward the objective of maintaining a racially mixed pattern. The biggest stumbling blocks to achieving this goal were the almost solid reluctance of white real estate brokers to show homes for sale to prospective white buyers and the ever present possibility of recurrence of panic selling, often inspired by Negro as well as white real estate operators. Even with the opposition from real estate operators, it had been possible to make sales to new white purchasers in some areas of racially mixed housing. In all new suburban areas, it is possible to control over-occupancy and associated undesirable property uses through occupancy standards and similar restrictions. This circumstance

---

[7] Arnold M. Rose, Frank J. Atelsek, and Lawrence R. McDonald, "Neighborhood Reactions to Isolated Negro Residents: An Alternative to Invasion and Succession," *American Sociological Review*, October, 1953, p. 499.

This is a familiar and oft-repeated pattern of behavior. In Syracuse, for example, the Friends Housing Committee released a survey of Negro families living outside the established area of non-white concentration. Among the significant findings were the following: "In view of this very high degree of community acceptance, the reader may wonder why more of Syracuse's higher-income Negro population has not moved out of the central part of the city. One reason, of course, is the very real difficulty encountered by a Negro in trying to find a home in a desirable neighborhood through a realtor or through a builder (practically impossible in the latter case, though the new Metcalf-Baker Law gives hope in this regard). . . . Finally, perhaps this study suggests that the greatest opposition to integration stems not from the average citizen but from the 'gatekeepers'—the realtors and builders, who *think* that the neighborhood will be less oriented toward a democratic housing pattern than it really is." (*Survey of Negro Families Living Outside 15th Ward Area in Syracuse, N.Y. and Surrounding Areas*, Friends Housing Committee, July, 1955.)

removes the greatest threat to a neighborhood incident to the entrance of a shelter-starved minority group.

In older sections of the city it has been a familiar pattern for non-white occupancy of a formerly middle-class white area to be typified by bad property uses, overcrowding, and physical decay. But where occupancy standards require single-family occupancy of single-family homes, prohibit cutting dwellings up into smaller units, and restrict undesirable additions, the market is limited, for the most part, to those who can afford to maintain the property and use it according to the standards for which it was designed. Thus in San Antonio, Texas, where Negro incomes were much lower than in New York State, colored families rapidly moved into the 200-unit Eastlawn Addition which was created in 1949 as an all-white project of $5800 to $8500 bungalows. Despite the fact that the development was directly east of the city's main Negro housing district, the rapid entrance of non-whites did not change the occupancy pattern save in the color composition of residents. As *House and Home* in the April, 1955, issue reported:

> The original white owners—civil service workers, policemen, railroad men, skilled labor—have now been largely supplanted by Negro civil service workers, ministers, railway postal clerks and skilled labor. Typically, most wives also work. Farm and Home Savings and Loan Association, which made many of the original loans, still holds many of the loans. Farm and Home's L. A. Lawlor says the mortgage payment record of the new owners has been as good as in any similar white area. And nobody, driving down the street, can tell which homes are white-occupied and which are not. Except for one thing: for-sale signs.

This experience is in striking contrast to the resentment and threat of violence in a lower middle-class neighborhood in Philadelphia when a low-income Negro purchased and moved into a house in the area. In this instance the Negro buyer was not economically able to restore or maintain his property, nor were occupancy standards applicable. His entrance did represent a threat to property values. Only alert action by the City's Commission on Human Relations and financial and other assistance from the Society of Friends and Negro citizens had been able to stem mass flight of white residents. "For sale" signs disappeared and, after this event, one real estate dealer alone sold twenty-six houses in the area, all of them to relatives or friends of the old-time settlers. Values didn't drop and the community seemed to have settled down to its old tranquillity.

On the other hand, the existence of "for sale" signs in the San Antonio suburb was inevitable. It reflected non-white inundation of a new source of relatively low-cost housing contiguous to, or close by, an existing ghetto. The concentration and intensity of non-white demand was due primarily to the fact that there were no other opportunities of this type available to Negroes. Had the area not been protected by adequate restrictions on use, in all probability Negro occupancy might have been accompanied by drastic changes in income level and occupancy patterns. All of these cases suggest that in adequately zoned, medium-priced developments removed from areas of non-white concentration, and where white owners resist appeals or urges for panic sales, interracial patterns can be stabilized, provided there are other similar areas open to non-whites.

In every discussion of non-white occupancy there is explicit or implicit reference to resulting fall in property values. We have much to learn about this relationship. Increasingly, however, recognized appraisers and real estate economists were, by 1955, accepting the dictum expressed by Oscar J. Stern in the January, 1946, issue of *The Review of the Society of Residential Appraisers:* "It is a fact, the axiom that colored infiltration collapses the market is no longer true." *House and Home* observed in the mid-1950s: "In recent years, more and more experts have put forth studies debunk-

ing the once widely-held notion that property values
slide in transition neighborhoods. Now evidence is ac-
cumulating that some city neighborhoods—at least in
the North—are ready to accept immigrant Negroes without fuss."

What then would be the effect of the new legislation?
Clearly, it would not, in and by itself, solve the housing
problem of non-whites. It would not even meet the
needs of the vast majority of middle- and higher-income
minority-group families seeking better housing in the
State of New York. Nor should its enforcement disrupt
or seriously affect the FHA- and VA-insured housing
market in the state. Still its impact should be appreciable; for it would not operate in a vacuum.

To a limited degree the new legislation should add
directly to the supply of medium- and higher-priced
shelter available to non-whites. At the same time, it
should accelerate acceptance of colored families elsewhere in existing medium- and higher-priced housing
both inside and beyond the city limits. From both of
these trends there should emerge additional experiences
of successful interracial housing. The fact that such case
histories emanate from the former citadels of racial exclusion will have repercussions throughout the housing
market. No longer will racially mixed housing be associated only with slums and public housing projects.

Basically, therefore, the effect of the law will be to
facilitate new patterns of racial occupancy. Reluctance
of non-whites to move in large numbers into developments far removed from existing areas of concentration and builders' preference for outlying sites will
combine in easing the impact as well as enforcement
of the Metcalf-Baker Law. As new patterns are established and accepted by occupants, the industry should
slowly modify its fears of, and concern with, non-white
occupancy. While this is occurring, new urban renewal
projects and expanding programs of state-aided limited
dividend housing will absorb a much larger segment of

the non-white demand for medium-rental units, since
they, too, are required by law not to discriminate. Concurrently, the non-whites' reluctance to venture into
what have been hostile areas will decrease. Conceivably,
a gradually growing effective demand for new suburban
dwellings on the part of minorities should coincide with
an increasing acceptance of such families by the developers and occupants of suburban areas.

An evolutionary process toward interracial living is
possible although, as in any instance of social change,
there will be problems. Economics, population movements, and response of whites to the slow infiltration of
minorities are all on the side of success. Profit-motivated
builders, too, have a real interest in achieving such results although established patterns of behavior will, of
course, be impediments to an easy transition. But this
change was being initiated at a time when the climate
in the United States was favorable; for there was growing evidence that new patterns and attitudes in intergroup relations were flowering in housing as in other
aspects of American life.

There has been a striking similarity between the reaction to the Metcalf-Baker Law in New York State and
to President Kennedy's Executive Order on Equal Opportunity in Housing. Reference was made at the beginning of this section to the prophets of doom who
greeted both actions. In addition, the initial impact of
both actions upon the volume of housing starts was also
similar. By early fall, 1963, there seemed to be realization in most segments of the housing industry that open
occupancy in federally assisted housing was here to stay.
The president of the Mortgage Bankers Association advocated extension of the order to include the savings
and loan associations and other institutions whose ac-
counts were insured by the Federal Government. The
National Association of Home Builders (whose 1962
president prophesied a one-third reduction in housing
starts as a result of the Order), in convention in Hono-

lulu in 1963, while divided on the Order, took positive action. By unanimous vote, it created a new committee on housing relations. The responsibility of the
committee was to develop NAHB policy on the Executive Order, collect pertinent data, and maintain liaison
with federal and private agencies involved. Of course,
the National Association of Real Estate Boards remained adamant, attacking governmental action to establish democratic patterns in housing at the national,
state and federal levels.

But even the NAREB could not ignore entirely the
trends of the time. Without retreating from its opposition to change, some of its leaders indicated that a
new era was in prospect. Thus Daniel F. Sheehan, president of NAREB in 1963, stated that "a change in our
conscience, a change in our thinking" is required incident to open occupancy. Significantly, he cited the instance of a Midwestern real estate agent who advised
a white homeowner not to sell when a Negro educator
moved into the neighborhood. Prices remained stable
in the area, Mr. Sheehan reported.

Most of the press and many of the trade journals accepted the fact that a new federal policy had been established and reported that the initial results had not
substantiated the notion that the Order would create
economic chaos. Some of the more liberal were attempting to allay the fears of those who saw in it a threat to
their economic interests. An outstanding example of
this was the *New York Times*, which, in a front-page
article in the Real Estate Section of the September 29,
1963, issue, carried an article titled "St. Albans Rises
Above Race Fears." It stated:

> . . . the integration of St. Albans [a section of Queens
> in New York City] occurred back in the nineteen thirties.
> What has happened in St. Albans since then, say pro-
> ponents of open-occupancy housing, could serve to allay
> the fears of many white homeowners who today are faced
> with the same situation.

Homes that sold for $9,000 in the late nineteen thirties and early forties in the integrated area of St. Albans are now selling for $20,000 or more. And despite the mixed racial character of the area, homes there, rather than deteriorating, are in great demand.

VI THE URBANIZATION
OF THE NEGRO

A Transitional Period of Population Movement

Between 1940 and 1950, over 7,000,000 people moved to the suburbs of this Nation. More than 2,000,000 whites deserted central cities at the same time that some 1,300,000 non-whites moved in. These figures, when they became available in the mid-1950s, gave rise to much speculation and apprehension about the future of American cities. Public officials, housing specialists, and journalists asked: Are the large cities in this Nation about to become non-white ghettos? Will the metropolitan areas of tomorrow have a core of low-income, colored families surrounded by middle- and upper-income whites in the suburbs? Does this mean Negro political domination in the larger urban communities? Will downtown businesses and cultural institutions wither away from lack of support?

Large-scale migration to cities is no recent phenomenon. In this country many nationality and ethnic groups have been involved, and each of these has at first gravitated to areas contiguous to downtown business. Every new group has been resented on the basis of imputed inferior status. Negroes, Puerto Ricans, and Mexicans are the most recent components in this process.

Middle- and upper-income families have been moving to the suburbs for decades, and the majority of the core areas suffered rather sizable out-migration during the depression and in the prosperous 1940s. Thus, for more than a quarter of a century, central cities have attracted fewer newcomers than their suburbs. Such growth as they experienced was due to the excess of births over deaths rather than to net in-migration.

Basically, therefore, the situation in the 1950s was a projection of trends which have been with us for some time. It did, however, have two peculiarities. It took place at a time when the exodus from the central city to the suburbs was at a peak, and a large number of the newcomers to the larger metropolitan areas belonged to readily identified minority groups. Both of these circumstances led to a considerable amount of distortion. Some have confused coincidence with causation. To them the desertion of the central cities by middle- and upper-income whites was purely and simply a means of escape from Negroes. Others seem to feel that large-scale movement of low-income families to industrial centers was peculiar to the migration of non-whites and that perpetual, enforced residential segregation was an inevitable consequence of such population movement.

Actually, this was not a new type of migration. Rather widespread enforced racial residential segregation had given a unique cast to a recurring phenomenon. Because metropolitan areas do not afford the most recent migrants free movement and equal opportunities for housing, their concentration in the core areas of many urban communities creates perplexing problems. What we do about the color line in shelter will determine whether these problems become chronic or dissolve into solutions which have typified earlier migrations to these same industrial cities.

Suburbanization through migration has been almost a universal phenomenon in the United States and a fairly general one in Canada during the last quarter of a century. Actually it is more than a phenomenon of the American hemisphere. Copenhagen, too, evidenced this development. There, as in this Nation, higher-income families are seeking shelter in the suburbs while low-income groups are finding shelter in the central city. A recent study of these movements concludes that "the central city may become increasingly the domicile of those whose income, type of work, and marital status makes residence in the more expensive and more family centered suburban areas economically impossible or socially undesirable."[1]

Here we have an instance of a European metropolis, with practically no non-white population, where migration is producing an increasingly (economically) homogeneous population in the central city, composed increasingly of low-income persons.

Many metropolitan areas in the United States where suburbanization of this type has occurred have extremely small non-white populations. Binghamton, New York; Brockton, Massachusetts; Cedar Rapids, Iowa; Duluth, Minnesota–Superior, Wisconsin; and Fall River–New Bedford, Massachusetts are just a few examples. Thus color alone cannot account for the migration of over seven million people to the Nation's suburbs in the 1940–1950 decade.

There are many and complex reasons for the movement to the suburbs. As in all migration, it has been in response to the "pull" of the attractions of the new locale and the "push" of the deficiencies of the old. Race became a factor only after technology had made suburban living possible for the great mass of Americans.

Had there been no migration of non-whites to urban communities, large-scale expansion of suburbia would have occurred in the post-World War II period, although, of course, the arrival of large numbers of less affluent migrants to central cities accelerated the process. Increased earnings made home ownership a more frequently obtainable goal, at the same time that larger families rendered suburban living more functional. Construction of a large volume of new, single-family

[1] Sidney Goldstein, "Some Economic Consequence of Suburbanization in the Copenhagen Metropolitan Area," *American Journal of Sociology*, March, 1963, p. 561.

homes in the suburbs with indirect Federal Housing Administration and Veterans Administration federal assistance accelerated movement to these areas. The overt and hidden persuaders, constantly competing for the consumers' dollars, were able to merchandise effectively new housing which had prestige and style. Negative forces operated, too. The most important of these were frustrations with the problems of living in the central city—old and neglected schools, inadequate public transportation, neighborhood blight, high taxes and architectural obsolescence of older structures, and lack of new construction of individual homes in the central city.

Not only did whites move to the suburbs for reasons unrelated to non-whites' migration, but other whites joined non-whites in augmenting the population of central cities. They, too, were resented. Thus, it was unrealistic to anticipate exclusive non-white occupancy of many core cities even if the 1940–1950 rates of migration were projected into the future. Besides, it was doubtful if non-white movement to industrial centers would long continue at the then current tempo, and recent data, cited subsequently, substantiate this notion. Rapid urbanization of Negroes over forty years drastically depleted the principal source of future non-white migrants; however, the natural increase in non-white population will in itself occasion pressure on housing accommodations unless this segment in the population achieves wider access to the market.

Although the proportion of non-whites among the migrants to the outer fringes of metropolitan areas was relatively small, actually one-third of a million colored people took part in this movement from 1940 to 1950. The majority of these were in the South. Here there is a paradox which is seldom appreciated. For the mass of Negroes, housing in the South was infinitely worse than in the North. Yet, for middle-income Negroes the reverse was often true. This followed largely because of regional differences in spatial distribution of non-whites. In the cities of the North, Negroes were concentrated in downtown areas far removed from suburban expansion. In the South, urban Negroes frequently lived on "the other side of the tracks" where there was the possibility of spilling over into outlying areas. Then, too, lack of access to public facilities and commercial sources of entertainment had established the home as a center of entertainment for Southern middle-class Negroes. Thus, for several generations, Southern Negroes with higher earnings placed greater emphasis upon upgrading the quality of their housing.

In the post-World War II period, these circumstances combined with higher incomes to facilitate new and larger Negro suburban subdivisions in the South. This trend had a precedent. In Washington, D.C., where a sizable number of Negroes had long had stable incomes, a central city suburb, Brookland, became an attractive, middle-class racially mixed neighborhood during the late 1920s and subsequently. In the District of Columbia the local savings and loan associations had a long tradition of financing home ownership by white-collar Negroes.

In the North, too, non-whites moved from the core cities when they could do so. For the most part this movement resulted in their concentration in a few Negro towns, ghetto areas in suburban cities, and Negro developments. Thus, much of the suburban non-white population in the Chicago metropolitan area resided in the all-Negro town of Robbins, Illinois. In the New York metropolitan area, the non-white population of Westchester County, which expanded significantly after 1950 and in 1959 totaled some fifty thousand, was concentrated in the cities of New Rochelle, Mount Vernon, White Plains, and Yonkers.

Despite the almost universal exclusion of non-whites from new housing in the suburbs, save in a few all-Negro developments, middle-class Negroes evidenced the same desire to escape from Manhattan as their white prototypes. This was demonstrated by their sporadic purchase of desirable second-hand surburban homes in Queens, Westchester, Long Island, and in those parts of New Jersey and Connecticut which were accessible, where they often faced a multiplicity of social, economic, and psychological rebuffs. The high cost of houses in the North further limited the extent to which non-white families could translate desire into fact, and long-term denial of housing outside established Negro areas had institutionalized somewhat limited outlays for shelter on the part of middle-income colored families in the North. Yet the presence of some non-whites in attractive suburban homes in all parts of the Nation indicate that, given increasing opportunities, non-whites would move to the suburbs at an accelerated rate.

As William H. Whyte, Jr., observed in the September, 1957, issue of *Fortune,* we must look beyond the ghetto.

> . . . the Negro middle-class will be constantly widening. No millennium in racial harmony is imminent, yet it should be remembered that much of the racial friction in cities today has less to do with skin color than the new arrivals' lack of knowledge of such rules of the game as not throwing garbage out the window. Middle-class Negroes, however, know the rules quite as well as middle-class whites, and the two can get along better than is commonly supposed.

The non-white population of our cities is heterogeneous. Some are new arrivals; some have urban backgrounds; some are financially secure; many are low-income; many are in the process of economic, social, and educational mobility. Census figures on migration, valuable as they are, do not tell the whole story. Dependence upon such restricted data is bound to give a distorted picture and blind us to the elements which offer the most promising avenues to solution.

Those who prophesy political domination by Negroes in American cities have failed to face up to the political realities of today or to realize that ghetto living limits greatly the political strength of minorities at the municipal level. For the present, Negro influence in local government is restricted by the fact that in over half of our larger cities candidates for the city council must run at large and on a non-partisan ballot. Numerical superiority of non-whites in central cities, at best a remote possibility in most localities for many decades, would be reflected in political control in other cities only if the colored population were dominant in a majority of election districts. Such dispersal, however, would greatly reduce the possibility of a bloc vote. To the extent that urban areas offer greater economic opportunities, less restriction on living space, and wider acceptance on the basis of individual worth, the non-white electorate will react as have earlier migrants to these same industrial areas. They will vote less and less on the basis of race and more and more on issues which affect them as they affect others. A minority vote is reflection of a consciousness of minority status.

The Impact of Urbanization*

Until fifty years ago, the Negro remained, for the most part, outside the process of urbanization. He was primarily an American peasant—perhaps the only basically peasant component in the Nation. In the last fifty years, however, he has joined the march to the cities and has caught up with and surpassed even the white rate of urbanization.

Negroes have become mobile, but their mobility is

* Copyright © 1964 by Robert C. Weaver
Copyright © 1964 by Wayne State University
The original version of this Section appears in *Assuring Freedom to the Free* by Arnold Rose and is used by permission of Wayne State University Press.

still very different from that of other Americans; it, too, is a search for a better life, but it is still a search more confined and bounded, more subject to disaster and tragedy and uncertainty than other Americans find. Urbanization has set the stage for a new and better life for Negroes, and over a third have realized this in economic terms. But the development of a really viable life pattern in the cities remains largely unfinished business for the majority of Negro Americans.

By 1960, 69.8 per cent of the United States population was urban; among Negroes, 72.4 per cent were urban. But even these figures underestimate the urbanization of Negroes, for while the vast majority of urban Negroes live in central cities, about a quarter of urban whites live in suburban areas. The movement out of the South, to the Northern and Western cities, has been steady from 1910, when 87 per cent of the non-whites lived in the South, to today, when slightly over half live in the South. Even in the latter region the majority of Negroes now live in cities.

The basic cause of the northward migration was undoubtedly economic. Great waves of Negro migration have been stimulated by periods of economic growth, particularly the expansion of assembly line production during each of the two world wars and the decades immediately thereafter. Northern industries actually solicited the migration of Negroes during World War I. But even without solicitation, it has been the search for full-time employment and higher wages that brought the Negro migrant to the city from the Southern farm. Within the South, too, it is the search for jobs that has urbanized the Negro population.

These great waves of migration may now be tapering off. The period from 1955 to 1960 appears to have been one of lessening movement from the South to the North. From 1950 to 1955, three and four times as many non-white males between the ages of 25 and 34 migrated to Chicago and Detroit respectively as entered in the next five years. Unemployment in these and other mass production cities of the North was clearly evident in the latter half of the fifties as automation grew more widespread and other technological changes occurred.

On the other hand, there were increasing employment opportunities in many parts of the South where new industrial and commercial activities were located. During the last decade, in the South, the rural Negro population declined by 11 per cent, but the urban Negro population increased by 49 per cent. Thus, while the tide of migration to the North subsides with decreasing job opportunities in that region, there is a strong rural-to-urban migration movement within the South in response to the decline of job opportunities in rural areas and expanding urban industrialization.

Viewed against the background of general population mobility in this country, the non-white rate of migration is not high. In the year beginning March, 1960, while 3.4 per cent of the white population moved from one state to another, only 2.3 per cent of the non-white population made such a move. Non-white migration is more apparent and more striking because until recently it has been directed to only a few destinations, while white migration has been composed of many more currents and crosscurrents.

There is another difference in the movements of whites and non-whites. Once the non-white arrives in the Northern and Western city, he moves around *in the city* more than the white does. In central cities of metropolitan areas, in 1960, 15 per cent of the white population moved from one house to another within the same county; but among the non-whites, 20.6 per cent moved to a different house in the same county. In Chicago and Los Angeles, more than one-quarter of the non-whites move in a single year from one house to another; less than one-sixth of the whites do so. This shuffling of one-quarter of the non-white population within some central cities represents, it seems, a desperate scramble for shelter among those who must play a game of musical chairs within a restricted supply of housing continuously affected by demolition, conversion, and losses for other reasons. For some, however, it also reflects a movement into areas of improved housing, particularly during recent years as more normal rates of vacancies have developed.

Once a new destination is reached, the non-white is apparently less likely to move again to another city or state than the white. The migration of the white population, on the other hand, is more often represented by a move to a new place where a job has already been secured and residence is easily exchanged. The white residential mobility in all the regions of the country reflects the availability of jobs and housing in the whole wide reach of the American scene. The mobility of the Negro is still a steady move to urbanization, relatively unmitigated by crosscurrents between urban areas. The white mobility contains many moves between areas by persons already urbanized, and one may conjecture that many white families move from one suburb to another without ever touching the central cities.

What is the effect of these great movements of people between rural areas, cities, and suburbs? For the white middle class, these migratory moves are probably beneficial. In addition to the economic gains, they probably contribute more to family stability than they take away. This, at any rate, was the point of view of the participants in a conference on American middle-class migration conducted by the Brookings Institution a while ago.

Another point made at the conference is of particular interest to this analysis. Two groups of long-distance movers, it seems, have difficulty in a Chicago suburb; New Yorkers, who were not accustomed to small town "mass participation in community problems," and

Southerners, who missed the "easy sense of community they left behind at home."

But if migrant white middle-class families in Park Forest, Illinois, have these difficulties, how much more serious must be the difficulties of a lower-class Negro rural family? For after the "urbanization" that is recorded in statistics—the simple move from country to city—must come the social and cultural "urbanization," the change in life patterns, the development of skills, and the evolution of values inherent in an urban way of life. And when this has to take place under conditions of hostility, overcrowding, and poverty, the adverse effects of the migration often balance out, at least for a time, the beneficial.

Urbanization for American Negroes has meant, as migration to our cities has always meant, bringing willing but unskilled hands into American cities. But we have less need for unskilled workers today than ever before in our history, and our new technology eats up unskilled and semi-skilled jobs at a frightening rate. The first Manpower Report presented to Congress by President Kennedy sums up the resulting situation authoritatively:

> In 1962 non-whites (nine-tenths of whom are Negroes) made up 11 per cent of the civilian labor force, but 22 per cent of the unemployed. On the average, there were 900,000 non-white workers without jobs during 1960, with an employment rate of 11 per cent, more than twice that for white workers. [Among adult men] the non-white workers' unemployment rate was two and one half times higher than that of the white. . . .
> In part, this is due to the heavy concentration of Negroes in occupations particularly susceptible to unemployment. . . . Nevertheless, within each broad occupational group, unemployment is disproportionately high among non-white workers, partly because these workers tend to be near the bottom of the skill ladder for their occupational group.[2]

[2] U. S. Department of Labor, *Manpower Report of the President* (Washington: Government Printing Office, 1963), p.

ple living in the same households; poverty and discouragement; and the observable consequences. And we can go further back, to seventeenth-century England. The rate of illegitimacy then was so disturbing that Sir William Petty, one of the fathers of political economy, proposed a system of government maternity hospitals for pregnant unmarried women, and urged that the illegitimate children born in them become wards of the state.

Today, the strains upon the non-white family continue to be aggravated by overcrowding. Thus, in the metropolitan areas in 1960, 28.5 per cent of the non-white households in rental units lived under crowded circumstances, compared to only 14 per cent of the whites. It is particularly significant that even at the income level of $6000 to $7000 the crowding remains just as high, and the disadvantage, compared to white households, as great.

If family stability is judged by the presence of both husband and wife, it declines with migration and increases with rising income. Among Southern rural non-whites, for example, there is considerably more stability than in Northern cities at every income level. And in both South and North, the stable non-white families become more numerous as income rises.

In the Northeastern and Midwestern cities, very high percentages of households with female heads occur among the poor non-whites. Thus, if households with incomes under $3000 and whose heads are in the 35- to 44-year age-bracket are considered, 1960 Census data reveal that over 50 per cent have female heads; for families with incomes between $3000 and $4000, the percentage drops, but is still over 20 per cent; for families with incomes between $4000 and $5000, the percentage drops further, to between 10 and 15 per cent.

Among Southern rural non-whites, in the poorest families with incomes under $3000, the percentage of families with female heads is only 20 per cent; and it falls in higher brackets to about 5 per cent. Thus, it may be said that in Northern cities there is, by one measure, approximately two-and-a-half times as much instability among non-white families as in Southern rural areas; and among the poorest families there is about four or five times as much instability as there is among those better off.

The 1960 Census figures for the District of Columbia (a locale often cited as the prototype of Negro crime and family disorganization), offer convincing proof that as the Negro acquires education and becomes integrated into the economic life of our cities, family life becomes more stabilized. Indeed, after Negro families achieved a relatively moderate income, $3000 to $5000 a year, the degree of family stability among Negroes in the District was as high as among whites, using our measure of proportion of husband-wife families.

The urbanization of the American population is an accomplished fact, yet our society still has a nostalgic longing for the rural life. The farm and its supposedly happy, well-adjusted family are still an ideal, presented weekly to the American public in the form of "Lassie" and "The Real McCoys" and the like. Reacting to our urban ghettos, it is easy to assume that nothing in a rural background could have been as bad; that the urbanization of the Negro in America has separated him from a source of strength, stability, and serenity. But it is important to view the relative merits of the urbanization of the Negro population, not because we can turn back the tide or change the fact, but because we can modify society's attitude toward this development.

The rural population of the South is undereducated, underemployed, and underpaid as compared with its urban counterpart. It is served with less adequate medical facilities and even in terms of minimal comfort it is poorly housed. If we look at education, for example, the Northern urban non-white has on the average three-and-a-half more years of education than the Southern rural Negro. And in terms of income, the relative position of the urban Negro, either in comparison with his white counterpart or Southern rural Negroes, is undeniably much superior.

Nor is this the only economic gain resulting from urbanization. The movement of Negroes to the North during World War I resulted in their entering American industry. True, they were concentrated in the heavy and dirty areas of production and in unskilled occupations, but even this type of employment represented a great advance over the status as a peasant. The Great Depression, of course, wiped out much of the gains achieved during the war and postwar periods, but these were recouped and extended during the defense and World War II economic expansion. By the end of the Second World War, Negroes had achieved a place in many light and clean industries; had become, in a significant measure, semi- and single-skilled workers; and were slowly moving into skilled jobs.

At the same time, the Negro became a functioning part of organized labor; and as of today, it is estimated that well over 1,750,000 Negroes belong to unions, most of which are positive forces for equal opportunity in employment. Concurrently, Negroes are entering engineering, technical, and white-collar jobs at a continually increasing rate. Since they started from a low base in these higher occupations, their proportions in the totals are still small. But it must be noted that in many of the highly trained occupations, there are more opportunities than qualified non-whites.

Under these circumstances, the transfer of disadvantaged Negroes to the areas where people have more advantages represents a gain. It brings the problems they face to light, forcing the attention of society to the contrasts they represent and causes acute discomfort. It is quite natural that society should choose to think that it is the transfer which creates the problems. It is important to recognize, however, that the transfer merely exposes the problems to view. In a word, the urbanization of the rural Southern Negroes has created a situation which has more potential for growth and improvement than their continued isolation from the mainstream of society.

But even for the Negro families themselves there are positive aspects of urbanization, despite the apparent misery of many in their initial situation. It is in the cities that many Negroes have learned the skills of the twentieth century and in increasing number have achieved middle-class economic status, if not social acceptance. The substantially higher educational attainment of the Northern urban Negro over the Southern rural Negro can be partially explained in terms of the increased educational opportunities available to the children of migrants and the longer period of schooling of the second and third generation of Negroes. This, too, is a result of their living in an area where the quality of education is of a higher level. It is in the cities that the broadened employment and education opportunities exist. And finally it is in the cities that the Negro population has been large enough to exercise political influence.

The last may well be the most important of the benefits of urbanization, although, as stated above, this will not occasion widespread Negro political domination in urban centers. James Q. Wilson's penetrating analysis of the methods employed in various cities in coping with their new Negro voters makes it plain that "Negro politics" is just a subdivision of the political apparatus in each city.[3] But the significant growth of Negro political power in the cities has been a comparatively recent thing. Today it is a fairly nationwide phenomenon, evidencing itself in the South as well as the North. For in large Southern cities almost one-third of the voting age population was non-white in 1960. In some Northern cities the proportion is one-quarter. Of course, the Ne-

[3] James Q. Wilson, *Negro Politics* (Glencoe, Ill.: Free Press of Glencoe, 1960).

ing the period of resistance to the Supreme Court decisions on this matter and of token compliance in some of the communities, housing patterns could be manipulated so that colored residents were concentrated in well-defined areas, there could be school desegregation with little or no mixture of the races in public schools.

Urban renewal offered new and undreamed-of possibilities in this direction. Its scope was so great that, given sufficient time, it could effect the relocation of a large part of the colored residents of Southern cities. Most of the existing concentrations of Negroes and racially mixed areas of living, as well as small clusters of whites or Negroes in neighborhoods predominantly occupied by the other racial group, qualified for clearance. Where this did not suffice to accomplish the end, location of highway programs, public improvements, or new industrial islands and commercial centers could go far to complete the process.

In certain Southern urban areas, like Winston-Salem, North Carolina, and Atlanta, Georgia, the development seemed well on its way. In these cities, as well as in Greensboro, North Carolina, and Austin, Texas, there has been a *quid pro quo* for the Negro community in that new and extremely attractive areas of housing for Negroes had been, and were being, created. New Orleans, Louisiana, too, had provided a most desirable site for similar housing.

While it is difficult to determine in each case that this new approach to non-white housing in these and other Southern cities was an integral part of the redevelopment program, there can be no doubt that in every instance it could and would make a major contribution to the institutionalization and perpetuation of residential segregation. Also, it appeared that the development of desirable residential areas for Negroes usually occurred in cities where the colored population has some degree of political power.

It is against this background that discussion of racial

policy in redevelopment occurred. The NAACP and other civil rights groups faced no problem. Their position, reiterated after an exhaustive analysis of the matter by the Commission on Race and Housing (composed of outstanding citizens drawn from all regions of the Nation and chaired by the Southern-born president of the country's largest savings bank), was that all housing facilitated by federal assistance should be open to all racial elements in the population. This position was motivated by its proponents' concept of the constitutional rights of Americans as well as by their conviction that in housing, as most other facilities, there is no such thing as separate but equal.

The President's Commission on Civil Rights also faced the issue and decided in favor of a federal open-occupancy policy. Southern Negro leaders, conscious of the need for more space and better housing among colored people, were troubled. Their dilemma was more acute in that they saw real progress in what has taken place in Atlanta, Austin, Greensboro, New Orleans, Winston-Salem, and a few other Southern cities.

If this was the best deal that could be made in these relatively progressive municipalities of the South, they asked, was it not visionary and foolish to hope for more in the rest of the region? As practical men they were impressed by the argument that a non-discrimination clause in urban renewal would simply mean that Southern cities would not participate and the much-needed improvement in housing standards of Negroes would be delayed. Some believed that this would increase the resistance to compliance with the non-segregation school rulings of the courts in that the impact of compliance would be greater as long as school districts include large areas of integrated living.

Social issues are usually more complicated than they appear on the surface. The question raised here is no exception. Those who, in all sincerity and concern for the housing of Negroes, advocated less than a national policy of non-discrimination in publicly assisted shelter made certain assumptions. The most important was that such a policy would result in a cessation of urban renewal and public housing in the South and a continuing neglect of the pressing housing needs of colored residents. Clearly, if this assumption were valid, one had to equate the immediate housing benefits possible under public housing, urban renewal, and associated construction activities against the dangers of further institutionalization of ghettos and *de facto* avoidance of school desegregation.

Actually these were not the real alternatives. Under the renewal program, the Federal Government takes up at least two-thirds of the public cost; in the federally assisted interstate highway program, the degree of federal participation is even larger. More important, the decay of the core areas is a real and increasingly recognized threat to central cities. A growing number of those who have entrenched economic, emotional, and cultural vested interests in the city, as well as a few of those who live in the suburbs, realized that the downtown areas must be revitalized. They knew that federal assistance is a must; many of them had come to recognize that something had to be done to improve and maintain housing standards among Negroes if the program is to succeed. While it is conceivable that public schools, traditionally financed primarily through state and local funds, might continue without a new federal aid program, it is inconceivable that any city could arrest urban blight in the absence of major federal assistance.

Traditionally, the South has not been hesitant to accept financial aid from Washington. It has, of course, attempted to condition the ground rules so as to avoid modification of the region's announced racial pattern. But few programs have been so vital to the communities affected as urban renewal; and few have been so dependent upon federal aid. The evidence was far from adequate to support the hypothesis that most cities in the region would elect to forego urban renewal if the financial assistance involved carried a non-discrimination clause. And as cities outside the South enjoyed a larger part of the funds available, there would develop an increasing amount of pressure for local participation. Regional pride alone would dictate this. Other factors would also operate.

Resistance to widespread school integration would, of course, inspire some of the affected cities to devise methods to use urban renewal to assure a minimum amount of racial mixture in the public schools. Thus, the probability was that some of the Southern municipalities would attempt to work out a compromise. This would probably be in the form of extending the type of residential pattern that has already appeared in the cities mentioned above. There would, therefore, be more and not less good housing available to Negroes. The main loss would be in the process of school integration. Paradoxically enough, non-discrimination requirements in urban renewal would probably accelerate the spread of token compliance with school desegregation.

One need not look far to discover what would occur if there were no federal regulation covering racial patterns in urban renewal. The consequences were clear. In *Barnes v. City of Gadsden, Alabama*, in the United States District Court for the Northern District of Alabama, there was impressive documentation. The record in this case indicated that both federal and local redevelopment officials were frank and candid in stating that the redevelopment plans contemplated residential segregation and the clearance of Negroes from a well-situated area which they had long occupied.

Throughout the South redevelopment plans and proposals involved either the concentration of displaced Negroes in existing ghettos or the expansion of racial ghettos in response to the pressure of numbers. Seldom did the supply equal the demand, and frequently there was greater overcrowding after the renewal process got under way. As in the past, the Negro residents of the affected cities had little or no say in the matter, and minority group leaders continued to be ignored in the development of plans and programs which determined the conditions under which they and their followers live.

The assumption of those who feared the consequences of pushing for a federal non-discrimination clause in urban renewal—that it would arrest the improvement of housing for Negroes—rested on very weak ground. Such results would have followed only if it were conceivable that the patterns of the more liberal Southern cities might be duplicated in the rest of the South. As a matter of fact, these patterns involved a vital process, consultation and bargaining with the representatives of the Negro community. This is exactly what the leadership of most Southern cities was dead set against doing.

The power structure in many Southern cities was, however, increasingly becoming committed to the need for, and the desirability of, urban renewal. The men and women who control the destinies of urban communities were the very ones who stood to lose the most through the continuing decline of the central cities. This was true regardless of whether they owned and operated stores and other commercial establishments, supported art galleries and museums, controlled local industries, or were affiliated with educational institutions. Chambers of commerce and others concerned with attracting new industries were no less directly involved. When the local situation had required them to bargain and negotiate with the Negro leadership, they did so in order to effect the purposes and goals they desired.

If the issues involved were basic to the interests of the control groups, the latter were usually successful in making their desires known to local political leadership.

Either under the guise of reluctant compliance with federal requirements or open action for a larger local objective, the political leaders "acted for the good of the community." In either event, consultation and co-operation between white and colored leaders emerged in Southern cities when it was required to secure money from Washington.

A non-discrimination clause in the urban renewal law would accelerate the process. Because of the requirement of open occupancy on sites redeveloped for residential purposes, these elements would attempt to minimize the effect of the provision. In most instances, this would involve provision of new areas of living for non-whites. Since demolition and relocation precede renewal by several years, a large segment of the Negro population eligible for occupancy on sites redeveloped would find shelter in the newly provided housing. The success of the latter, however, would require consultation and cooperation with the Negro community. Necessity would, even in the then strained condition of race relations in the South, have required re-establishment of communication between the races.

More important, from the point of race relations in the region, the complete institutionalization of residential segregation in the center of the city (a traditionally desirable location of Negro homes) would be avoided. There would be a basis for negotiation and expansion of spatially integrated living expressed in a legal requirement and often based upon token participation in the new development. The school, too, would often accommodate a few Negro pupils whose presence would provide the starting point for making more real the legal rights delineated by the courts.

It is difficult to envision any real improvement in the housing condition of urban Negroes in the South or elsewhere unless the land space and dwelling units available to them are materially increased. That the process is a real possibility in the cities of the South had been demonstrated in the postwar years. Urban renewal, which has a vital appeal to Southern as well as Northern cities, is the most effective vehicle to extend the benefits elsewhere throughout the region. It will not be so employed unless the Federal Government sets forth adequate ground rules.

There are, of course, many other considerations which demanded such affirmative action from Washington. As the Commission on Race and Housing delineated, it is one thing for private industry to establish and maintain enforced residential segregation and another for the Federal Government to do the same thing. In the latter situation, the Nation puts its official stamp of approval on a pattern which violates the law of the land. It says to the world and to the American people that there are second-class citizens, creating a situation under which a segment of the population is subjected to exploitation and substandard living conditions. The Federal Government cannot be neutral in this matter. By failing to act, it was supporting forced residential segregation.

Because housing is competitive, there must be a general non-discrimination clause in urban redevelopment. Otherwise, in any given community the one redeveloper who has the courage to establish democratic patterns of living will be subject to attack and unfair competition from others who advertise and sell racial exclusiveness. Of course, there can be no national policy which recognizes regional differences in constitutional and legal rights.

With or without urban renewal, many Southern cities will use every means to accelerate residential segregation. Historically, the continuing existence of racially mixed areas of living in many of the older Southern cities and towns posed no problem of Negroes' participation in most phases of community life. Segregation laws accomplished this. Now that school segregation is doomed, it is inevitable that these urban communities will have a new and intense interest in manipulating residential racial living patterns so as to perpetuate traditional exclusion.

The real problem, therefore, was not one of better housing for Negroes *versus* integrated living. It was whether the decisions of the Supreme Court regarding tax-supported schools were to be evaded in fact through federally supported action on the housing front.

And the matter was complicated by the very nature of the social and economic forces which operate in the Negro community. The middle- and upper-class Negro families, which of necessity occupy accommodations provided in any areas of new housing for non-whites, exclusive of public housing, are the households most apt to press for integrated schools. Their children are the ones most likely to qualify for immediate transfer on placement and associated tests. By concentrating these families in separate sections, school integration will be delayed and frustrated in large measure.

There was real Southern comfort in this possibility. Surely, if it were facilitated by urban renewal and unquestioned by the federal housing agencies, it represented a serious misuse of federal funds.

This section was written in 1960, appearing in the summer issue of the *Journal of Intergroup Relations* under the title, "Southern Comfort: A Possible Misapplication of Federal Funds." Since then, time and events have provided a basis for testing its validity. On November 20, 1962, President Kennedy issued his Executive Order on Equal Opportunity in Housing. Among its provisions was the banning of discrimination in federally assisted housing, including that constructed on urban renewal sites. In the first eight months subsequent to the Order's promulgation, there was no appreciable decline in the initiation of new urban renewal applications for projects in the South, or elsewhere in the Nation.

Emerging Trends in Housing

By 1960 it was clear that although there had been shifts in the regional intensity of residential segregation, its incidence remained universally high throughout urban areas of the Nation. There was a slight decrease in spatial segregation in Northeast and North central cities from 1950 to 1960. Residential segregation in the urban South, however, increased, so that by 1960 it was more pronounced in Southern cities than in those of any other region. Although the decline in spatial segregation in the North was small, it took place in the face of large increases in the non-white population. In the absence of future large-scale in-migration this could represent a trend, and there were institutional reasons for believing that it would. Clearly the impact of new federal open-occupancy policy, more effective enforcement of state and local fair housing laws (which existed in nineteen states and over fifty cities as of July, 1963), the existence of some three hundred citizens' fair housing committees working toward open occupancy in white neighborhoods, and the pressures of the Negro people will combine to accelerate the reduction of enforced residential segregation, primarily in the North and border cities.

The situation in the South seemed to reflect projection of a trend which had become apparent soon after the Supreme Court school decision of 1954, when residential segregation became a means of evading the court order. At the same time, as has been delineated, the spatial distribution of urban Negroes combined with the growth of the middle class in facilitating the development and expansion of new Negro suburbs in the South and border states. This trend toward increased residential segregation will probably be offset somewhat in the border states and upper South by the impact of President Kennedy's Executive Order for Equal Opportunity in Housing. It will also be reduced by *de facto* desegregation of school and other public facilities. Only time can tell how fast the process will occur.

As was suggested above, dislocation of non-white families incident to urban renewal, highway construction, various public works undertakings, and private decisions in the market, as well as population growth, increased their demand for public housing. At the same time, the greater economic upward mobility of whites and their access to a much wider housing market reduced their demand for public housing. As a consequence, the proportion of non-whites in this housing increased during the decade from 1950 to 1960. In the former year, 35.6 per cent of those in federally assisted public housing were non-whites; by 1960 the figure was 45.8 per cent. Thus, although these public housing units were but 0.8 per cent of all dwelling units, they were 3.9 per cent of the housing stock available to non-whites. Since 1960, the trend has continued. As of June, 1963, of the 494,-000 units of federally assisted public housing in occupancy, 49 per cent were occupied by non-whites.

Public housing continued to play a peculiar role in influencing racial occupancy patterns. It is still instrumental in occasionally introducing non-whites into neighborhoods where they had previously not lived. At the same time, an increasing number of formerly integrated public housing projects are becoming all, or practically all, non-white in occupancy. To complicate the picture further, in the first few months after issuance of President Kennedy's Executive Order, several housing authorities in the Midwest, long urged to integrate their programs, did so, and in the upper South one city in which there had been continuing vacancies in a "white" public housing project adopted an open occupancy policy.

As long, however, as there is a disproportionately intense demand for low-rent public housing on the part of non-whites, the limited supply will be increasingly

improving the quality of shelter occupied by non-whites.

The impact of the Section 221(d)(3) housing program is already evident in Southern cities. In a growing number of localities in the region, this program was supplying a new type of housing available to Negroes. A typical case, from the point of view of sponsorship, upgrading of amenities, and cost, occurred in Dallas, Texas. A new residential community was developing around the campus of Bishop College in South Dallas, where the St. John Missionary Baptist Church of the city sponsored Highland Village, a 300-unit Section 221(d)(3) rental apartment development.

The new living facility will have central heating and air conditioning; pile carpeting and draperies; completely equipped kitchens with electric ranges, refrigerators, and garbage disposal units; tiled baths; and a child care and day nursery center. Rents will range from $75 a month, including utilities, for a one-bedroom unit to $90 a month for a three-bedroom, one-and-a-half-bath apartment. It is expected that there will be tax abatement resulting in a $5 a month reduction in rentals. The forthcoming accommodations will set a new standard of comfort for those moderate-income families which qualify for occupancy in the garden apartments.

Early results were no less striking in urban renewal areas. Philander Smith College is sponsoring a three-million-dollar, 240-unit apartment development in the Dunbar Redevelopment area of Little Rock. Rents begin at $55 for a one-bedroom unit, will be as high as $88 for three bedrooms. The Wheat Street Baptist Church is sponsoring a 520-apartment development in Atlanta's Butler Street Urban Renewal; there rents will start at $70. In Cumberland Urban Renewal in Greensboro, North Carolina, a non-profit group is undertaking a similar development; rents will range from

$60 for a one-bedroom unit to $77.50 for three bed-rooms.

In contrast to the situation in the low-income groups, non-whites are far from being a principal source of ef-fective demand for moderate-income housing, even in cities with large non-white populations. Thus, if favor-ably located (from the point of view of attractiveness to white families) moderate-income housing is well de-signed, it will be bi-racial in many sections of the Na-tion. This already exists in urban renewal areas in San Francisco; New York; Paterson, New Jersey; Madison, Wisconsin; Cincinnati; and Minneapolis. It is sug-gested by token non-white participation in moderate-income redevelopment projects in Brookline, Massa-chusetts, and the beginnings of white participation in Marine City, California. Existing allocations and com-mitments for Section 221(d)(3) housing suggest that additional bi-racial areas may be developed in Los An-geles, New Haven, Chicago, Boston, Detroit, Kansas City (Missouri), St. Louis, Madison, Denver, Hartford, Binghamton (New York), Bridgeport, and a score of other cities.

In addition, of course, a larger amount of Section 221(d)(3) housing is planned or under construction on sites outside of urban renewal areas, primarily in cit-ies with sizable non-white populations. The resulting housing, too, will upgrade the quality of shelter avail-able to non-whites in many instances. Much of this new construction will be in developments where whites and non-whites will reside as neighbors.

There are several major forces working to extend the housing choices available to non-whites of higher in-comes. First, the increasing number of state and local open-occupancy laws and their constantly broadening coverage is important. Secondly, the Executive Order on Equal Opportunity in Housing banned racial dis-crimination in housing financed with FHA- and VA-underwritten mortgages, and these two agencies had title to over 90,000 dwelling units which were immediately available to non-whites. Concurrently, between November 20, 1962, and October 15, 1963, some 55,000 completed FHA-aided units were subject to the non-discrimination order. Thirdly, applications for 169,000 FHA-aided new homes and 78,000 units of new multi-family housing, as well as about 100,000 VA-aided units, were pending; those in this group completed and financed with FHA- and VA-underwritten mortgages would be similarly affected. Fourthly, Negro pressure for equality included housing on its agenda, and results were apparent as early as mid-summer. Finally, and perhaps in part as a consequence of the first four developments, hundreds of fair-housing groups were actively encouraging Negroes to find homes in the suburbs.

The situation in the New York City metropolitan area has been summarized:

> Two developments are expected to accelerate the movement to break the color line in New York suburban housing. One is the national surge to obtain equal rights for Negroes and the other is the adoption of legislation this year by New York and Connecticut.
>
> The legislation, effective September 1 in New York and October 1 in Connecticut, bars discrimination on account of color in the sale or rental of virtually all housing. A similar measure is pending in the New Jersey Legislature.[4]

As the article quoted above reports, there are more than fifty fair-housing groups in the New York City area. These groups had been effective in extending help

[4] Clarence Dean, "Drive for Homes for Negroes in Suburbs Will Be Intensified," *New York Times*, August 14, 1963, p. 19. In a Maryland suburb of Washington, D.C., a fair-housing group had similar successes as those set forth in the text for New York City. The income groups involved, neighborhood reactions, and techniques were substantially the same as those reported for New York. See Robert E. Baker, "Suburbs Opening Up for Negro Housing," *Washington Post*, October 17, 1963, pp. 1, 8.

to, and securing acceptance of, non-whites in new areas of living. The significant social factors incident to their work were: (1) the number of non-white families which elected to move into the new areas was small; (2) although there had been great apprehension on the part of white owners to the prospect of a Negro neighbor, once the individual, as contrasted to the concept, became a reality, there was little opposition; (3) the non-whites involved (and they were relatively high-income professionals) found warm acceptance on the part of their new neighbors.

All of this suggests that the American people are capable of adjustment to new racial patterns when and if they realize these are inevitable. This was true in employment during World War II, and it will be true of housing in the decade ahead,[5] although in shelter

---

[5] As 1963 came to its close, there were evidences of realization that the homebuilding industry would have to adjust to open occupancy. The editor of *Practical Builder*, addressing himself to homebuilders, observed: ". . . Limited experience in 1963 indicates that open occupancy need not be an important handicap for builders. Most problems have been settled according to law and local opinion. We believe that most of the few incidents that have occurred have been the result of hasty or ill-considered reaction on the part of the builder or his employees.

"Builders have learned that this problem cannot be evaded or solved by avoiding the prospect. It has also become apparent that complacent local authorities do not have the final answer to a national problem. The builder's decision may vary according to the community where he builds, but the need for full information, tact and decisive action applies everywhere.

"Every builder should know the laws under which he operates and the temper of his community. He knows what he should do and what he must do. Equally important is a well prepared advance plan of how he will do it.

"Until you have planned what you will say and do as you meet each problem of open occupancy—and until each of your representatives to the buying public is thoroughly trained according to your plan—you are not ready for 1964" (Larry Drake, "Open Occupancy in 1964," *Practical Builder*, December, 1963, p. 6).

the initial opposition will probably be greater, as it has been in school desegregation.

A significant development during the decade from 1950 to 1960 was the increasing utilization of government-underwritten mortgages by non-whites. This was one of the few areas in which minorities had improved their relative status during the period. Thus, in 1960, some 43 per cent of white and 29 per cent of non-white owners of mortgages had availed themselves of FHA-insured and VA-guaranteed mortgages, compared to 32 per cent and 18 per cent, respectively, in 1950. Involved in this development was an increase of 145,000 non-white homeowners with government-underwritten mortgages, for the most part under the VA program. Over the decade, there had also been an increase of 254,000 in the number of non-white homeowners with conventional mortgage loans.

These developments were encouraging because prior to 1950, non-white participation in governmental programs designed to encourage and financially ease home ownership had been minimal. In 1950, for example, 22,322 non-whites had VA-guaranteed first mortgages, and non-whites represented 2.2 per cent of those having such mortgages. By 1960 some 124,000, or 3.7 per cent of the total, were non-whites. For the FHA, comparable figures were 24,407, or 2.3 per cent, in 1950; and 68,000, or 2.5 per cent, in 1960. No doubt the 1960 figures reflected the availability of a sizable amount of older urban housing to non-whites in all parts of the Nation, the rise of Negro suburban developments in the South and border states, access to increasing but still greatly limited suburban areas in the North (as a consequence of fair-housing laws), and rising incomes among middle-class Negroes in all parts of the country. They also indicated that non-whites still benefited much less from FHA and VA mortgage programs than did whites.

It is revealing that the median incomes of whites

and non-whites having FHA-insured first mortgages were substantially the same in 1960—for whites, $6900; and for non-whites, $6800. For homeowners with VA-guaranteed first mortgages the figure for whites was also $6900, but for non-whites it was $5000. For conventional loans, there was the greatest discrepancy: $6500 for all, and $4200 for non-whites. These relationships occurred in a situation where median incomes for those with all types of mortgages were as follows: for whites, $6800; and for non-whites, $4500. The consequences are what would be expected. In the FHA and VA programs whites and non-whites paid the same median interest rates. On conventional loans, where 70 per cent of the non-white financing was concentrated, the median for non-whites was .5 per cent higher than for the total. Since the non-whites were such a small proportion of the total number of mortgagors, it works out that, for all loans, non-whites paid a median rate almost 1 per cent higher.

The relative extent and proportion of non-white participation in government-underwritten first mortgages is set forth in detail in the table on the next page. With the exception of the $3000 to $4000 income bracket, only non-whites with incomes of $10,000 or more had as large a proportion of government-underwritten mortgages among the total held by the group as did whites. Interestingly, at the $10,000-and-over income level, this non-white rate of participation exceeded that of whites. Here, too, there was another peculiarity: the rate of this participation of non-whites at this income level and at the $7000 to $10,000 level was greater than for whites in FHA and lesser in VA. It was at the $3000 to $4000 and the $4000 to $5000 income levels that the rate of non-white participation in VA-guaranteed loans exceeded that for whites. In order to understand the figures set forth in the table, it must be realized that the downpayment required for VA-guaranteed loans has consistently been lower than

NON-FARM HOMEOWNER PROPERTIES WITH GOVERNMENT-UNDERWRITTEN FIRST MORTGAGES, BY COLOR AND INCOME OF MORTGAGOR, UNITED STATES, 1960ᵃ (Number of Properties in Thousands)

	White—Properties with				Non-white—Properties with			
Household Incomeᵇ	All Mortgaged Properties	Government-Underwritten First Mortgage	FHA First Mortgage	VA First Mortgage	All Mortgaged Properties	Government-Underwritten First Mortgage	FHA First Mortgage	VA First Mortgage
Number Totalᵈ	13,805	5,857	2,600	3,257	648	192	68	124
Less than $2,000	524	110	64	46	89	10	3	7
$2,000 to $2,999	425	129	70	59	85	14	7	7
$3,000 to $3,999	774	235	96	139	92	29	8	21
$4,000 to $4,999	1,457	577	255	322	113	33	6	27
$5,000 to $6,999	4,245	1,985	838	1,147	133	47	13	34
$7,000 to $9,999	3,897	1,933	849	1,084	89	42	22	20
$10,000 or more	2,483	888	427	461	47	18	10	8
Median	$6,800	—	$6,900	$6,900	$4,500	—	$6,800	$5,000
Per cent Total	100	43	19	24	100	29	10	19
Less than $2,000	100	21	12	9	100	11	3	8
$2,000 to $2,999	100	30	16	14	100	16	8	8
$3,000 to $3,999	100	30	12	18	100	32	9	23
$4,000 to $4,999	100	40	18	22	100	29	5	24
$5,000 to $6,999	100	47	20	27	100	36	10	26
$7,000 to $9,999	100	50	22	28	100	47	25	22
$10,000 or more	100	36	17	19	100	38	21	17

ᵃ One-unit owner-occupied non-farm properties. ᵇ Income of owner and relatives living with him. ᶜ Derived by the Housing and Home Finance Agency. ᵈ Totals may not add to sum of components due to "rounding."

SOURCE: Department of Commerce, Bureau of the Census, *1960 Census of Housing*, Volume V, Part 1, Table 2 and Part 1, Supplement, Table 2.

that required for FHA-insured loans. As a matter of fact, downpayments have been required for VA loans only during two limited periods since 1950—July, 1950, to September, 1952; and April, 1955, to April, 1958.

These data suggest certain conclusions. It is obvious that as non-whites had access to a wider segment of the housing market and achieved higher incomes, they secured better mortgage terms. This was accomplished, primarily, by their qualifying for a larger volume of government-insured and guaranteed mortgages. The new Executive Order should accelerate this development. Of equal immediate impact will be the continuing expansion of the new FHA-insured low- and moderate-income housing programs, provided for under the expanded Section 221 in the Housing Act of 1961 and set forth in Chapter V. These new programs are already providing mortgage insurance for scores of thousands of new dwelling units that will be occupied by non-whites. The utilization of Section 221(d)(3) for rehabilitation in the gray areas, described in Chapter III, will, if successful, also accelerate non-white participation in the benefits of FHA mortgage insurance activities.

Ironically, the least affluent among non-white home purchasers have traditionally benefited least from lower-cost government-underwritten mortgages. This was typical of the programs, and applied to whites as well as non-whites. However, the degree of lack of participation was almost twice as intense for low-income non-whites in 1960. Clearly this reflected the latter's concentration in the older areas of core cities, their consequent restriction to a limited and generally less desirable section of the market, and the long-established expensive forms of credit available to them. Here, too, recent developments should provide some relief.

In this situation, we shall probably see in the next decade, a continuing upgrading in the amount and quality of shelter available to low-income non-whites. This occurred during the decade 1950–1960, although during that period the average upgrading of housing at all price ranges for whites outstripped that among non-whites.[6] Whether or not this qualitative gap will close in the current decade depends primarily upon the relative income structure among non-whites (as compared to whites) and the degree of access non-whites have to the total housing market.

Higher-income non-white families will probably make the most significant gains in terms of better facilities and wider choices in the housing market. This will reflect their ability to pay for good accommodations and their desire for racially integrated neighborhoods, no less than the wider receptivity on the part of whites to a limited number of middle-class colored neighbors as contrasted to the fear of inundation by a large number of low-income non-whites. It is also in the American tradition, which has afforded the descendants of the newcomers greater access to better housing in the total market as they have effected significant economic, social, and cultural improvement.

Insofar as wider opportunities for housing available to non-whites are concentrated in the suburbs, they will provide an additional dividend benefiting the whole urban complex. As was observed in Chapter I, an important impediment to metropolitan approaches to area-wide problems of community development and housing has been the residential racial distribution of our population. Any modification in these patterns will facilitate greater cooperation between the core areas and the suburbs that surround them.

The most stable interracial neighborhoods will be those of relatively high-cost and the well-located moderate-cost, new developments. It has been indicated that

---

[6] For an analysis of the changes and relative status of housing among whites and non-whites from 1950 to 1960, see Marion P. Yankauer and Milo B. Sunderhauf, "Housing: Equal Opportunity to Choose Where One Shall Live," *Journal of Negro Education*, Fall, 1963, pp. 402–414.

the income distribution and the effective demand for high-cost shelter among non-whites is such as to limit the volume of colored residents in this price range, while in the moderate-income sector, the effective demand is bi-racial. Ironically, in light of its image and early history, urban renewal, in all probability, will facilitate the greatest advances. Already it has introduced a new phenomenon: a growing number of whites living next door to non-whites of comparable income by choice.

At the same time, the recent Executive Order and the work of the fair-housing groups and others are gradually opening the suburbs to non-whites. In this segment of the housing market, progress will be somewhat slower initially (for reasons set forth in Chapter II). In proportion as desirable high- and moderate-cost new housing in the core cities is available to minorities, their demand for suburban facilities will be lessened. While in moderate-cost housing the pressure of numbers may result, in some instances, in non-white occupancy of most of the available units in a development, such a situation is highly improbable in the higher-cost counterparts. And, as indicated above, many of the moderate-income developments in the central city will remain bi-racial.

Low-income non-whites will get a larger supply of housing, too, but it will probably be in a market that is either now, or will soon become, racially homogeneous. Some of the forthcoming low-income public housing will initially be racially mixed. Much will be predominantly or exclusively non-white in occupancy. Simultaneously, many of those displaced will gravitate to existing areas of non-white concentration or to contiguous areas. For class as well as color reasons bi-racial areas with large numbers and proportions of low-income non-whites will tend to lose their racially heterogeneous character. But for most low-income non-white individuals and households involved, the latter circumstance will be of secondary importance. In time two factors will serve to accentuate low-income non-whites' desire for residential integration: the qualitative and quantitative limitations inherent in ghetto residential patterns and the paucity of public facilities (especially schools) characteristic of racially segregated low-income neighborhoods.

Of course, a large part of non-whites' housing problems stems from their low incomes and resulting restricted purchasing power. There is, however, another recent development which has great pertinence to the housing, no less than the general status, of non-whites. It is the pioneering efforts to deal with the human problems of urban living. The nature of these problems as they relate to housing and urban renewal was delineated in Chapter I, and our initial efforts and plans to meet them were set forth in Chapter III. The next section of this chapter treats the more general disabilities of our newest migrants to urban areas. Success in dealing with these needs can, in the long run, be the most significant single force in upgrading housing and living conditions of all low-income families in our society. Clearly, neglect of these human needs will not only prevent success in meeting the housing requirements of low-income families but will also delay, complicate, and, perhaps, ultimately destroy urban renewal.

The Most Recent Newcomers

In post-World War II, the economic environment has become vastly different. The shift in emphasis from industrial to service employment has continued and, more recently, automation and other technological advances have been introduced and expanded. We now face a complex situation in which the economy produces more and more goods with fewer and fewer workers. These developments occasioned a radical change in the nature of the demand for labor, involving a significant decline in the need for unskilled workers in the industries of this Nation. *Most of these forces would have been operative regardless of the ethnic composition of the migrants to American cities.*

One of the great disabilities of the Negro is his lack of resources to meet the more difficult problems of upward mobility. An obvious manifestation of his paucity of internal resources is the absence of widespread internal patterns of voluntary organizations. The latter contributed greatly to the adjustment and assimilation of European immigrants. But the Negro's heritage under slavery and the nature of his migration *within* the United States militated against his development of similar self-help institutions. More important is the fact that the current adjustment of the Negro to an urban environment is occurring at a time when public agencies are rapidly supplementing private voluntary organizations.

The history of most ethnic minorities in urban centers of the North and West has been one of initial rejection, gradual acculturation, and eventual absorption. Peoples with different customs and values who were exposed to the process of Americanization modified their beliefs and behavior and thereby achieved a new position in society. Starting, for the most part, as low-income workers, they have been able, in large numbers, to acquire education, obtain better jobs, and achieve higher social status. They have moved out of the slums of yesterday into the suburbs and middle-class neighborhoods of today. This Nation offered them middle-class status when and if they evidenced adherence to the dominant culture. For them, there were and are real, tangible, and demonstrable rewards for industry, conformity, and ambition.

Similar rewards are far less general for non-whites. Thus, the degree of social and economic mobility among this group is less. This circumstance, in turn, is used as justification for perpetuation of second-class status for colored citizens. Yet the fact of the matter is that the immigrant was criticized because of difference in culture, behavior, and appearance which he could and often did change. The non-white, even when he has modified cultural and behavioral patterns, is stuck with pigmentation which in our society is a badge of difference and inferiority.

Before the complex nature of the situation occasions despair and hopelessness, let us view briefly the other side of the changes in our society which have brought about these more intricate problems. Concern for slum clearance, effectuating a solid economic base for our central cities, and arresting the spread of blight have created new, if reluctant, allies in meeting these problems. Increasingly, it is apparent that slum clearance, rehabilitation, and urban renewal must come to grips with the human problems involved. Either we increase appreciably the social, economic, and residential mobility of non-whites and other ethnic minorities, or we will continue to tear down one slum only to create others and spread blight. Programs in this field are threatened by large elements in the society relegated to a perpetual submerged status.

Cities seriously concerned with urban renewal are being made to appreciate that, both in terms of human potential and dollars and cents, there are sound grounds for public programs designed to accelerate the participation of those who are now rejected from the mainstream of modern urban life. Herein lies another significant change in intergroup relations. For generations, many Americans have been troubled by the constitutional issues inherent in racial discrimination. Gunnar Myrdal identified the color problem in this Nation as a moral issue. The cold war has made race relations a crucial international concern. Current events are adding a new dimension. Now it is becoming apparent that there are significant economic and political reasons for action to accelerate the effective participation of the latest newcomers in urban life. No doubt, we will have to do much experimentation in this area, but once there is a commitment to meet the issue, productive techniques can and will be developed.

There will be those who advocate a program of exhortation, believing that people can be high-pressured into making sacrifices for goals that their experiences have proven to be unobtainable. There is little factual basis for this point of view. We must learn how to motivate those who are now the low men on the totem poles. At the same time, no effort will be worthwhile unless it combines two features: continuing evidences that preparation and ability are rewarded; and appreciation for the values which have developed among peoples who have suffered generations of discrimination and segregation, and are still largely on the sidelines of the society. The first of these is necessary if an effective job is to be done in really raising horizons of hope or inspiring greater motivation, thereby increasing the number of middle-class persons among non-whites. The second is necessary in order to make effective communications with those who are involved.

In this connection, our constitutional guarantees are unequivocal. Every citizen, regardless of race, creed, color, or status, has certain civil rights. When, because of ethnic or religious identification, anyone or any group is denied these rights, such a person or group has less reason to aspire for what this Nation is supposed to offer all its citizens. These civil and constitutional rights are, therefore, a basic part of the motivation of our citizens.

Increasing the number of those among the newcomers to our cities who adopt dominant cultural patterns should not imply a value judgment concerning the virtues of such patterns. Rather it is a pragmatic recognition that ours is a middle-class-oriented society and those who conform to the dominant standards are quickest to gain acceptance. This has been the route of mobility and advancement for earlier migrant groups. It is a step toward that status for non-whites although for them it will not be the whole answer for a time. Simultaneously, if it is clear that middle-class status is not regarded as an end in itself but a means to mobility, it will be possible to work on the other side of the problem. That involves facilitating the minimum adjustment of values and concepts on the part of those who are not now and will not soon become counterparts of middle-class Americans. The problem is one of delineating the grosser impediments to adjustment and discovering the deviations from dominant values and conduct which are not inconsistent with a productive and healthy life in modern cities.

Despite the universal urge toward proselytizing, history casts grave doubts on the assumption that the values and practices of any one culture or class are universally superior or inferior to those of another. Certainly we recognize the dangers to human personality inherent in destroying accepted values without providing the opportunity, impetus, and resources necessary to sustain values which are compatible with an integrated system.

To most Americans, lack of willingness to postpone immediate satisfactions for more significant future rewards and security seems improvident and shortsighted. But those who hold this view live in a world where education is closely correlated with social and economic upward mobility and where there is sufficient job security to render savings meaningful. Before such behavior can gain adherents among a large number of newcomers, the latter, too, must experience or envision such a world. For a man or woman who lives "from hand to mouth" and knows not how long his job will last or sees little or no prospect for increasing his earnings, consumption for today and enjoyment now makes a great deal of sense. Were he to postpone these pleasures, he might never know them and his experience and observation suggest that postponement would not spell security for him.

The complex problem of acculturation in a modern industrial community involves more than imposing one's values upon others, or attacking others' values with hammer and tongs. Rather it should emphasize the positive existing values and an appreciation for the different, but frequently extremely utilitarian, patterns of thought and behavior which exist among those who differ from ourselves. New opportunities must go hand in hand with new values and aspirations, if a society is to remain healthy.

Every individual has a responsibility for achieving and maintaining good citizenship, and groups which press for rights must stress internal development. But it is both unrealistic and an evidence of the projection of one's own middle-class values to expect most of those who are denied middle-class rewards to strive for what experience has demonstrated to be unobtainable to them. People who do not respond to exhortation and suggestions of self-improvement are behaving in a realistic fashion. Were they to do otherwise on a large scale, under present conditions there would be greater mass frustration and hostility.

If we had the time of several generations to solve the problem, greater dependence could be placed upon minorities' readying their own members for more effective functioning in our cities. In the American tradition, opportunity and readiness to accept it, go together. As the Negro presses for equality, he must be ready, willing, and able to perform on the basis of national norms. Given time, this would probably emerge in the nonwhite population. But we do not have the required time to wait for its development.

Clearly, there is an important role that non-whites have not adequately performed and should more fully perform. But they alone have neither the resources nor the know-how to do the total job within the foreseeable future. Just because society is slowly realizing that time is of the essence, society must assume the principal responsibility for dealing with the problem. If involvement, participation, partnership, and recognizable rewards are a part of the concept of self-improvement, it can, and will, become an effective instrument for achieving a desired goal.

Of course, we are concerned here with more than a racial problem. Although there are some 30 to 40 million Americans living in poverty, this is not a non-white universe since the non-white population numbers only some 20 million, and at least a third of those in urban areas are well above the poverty level. Even if one adds the Puerto Ricans and Mexican-Americans (identified as white by the Census some thirty years ago), some three-fifths of those economically deprived are white. But poverty, although it exists in all parts of the Nation and among all major groups in the population, is concentrated among certain groups, especially those residing in rural areas, and non-whites. Thus, while non-whites constitute only a third of the poor, about a half of all non-whites are in this category. Any effective program to deal with poverty must be a national effort. Its benefits will, inevitably, affect a large proportion of the official and non-official non-whites, but these groups will not have a monopoly.[7] Indeed, their component of those assisted would constitute a decided minority of the people involved.

There is still another imperative for action. The recent tendency toward widening the gap in economic status, as between the upper and lower classes among non-whites, has serious implications, as was set forth in

[7] The Johnson Administration recognizes this. Thus it has announced an attack on poverty. This will include greater and more meaningful public educational advantages, improved welfare and social services, assistance to migrants in adjusting to urban life, and expanded programs of vocational training and counseling for the disadvantaged.

the earlier discussion of urban renewal. They are apparent in the rise of the Black Muslims, which reflects a disenchantment with dominant values and goals on the part of a segment—still small—of the Negro population. The extreme militance among certain other groups, too, suggests the possibility of the development of class conflict within the non-white community and, ultimately, throughout our society. Only the success of the recent direct action programs, which have involved all classes, has delayed the hardening of the dichotomy of outlook within the non-white community. But there are already the ingredients of serious class antagonisms and conflicts. They will evolve into anti-social forces unless there is a significant acceleration of gains toward realization of equality of opportunity for all and unless the high rates of unemployment, particularly among non-whites, are appreciably lessened. Clearly the basic issue is economic.

Largely because of the continuing publicity given to the Black Muslims, there is a tendency to view that group as typical of the disadvantaged and discouraged Negroes. This is unfortunate on several grounds. It greatly exaggerates the current importance of this new cult; it tends to strengthen a movement which actually still has a limited following; and it ignores the long-run implications of class unemployment. Insofar as the latter situation reflects discrimination, it breeds demonstrations and direct action on the part of those affected. This, in turn, extracts a real economic toll from the community: witness the cost on a single project. As of the end of October, 1963, the dispute on racial employment discrimination on the Harlem Hospital annex had run on for four months. The *New York Times* for October 28, 1963, estimated that the dispute cost the city between $500 and $850 a day and that the contractor could be expected to bill the city for between $68,000 and $115,000 as of the end of October.

The potential cost of continuing class unemployment

is much greater. It involves the possibility of competition and conflict between unprepared, unwanted, and unemployed white and non-white workers.[8]

The future of this Nation will depend in large measure upon what we do in this area. Success in meeting this issue involves achievement of full employment, development of effective programs for training and retraining our labor force, and concern for the new phenomenon of class unemployment. Also, of course, we must learn how to accelerate the urbanization of our newest migrants. The urban complex is composed of all its people. It and society can never escape the economic and social problems they have created.

[8] Over fifteen years ago I wrote, "The Negro is dedicated to fight for the right to work [not, of course, for "right to work laws"]. In doing this he is simply expressing a universal desire to survive. The danger ahead is that his fight to work and that of his white prototype may occur in a society with not enough jobs to go around and result in racial conflict. In the past, this has often happened. . . . In the United States, it's work or fight on the color line." (R. C. Weaver, *Negro Labor: A National Problem* [New York: Harcourt, Brace and Co., 1946], pp. 315–316.)

VII FUTURE DEVELOPMENT OF
THE URBAN COMPLEX

Just as problems of race harass many central cities and
knock at the doors of the smaller communities that
surround them, land and its utilization and development are basic concerns of the suburbs. The central
cities, too, have land problems; but, as has been suggested above, these relate primarily to reuse rather than
initial use. The entire urban complex is threatened by
traffic congestion, and a balanced system of adequate
highways and mass transit is an indispensable element
for efficient development of major urbanized regions. At
the same time more rational development of the suburban areas would minimize transportation needs and
utility line extensions. And, too, the development of
satellite communities affording employment opportunities, and educational—as well as recreational and commercial—facilities, would serve the same purpose.

The questions before us have been suggested above.
They include:
Will scatterization continue?
Will we saddle a new generation of Americans with
having to make lengthy journeys to and from work only
to arrive at the end of the day in a culturally sterile
community devoid of shops, theaters, libraries, and parks
within easy access?
Will we go on developing new subdivisions at random
—uncoordinated to any area planning—and dependent
upon septic tanks and wells which are destined to be replaced, thereby occasioning unnecessary expense?

Will we act to provide basic facilities, such as sewerage and water systems, of sufficient size and capacity to satisfy existing and anticipated needs and to facilitate optimum efficiency in operation?

Before attempting to discuss the issues suggested by these questions, reference must be made again to the nature of our governmental structure. The locale where most of the problems of land planning and development are concentrated is generally outside the jurisdiction of city government. This locale is the area lying in the county, in a small township, or in an unincorporated village. Thus, in the case of many subdivisions, there will be a viable urban-orientated government only after most of the basic planning and development determinations have been made.

Because of these circumstances, two results seem self-apparent. First, unless the state government establishes programs and procedures for meeting these issues, the Federal Government will assume primary responsibility in this field or else it will remain neglected. Second, in the absence of adequate local controls and inducements, efforts to achieve better land uses must flow through indirect mechanisms, primarily federal inducements to the private developer.

Our concern must be to discourage, to the maximum extent possible, the mistakes of the past, such as the destruction of scenic attributes, while encouraging positive actions that will provide a better physical environment for the homes of tomorrow. Better utilization of sites will allow utilities to be provided more economically. In the process, larger and more meaningful open spaces could be provided. If clustering of houses, utilization of town houses, and multi-family units are incorporated in the large subdivisions of the future, it will be possible to provide sites at lower costs to homebuyers.

The new community concept, involving thousands of dwelling units and varying mixes of industrial and commercial facilities, has even greater potentialities. As this is written, some seventy-five such large-scale developments are in various stages of execution and planning in the Nation. Because of their size and scope, the new communities afford a setting for advanced site and architectural design at the same time that they facilitate maximum economies in basic facilities, such as water and sewerage systems. In addition they utilize land more remote from population concentrations, and consequently less expensive than that which is closer to urban centers.

These large new communities can and should provide site employment and diversified shopping, as well as comprehensive educational, recreational, and cultural facilities. In addition, they present an opportunity for planners to reappraise man's varied needs and devise new modes of satisfying them.

New communities have many unrealized potentialities. They could, and should, be, but, to date give little promise of being, the setting in which truly democratic communities are developed. This means that they should demonstrate how families and individuals of a wide variety of incomes and ethnic attributes can live together. In addition, they should be laboratories where we can develop performance standards for building codes, more realistic and efficient zoning, and experiments in utilization of new materials and construction methods. In the new environment which they create, it should be possible to experiment with new approaches to housing for low- and moderate-income households and develop exciting and novel arrangements for communication and transportation.

Most important, however, is the opportunity that new communities afford to demonstrate to the American people that a better life is possible. This involves all that has been suggested above as well as the creation of aesthetically attractive and pleasing areas of residence. It also implies increasing opportunities to work in the community where one lives, to find recreational and cultural outlets there, and to enjoy to the maximum degree the beauties of nature which reside in the countryside of this Nation.

In all of these matters, the new community enjoys a unique advantage. It is unencumbered by existing social or economic vested interests or by a physical pattern which restricts creative departures from the *status quo*. So far, however, there is only one of the seventy-five new communities in planning or execution which seems to be moving in this direction. Some others are attempting to realize better site planning and a full component of community services and facilities, but the vast majority appear destined to become country-club communities for upper-income families.

The future potential for the urban complex is great. Our tools for achieving this potential are imperfect and still in the process of development. But a nation which is affluent, which is willing to face up to social problems, and which is excited by its possibilities has a real future.

Urban renewal is demonstrating that for many elements in our population the central cities can be attractive. These central cities are becoming economically more healthy, aesthetically more appealing, and culturally more vital. There is no need to despair of them; nor are they threatened by the possibility of better subdivisions and of new communities in the outlying areas. Indeed, the new communities will strengthen the central cities if they face up to the social issues and become truly democratic institutions with a racial and class mix, if they develop new and better approaches to low-income housing, and if they establish novel and more satisfying modes of meeting man's many needs.[1]

[1] President Johnson's housing and community development proposals would accelerate and encourage this process by providing financial assistance to new communities while requiring that they house multi-income groups, conform to area plans, and accomplish effective utilization of land.

We have been shown that the residential environment in all parts of the urban complex can be improved. The task ahead is to raise our sights and create the excitement and the expectation which inspire new approaches and successful breakthroughs. The American consumer is exposed to constantly improved products, which affect his tastes. He rapidly demands more and more as he is conditioned to expect more. When, therefore, we are able to provide him with wider choices and new horizons of expectation, he will exert pressure for continuing experimentation and improvement.

In the years ahead, therefore, the housing industry, in all its branches, and government, at all its levels, should strive to whet the appetite of the American people for better housing and community development.

Today, as we stand at the threshold of a new population explosion, involving another major expansion of suburbia, there is a unique opportunity for action. It is vital that the American people be attuned to this possibility; and it is incumbent upon those who value our culture to press for results. Never before has there been such a fortuitous combination of economic resources, technical knowledge, and urban concentration. What we do with these resources will fashion the urban complex in our times and for years ahead.

APPENDIX A

The Low-Income Housing Demonstration Program

The Low-Income Housing Demonstration Program was created by Section 207 of the Housing Act of 1961. The Act authorizes the Housing and Home Finance Administrator to enter into contracts to make grants, not exceeding $5,000,000, to public or private agencies for the purpose of developing and demonstrating new or improved means of providing housing for low-income persons and families.

Eligibility is confined to proposals for demonstration of new or improved ways of providing housing for low-income families or persons. In addition, proposals must give promise of results useful in other communities, either directly or once the necessary legislative aid has been provided.

Section 207 grants are used generally to pay or help pay for the cost of the conduct of the demonstration, its evaluation by a competent objective organization (most often a university or university-affiliated unit), and the publication of a report on its results. Financing of the development, purchase, or rehabilitation of the housing which provides the setting for the demonstration is provided from the grant only when such financing cannot be readily obtained otherwise. In these occasional instances, the housing is to be sold or refinanced upon conclusion of the demonstration, with the resultant proceeds payable to HHFA. Moreover, financial assistance is limited to the cost of applying the new method to the minimum number of dwellings required for effective testing, and cannot be used for activities for which funds from other established federal programs are available.

Program Summary

At the end of June, 1963, twenty-three low-income housing demonstrations were under approval and nearly thirty proposals were under consideration. Demonstrations have been approved for conduct by public or private bodies in twenty-one municipalities in sixteen states, ranging (not, of course, without gaps) from Massachusetts to California and from Alaska to Florida.

The demonstration proposals approved to date comprise a considerable variety of new approaches. Several are centered on design and construction techniques for achieving better housing at less cost. Methods for increased utilization of the existing housing supply, particularly by local housing authorities, are to be tested. Public supplementation of rents for families placed in private housing, both existing and new, will be demonstrated. Rehabilitation and upgrading of existing dwellings are approached with sharp focus on avoiding the economic displacement of the low-income family. Newer means for facilitating low-income family purchase of housing are to be tried out. A test of self-help in providing housing is also included, with emphasis on maximizing the productivity of self-participation and minimizing financing need.

Demonstration Types

1. DESIGN AND CONSTRUCTION TECHNIQUES

Four demonstrations are addressed to new construction techniques. Based on a body of previous research, Pratt Institute, New York, will test new methods for lowering the cost of high-rise apartments through the use of "box frame," lightweight steel, and reinforced brick construction. Housing Research, Inc., in Michigan City, Indiana, will demonstrate multi-dwellings at lower density through "stacking" manufactured dwelling components.

The University of California at Berkeley will develop a low-cost house for comfort in a hot-dry climate, through design rather than the use and cost of mechanical refrigeration. On the other hand, the Alaska State Housing Authority will develop a low-cost dwelling for comfort under extremely cold and windy conditions, while also countering such higher-cost factors prevalent in Alaska as scarcity of building materials, limited building season, and short supply of skilled workers.

2. UTILIZATION OF THE EXISTING HOUSING SUPPLY

Five local housing authorities are bent upon experimental use of various types of existing structures—both multi-family and single family, hotels, and even structures initially built for combined commercial and dwelling use.

The New Haven Housing Authority will house larger families in private rental apartments, while the Chicago Housing Authority will place elderly households in such units.

In the District of Columbia, the National Capital Housing Authority will use vacancies in single-family dwellings to serve larger family needs.

The Detroit Housing Commission intends to use an older but structurally sound hotel to try out better methods of housing males of low income, particularly the former residents of skid row.

In Philadelphia, the Housing Authority will expand and evaluate its program for the purchase and rehabilitation of existing dwellings to serve as public low-rent resources. The demonstration will cover the standards, procedures, and costs of property acquisition, rehabilitation, management, and maintenance; the livability results; the effects on neighborhoods; and a number of related questions.

The New York City Housing Authority will combine the second and third floors of old three-story houses into large units for large families, while the first floors, formerly stores, will be converted into smaller apartments.

In addition, Kundig Center, a settlement house in Detroit, will have an analysis and report prepared on its system of leasing rooms within walking distance of the Center and subleasing them, without profit and at low rents, to the very low-income elderly.

Here is a common search for a more varied and flexible low-rent housing supply; housing resources which can be provided faster and more cheaply than new construction, while also avoiding the increasingly difficult site problem; and dwellings in less institutionalized settings than "project" housing.

3. RENT SUPPLEMENTATION

Rent supplementation—the payment directly to the private landlord of public subsidy covering the difference between market rent and what the low-income tenant can afford to pay from income—is to be tested in three different situations. It will be used with larger families in private apartments in New Haven and elderly households in private apartments in Chicago, as mentioned above. It will be tried also in St. Louis County, Missouri, where the Redevelopment Authority will place a limited number of rent-assisted families among those paying full rents in a new garden-type moderate-income development, financed under FHA's Section 221(d)(3) program.

Thus tests are being made of the provision to low-income families of private housing which meets decent standards and is located in a non-project setting. Rents are kept in line by agreement between the public agency and the private owner. Owners and managers of

private rental housing are assured of an outlet for sur-
plus shelter, if it is kept in good condition. In addition,
the community is provided a means for obtaining additional low-rent housing resources quickly, in various
neighborhoods, with greater locational choice to the
families.

4. REHABILITATION

The four rehabilitation demonstrations under the
Program emphasize methods of (a) minimizing economic displacement of the family as a result of the cost
of the physical improvement and (b) producing dwellings large enough for larger families.

The Flanner House unit of the Board for Fundamental Education in Indianapolis, Indiana, will test guided,
team-based self-help by low-income occupants in rehabilitating their dwellings.

The Rent and Rehabilitation Administration in New
York City will demonstrate techniques of limited rehabilitation that will avoid altogether the physical displacement of the families during the repair work, while
keeping within the means of tenants any rent increases
that may be necessary.

5. HOME OWNERSHIP FOR LOW-INCOME FAMILIES

Four demonstrations, each differing in detail from
the others, have been approved in this area of the low-
income housing problem.

The University of Florida, at Gainesville, will test
the use of criteria and procedure for mortgage credit
analysis that have been especially modified to facilitate
qualification of low-income applicants as acceptable
risks. Since in some market situations the identification
and qualification of low-income families for mortgage
credit have been more successful than in others, systematic effort to discover and test the distinctive factors and procedures involved is being undertaken.

In Tulsa, Oklahoma, the city will enable displaced
families to prepare themselves for and gradually as-

sume home ownership responsibilities, by providing them housing under a lease with an option-to-buy, or "conditional purchase," plan. The families will first occupy the new Section 221(d)(3) dwellings as tenants, then accumulate their downpayments as their incomes are improving, and thereafter purchase the same dwellings.

A third application of lease with option-to-buy will take specially selected and prepared families into cooperative and condominium ownership of apartment units. The San Francisco Development Fund will place the families in dwellings that are part of developments located in three different renewal areas in that city.

Another demonstration in the home ownership group is addressed to a serious problem accompanying urban renewal and other public improvement programs. This is the plight of the displaced homeowning families with too little income for purchase of homes in other areas. In Glassboro, New Jersey, the Housing Authority will guide low-income families, forced to sell their homes because of urban renewal, in escrowing the proceeds from the disposition of their properties to be demolished, so that they can serve as downpayments on new dwellings built in the same area. Because the downpayments will be heavier than usual, the monthly payments for housing will be lower. In addition, tenure will be cooperative, an approach facilitating participation of the people in planning housing to meet their tastes and pocketbooks, while buttressing the protection of assets through the escrow deposit.

These home ownership projects are not promotional. Instead they carry in common three assumptions about low-income families who typically have strong desires for home ownership, will be tempted to and do undertake it, but are often ill-equipped to assume its risks and responsibilities. First, it should be possible to identify families which are on their way up and will improve their incomes. Second, once this step is taken, they can be provided with systematic support to assure both increase of income and better financial management, focused on housing. Thirdly, the preliminary leasehold can be used as a period for practice and proof of capacity for home ownership responsibilities.

6. SPECIAL GROUP NEEDS

There is also a group of eleven demonstrations each of which is oriented toward potential repetition in meeting a special segment of low-income housing need as well as testing a particular method of providing housing.

Large families are to be accommodated in the demonstration housing provided by the National Capital Housing Authority, the New Haven Housing Authority, and the New York City Housing Authority.

Solutions to the housing problem of elderly persons and families are being sought under the Chicago Housing Authority and Kundig Center demonstrations, described above.

The special needs of physically handicapped persons will be met under a demonstration of the Toledo Housing Authority.

Alaska will provide housing not only suitable for cold climates, but within reach of Indians of very low income.

The rural in-migrant, new to an urban environment, will be assisted in Cincinnati.

The Fair Housing Inc., demonstration, being carried out in the metropolitan area of Boston, intends to provide to non-white and other socially disadvantaged families housing which is located closer to places of employment of the family heads. For some families such housing will only be found in suburban communities. The sponsoring group is an organization created particularly to provide brokerage and other services for closing rental and purchase transactions between willing landlords in the suburbs of Boston and selected low-income purchasers.

Citizens for Better Housing in the District of Columbia is also a specially created non-profit organization, to provide to investors in and developers of private low-income housing, anywhere in the metropolitan area, assistance with land acquisition, financing, market analysis, construction cost-cutting, and other technical problems. It is expected that through this mechanism the resources of churches, labor unions, and other groups interested in providing Section 221(d)(3), Section 202, and other low-cost housing will be effectively marshaled.

APPENDIX B

The Mass Transit Demonstration Program
(as of September 30, 1963)

A grant was made to the Commonwealth of Massachusetts for a variety of service improvement and fare experiments in the Boston metropolitan area and the urban areas of Fitchburg, Worcester, and Pittsfield. The project involves the Boston & Maine and the New Haven Railroads, the Metropolitan Transit Authority, and about a dozen private bus companies.

Despite restoration of peak-hour fares (reduced in the initial phases of the demonstration) to the predemonstration level, patronage on the Boston & Maine continued its upward trend. Total ridership in the fall of 1963 was about one-third above that of the preceding year, with off-peak riders up about 85 per cent. The New Haven Railroad showed a much smaller increase, and a passenger survey was under way to discover the reasons for this result. Bus and parking-lot experiments continued to show a mixed result, and some of the least productive were being discontinued. In a few cases, it had already been determined that the experimental service would be continued after the test period.

The City of Detroit received a grant of $224,400 for an eight-week demonstration on the Grand River Avenue bus route to determine the effects of a substantial increase in service on passenger volume and traffic flow. The final report, published in February, 1963, showed a progressive daily increase in passenger volume and revenue—rising, by the eighth week, to a level of 12 per cent for passengers and 8.6 per cent for revenue, over the comparable 1961 base period. Although costs of the increased service greatly outran additional revenues, the experiment yielded valuable information on the characteristics of bus patrons in the service area and provided a test of certain survey techniques. This demonstration also clearly indicated that experiments of this length could not be expected to produce significant changes in rider habits.

A grant was made to the District of Columbia government to test the operation of a "minibus"[1] service within the downtown business district. A two-month preliminary test of a prototype vehicle, completed in March, 1963, will be followed by a one-year demonstration of a fourteen-vehicle fleet beginning in November, 1963.

Kansas State University received a grant to design and demonstrate in actual transit operations a system for using the digital computer in scheduling vehicles and manpower. Transit systems in Kansas City (Missouri), St. Louis, Cincinnati, and Omaha are cooperating. Preliminary data on existing systems have been gathered and are being collated; the field demonstration is scheduled for the summer of 1964.

A grant was made to the Memphis Transit Authority for a demonstration to determine whether the pattern and volume of transit ridership can be influenced by establishing immediate full-scale bus service in new or rapidly developing suburban areas. Three representative types of suburban areas are being tested. Preliminary results show the service in one area doing better than expected, one worse, and one about as estimated.

The Metropolitan Transit Authority of Nashville–Davidson County was given a grant to test revisions in transit-service patterns to meet changing land-use patterns. These include the provision of combined local

[1] Minibuses are small motor vehicles designed for short runs.

and feeder service in satellite communities, and the establishment of circumferential connections between built-up areas now served only by radial routes from the central business district. The new service began October 28, 1963.

Five demonstration projects have been approved for the New York metropolitan area. Four of these are being undertaken by the Tri-State Transportation Committee—including a park-and-ride facility on the Pennsylvania Railroad at New Brunswick, improved service and facilities on the Harlem Division of the New York Central, feeder bus service to the New York Central in southeast Rockland County, and a test of fare collection equipment on the Long Island Railroad. The Rockland County project is in operation; that at New Brunswick will begin operations shortly.

The fifth grant was to the City of New York for a study and test of the means of expanding the capacity and potential of existing commuter facilities in the Queens-Nassau sector of the Long Island Railroad. The City is in the process of selecting a project director for this demonstration.

Two grants have been made to the Southeastern Pennsylvania Transportation Compact (SEPACT), serving the Philadelphia area. One project, approved on October 22, 1962, seeks to attract new patronage to the Pennsylvania Railroad and Reading Co. lines by experiments with increased service, lower fares, better parking, and feeder bus service. This demonstration, for the January–July, 1963, period, shows an increase in passenger volume over 1962, of 83.4 per cent for the Pennsylvania Railroad and 34.5 per cent for the Reading.

The other project is just getting under way. It will demonstrate how, by a series of integrated analytical studies, the improvement needs and potentials of rail commuter facilities can be appraised and evaluated in relation to present and future travel demands.

A grant was made to the Port Authority of Allegheny County to construct and operate a one-mile section of a new type of rapid transit system using trains of small, lightweight, rubber-tired, electrically powered cars. Preliminary engineering is now under way. This is the first "hardware" project under the demonstration program.

A grant was made to the San Francisco Bay Area Rapid Transit District to assist in a 28 million dollar program for the development and testing of new concepts in rapid transit design. Preliminary work on this program, including wind tunnel tests, test track engineering, and the negotiation of various test equipment contracts, is now under way.

The University of Washington was given a grant to prepare a report on the Seattle Monorail. The report, published in November, 1962, covered engineering and cost characteristics of the installation. Some data were also obtained on public acceptance.

INDEX OF NAMES

INDEX OF SUBJECTS